A Different Approach to Work Discipline

Marek Bugdol

A Different Approach to Work Discipline

Models, Manifestations and Methods
of Behaviour Modification

palgrave
macmillan

Marek Bugdol
Human Resource Management
Uniwersytet Jagiellonski
Krakow, Poland

ISBN 978-3-319-74007-2   ISBN 978-3-319-74008-9   (eBook)
https://doi.org/10.1007/978-3-319-74008-9

Library of Congress Control Number: 2018938221

Printed on acid-free paper

This Palgrave Macmillan imprint is published by the registered company Springer International Publishing AG part of Springer Nature.
The registered company address is: Gewerbestrasse 11, 6330 Cham, Switzerland

Contents

List of Tables

1

The Definitions, Types and Functions of Discipline as Well as Factors Influencing Discipline

1.1   Introduction

Very many interesting observations concerning work discipline and employee punishment can be found in the opinions of the forerunners of management. Their views proved that management sciences develop on a continuous basis. Contrary to appearances, there are no revolutionary ideas here. Even re-engineering hailed as a business revolution has its roots in the accomplishments of K. Adamiecki. The same can be said about the model of positive discipline proposed by D. Grote.

It is the Michelin brothers and H. Emerson who can be regarded as the forerunners of positive discipline. They opposed the automatic punishment of employees and the advocates of learning from one's own mistakes. Nowadays these solutions are used practically in the whole automotive sector; what's more, they are included in standardised quality management systems, which should be dominated by corrective and preventive actions. A short review of the achievements of the precursors of management will be followed by a presentation of the definitions of discipline. In the previous literature on the subject (Schoen and Durand

© The Author(s) 2018
M. Bugdol, *A Different Approach to Work Discipline*,
https://doi.org/10.1007/978-3-319-74008-9_1

1979; Boyd 1984; Catt and Mille 1985; Torrington and Hall 1991; Haimann and Hilgert 1997; Morgan 1999; Guffey and Helms 2011), discipline is identified with obedience, proper behaviour and action taken against employees who do not comply with the organisation's rules. It is even believed that disciplining is connected with the use of force and formal authority; however, simultaneously there appear opinions arguing that discipline means "the strengthening of morale and self-control" (Boyd 1984: 202).

Discipline may be analysed based on the normative approach and the broader cultural approach. It should be stated unequivocally that employee behaviour is not dependent on formal, informal, group, qualitative or technological norms (after all, norms are one of the elements of culture), but is embedded in a particular environment or organisational culture.

There exist various types of discipline. In the literature (Leonard 1968; Schoen and Durand 1979; Torrington and Hall 1991), it is possible to find a division into managerial discipline and group discipline as well as self-discipline, strong discipline, weak discipline and group discipline. In reality, there are very many types of discipline. Besides generally known and accepted types of discipline such us budgetary discipline, we can distinguish other types, for example, ethical, unethical, motivational, cultural, conscious, unconscious, trust-based, etc.

Work discipline fulfils numerous functions (deterring, motivational, insuring, educational, corrective, integrating, internalising, socialising or destructive functions) and has to be maintained in compliance with many principles (e.g. the principles of transparency, inevitability, justice). The research conducted so far indicates that personality traits (e.g. Argyle 1989; Michel and Bowling 2013; Scott and Judge 2013; Wei and Si 2013), organisational structures (e.g. Priesemuth et al. 2013), and management styles (Tepper 2000; Ertureten et al. 2013) may be relevant for work discipline. Apart from these factors, it can be assumed that work discipline depends also on the ownership form of an organisation, the type of an organisation, technical equipment and infrastructure.

1.2 The Views of the Forerunners of Management on Work Discipline

It is difficult to determine the origins of what we refer to nowadays as work discipline. In the Bible, God tells Adam to comply with particular rules—he must not eat the fruit from the tree of knowledge of good and evil. Due to his disobedience, Adam loses eternal life, has to be punished for his sin, begins to experience shame and is forced to work hard. It can be said that God did not go easy on Adam—he must not have known the rules of positive discipline.

In 1776 Adam Smith wrote *The Wealth of Nations*: the division of labour becomes more and more specialised and factory owners attempt to restrict the freedom of labour by means of the technical system (tying an employee to a machine) and by introducing strict supervision. According to G. Morgan, "in order to get workers accustomed to the new and rigorously obeyed factory production routine, new work methods and procedures were introduced" (Morgan 1999: 21).

Some models of dealing with workers were adopted from the military. G. Morgan claims that the school of a mechanistic organisation[1] owes a lot to Frederick the Great, whose principle was for soldiers to fear their officers more than their enemy. Absolute discipline and obedience was required, but also specialisation and standardisation—all these features of the Prussian army were replicated subsequently in "mechanised" organisations. The German sociologist Max Weber also made a significant contribution to the development of knowledge of the methods of discipline. His ideal bureaucratic machine indicated the need to introduce hierarchical supervision and detailed regulations; it also stressed the importance of reliability and regularity.

As a matter of fact, the classical theory of organisations did not refer to work discipline, but its basic rules were shaped by:

- determining a single source of instructions (every employee receives instructions from one boss only);
- determining the scope of control (the number of subordinates cannot be too large in view of the requirements of communication and coordination processes);

---

[1] In mechanistic organizations, employees perform routine actions; mechanical work consists in performing repetitive activities.

- assigning responsibility and authority (everybody knows their authority and thus can demand obedience; entrusting somebody with authority means allowing them to take disciplinary actions).

The importance of work discipline was emphasised by F.W. Taylor, who directly formulated the proper features of discipline, i.e.:

- justice (remuneration adequate for efficiency);
- reason (reasonable administration of punishments);
- quality of management (good management guarantees discipline).

According to the school of a scientific organisation (represented by Taylor, Fayol, Gantt), discipline results also from the necessity to subordinate personal interests to those of the whole organisation.

Taylor claimed also that workers should be permanently controlled. Only compliance with procedures leads to improvement in their work efficiency.

Although strict discipline prevailed in Henry Ford's factories, his employees did play various organisational games (necessitated by the monotony of the work). They were subjected to centralised control and dismissals were effected immediately (Martyniak 2002).

Even today, many people tend to associate discipline with punishing employees. Therefore, the views of H. Emerson on disciplining employees should be regarded as revolutionary. He believed that the punishment of employees by people who had power was a short-sighted policy. For Emerson, discipline meant a certain order in life (Martyniak 2002). He paid attention to the cultural aspect of discipline and concluded that an important role in maintaining discipline was played by an organisation's spirit and customs.

An interesting method of ensuring discipline was also used in the factories owned by the Michelin brothers. An employee who had made a mistake was not punished automatically, but had to go to their boss in order to discuss possibilities for improving their work (Martyniak 2002). Nowadays similar solutions are used where quality management systems have been implemented correctly and where quality is being improved comprehensively by means of corrective and preventive action.

O. Sheldon noted that the notion of justice played an important role in people management. His views on this matter have been confirmed by many studies. A sense of justice is important for the further motivation of work. It is of enormous importance in work discipline systems.

The views of the forerunners of management on work discipline and control are presented in the table below (Table 1.1).

A brief review of the achievements of the outstanding forerunners of scientific organisation of work provides us with interesting observations. It turns out that in the past, discipline was not connected with punishing employees only. In the first half of the twentieth century, famous authors specialising in the area of organisation and management paid attention to the fact that:

- In the shaping of organisational behaviour, an important role is played by "the organisational spirit" (cf. Emerson).
- Justice as perceived by employees is very important for discipline (cf. Sheldon).
- Management plays the most important role in the maintenance of discipline favourable for quality (cf. Bata).
- Too much control is harmful (cf. Kotarbiński).
- People may obediently meet legal requirements irrespective of the will of management (cf. Weber).
- Spontaneous discipline plays an important role in organisations (cf. Dubreuil).
- Discipline is one of the elements of a general management model (besides others such as equality of opportunities, punishments and rewards, initiative, proper improvement and deployment of employees, sense of belonging, stability) (cf. Urwick).

1.3 Definitions of Discipline

The literature on the subject does not tell us how discipline should be defined. There are few publications in which attempts were made to define the notion of discipline (e.g. Catt and Mille 1985; Morgan 1999; Guffey and Helms 2011). According to the classical principles of the

Table 1.1 The views of the forerunners of management on work discipline and control

Author	Views	Notes
F.W Taylor	Formal control should be exercised by foremen; their role consists in maintaining work discipline. Good management guarantees discipline. Reason plays an important role (e.g. in the administration of punishments). The card system informed employees whether tasks were being carried out correctly (a yellow card meant a warning)	Taylor's views on reason and good management are still valid. However, the discipline of work is not just about applying penalties. Nowadays, unfortunately in the theory of management only, and rarely in its practice, great importance is attached to self-discipline and a proper organisational culture whose elements include expressing respect for employees and taking advantage of their competences. Taylor's follower, C.B. Thompson, talked already about taking advantage of employees' experience
F.B. Gilbreth and L.Gilbreth	They introduced the notion of competition (with oneself, colleagues at work and standards). The attitude towards discipline changed. It was not only compliance with standards but also motivation to change (sharing in profits, methods of remuneration) that were to encourage people to increase their efficiency	Today the Gilbreths' views may be useful particularly in maintaining self-discipline by continually improving one's own work (competing with oneself)
A.P. Sloan, Jr.	He looked for methods to achieve balance between extreme centralisation and decentralisation. He concluded that what was necessary was the centralisation of control over all functions of an organisation. Such control was to be exercised by a president or managing director. He introduced coordination committees	Sloan's views today allow us to understand relationships between organisational structures and control

(continued)

Table 1.1 (continued)

Author	Views	Notes
H. Ford	As W. Krzyżanowski observes, discipline prevailed in Ford's factory. The employer was to pay good wages, but also administer discipline themselves. Disputes between superiors and subordinates were settled by labour inspectors. Ford was an opponent of excessively developed structures. In his company, every employee could contact the chief manager about anything. Ford was very suspicious; therefore, in his company, he maintained a special service that Z. Martyniak calls "the secret police". Dismissals from work were immediate and irrevocable	Power centralisation and information barriers do not favour the quality of management. Nevertheless, some of Ford's ideas can still be applied today in developing discipline systems (e.g. teams of inspectors dealing with dispute resolutions)
A. Michelin and E. Michelin	These great industrialists and forerunners of a science-based organisation introduced a system that resembles the principles of positive discipline. An employee who had made a mistake was not punished automatically, but had to go to their boss in order to discuss possibilities for improving their work	The Michelin brothers can be regarded as both the forerunners of positive discipline and the originators of contemporary quality management systems (which should be dominated by improvement activities)
K. Gastiew	He paid attention to the following two dimensions of discipline: self-control and order in the workplace A manager was not a controller only; they were supposed to learn and control themselves. Gastiew introduced particular rules of discipline (e.g. employees were not allowed to smoke or eat during work time)	Even nowadays the supporters of lean management and other approaches agree that order in the workplace (which prevents wastage) plays a considerable role in the maintenance of organisational order The rules of self-control remain very much topical

(continued)

Table 1.1 (continued)

Author	Views	Notes
K. Adamiecki	The outstanding Polish precursor of scientific work organisation did not deal directly with work discipline. Nevertheless, his research contributed to the better understanding of the principles of inter-operational control. Adamiecki observed that production processes lacked harmony and were fraught with unnecessary stoppages, generating losses. He also paid attention to the role of social relations, in particular the problem of prejudices	One may risk the thesis that if it had not been for Adamiecki or Taylor, the concept of lean management would not have been developed According to Adamiecki, for people dealing with discipline, it is important not to be influenced by prejudices or stereotypes in making assessments
H. Fayol	In Fayol's concept, discipline plays an important role—it is one of the principles of management (besides unity of command, stability of tenure of personnel, humaneness, division of work, authority and responsibility, unity of direction, order, remuneration, scalar chain)	Fayol's views allow us to understand that discipline is not the most important. Organisational order and humaneness are equally significant
H. Emerson	Discipline and reason are the basic principles of efficiency According to Emerson, there are three meanings of discipline. Firstly, it means adjusting to the requirements of the environment; secondly, it refers to order in life; and thirdly, it is punishing He believed that punishing employees by people who had power was a short-sighted policy.	He paid attention to the cultural aspect of discipline and concluded that an important role in maintaining discipline was played by an organisation's spirit and customs

(continued)

Table 1.1 (continued)

Author	Views	Notes
M. Weber	He thought that subordinates' obedience consisted in compliance with the law, and not with the will of the leader (in the rational type of authority). In his bureaucratic organisation (in the system of legal authority), employees had to have a specified scope of giving orders or instructions and use coercive measures. According to Weber, people holding administrative positions are subjected to strict discipline and control	Subordinates' obedience consists in following the law, and the will of the leader. This view lies at the foundation of the behaviour of contemporary whistleblowers (who are frequently punished without justification)
L. F. Urwick	Discipline is one of the elements of a general management model (in the same area as equality of opportunities, punishments and rewards, initiative, proper improvement and deployment of employees, sense of belonging, stability). In the detailed management principles, discipline is a process, and its results include the personnel's morale, stability and initiative. Both punishments and rewards constitute a process	Urwick's views make us aware that, without a previous diagnosis (deployment of resources), without stability and a sense of belonging, discipline is deprived of any sense
A. A. Bogdanow	Bogdanow focused on two important issues: firstly, on the notion of organisational standards which, as K. Perechuda writes in his doctoral dissertation, are a set of restrictions hedged with sanctions and incentives; secondly, on the active role of workers in handling emergencies and making independent decisions	Bogdanow's views are nowadays used universally in emergency response procedures. The theme of the active role of employees in handling emergencies is developed in the idea of comprehensive responsibility for made mistakes (according to organisational rules, an employee who has made a mistake has to receive support from all their colleagues)

(continued)

Table 1.1 (continued)

Author	Views	Notes
T. Kotarbiński	He introduced the notion of pure and interventionary surveillance. Pure surveillance consists of applying strict control and restricting actions to control only. Interventionary surveillance manifests itself when the employee sporadically participates in an action. Kotarbiński was convinced that good results could be achieved by minimising intervention	Kotarbiński's views allow us to understand better the mechanisms of control or rather the scope of control (e.g. at the initial adaptation stage control is a mistake)
O. Sheldon	Sheldon did not deal with discipline directly, but in his guideline he referred to the notion of justice, particularly in contacts among employees and managers	In the 1990s researches confirmed that organisational justice was of considerable importance for effective work discipline
F.R. Roethlisberger	F.R. Roethlisberger was not involved particularly with work discipline issues (although he was the first to introduce the teaching subject of organisational behaviour), but his views on the functioning of organisations are important for the understanding of how discipline occurs. He introduced a simple division into the social function and the economic function. He had enough courage to admit that the economic function dominated over the social function	His views are still valid. It is very often the economic function, sometimes understood incorrectly as pursuit of immediate profits, which shapes the social relations in organisations and leads to strong and dehumanised discipline

(continued)

Table 1.1 (continued)

Author	Views	Notes
T. Bata	Bata introduced a new system of punishing managers. It consisted of the administration of financial penalties. In the event of any losses, managers assumed complete financial liability for them	It is a pity that Bata's recommendations are not always followed. Just the opposite; at present many organisations are introducing systems of financial penalties for their employees or contractors, ignoring the fact that efficiency and quality depend to a larger extent on the management (which was also observed by E. Deming)
H. Dubreuil	In his views, he referred to the notion of spontaneous discipline and antinomy—a logical contradiction. Spontaneous discipline cannot be imposed; it results from the fact that employees, who know their potential best, should decide the division of work. H. Dubreuil was interested in the issues of the antinomy between "order and the individual's freedom; between discipline and individual initiative" (Martyniak 2002: 196)	Unfortunately, his opinions on spontaneous discipline were not the subject of further research. However, relations between discipline and initiatives are reflected in theories concerning employee commitment and citizenship behaviour
Ch.I. Barnard	According to Ch.I. Barnard, disciplinary measures, supervision and control are managerial sub-functions	He referred not only to the maintenance of order but also to the maintenance of morale. For him, discipline was one of the sub-functions only, not the dominant one

Source: The author's own work based on (Martyniak 2002)

theory of management, discipline means "obedience, diligence, energy, proper behaviour and clear indications of respect consistent with the established rules and customs" (Morgan 1999: 25). Discipline is "all actions taken against employees who do not comply with policies, standards and rules in place in the organization" (Catt and Mille 1985: 261). Discipline, or strictly speaking, disciplining employees, "is connected with the use of force in combination with formal authority" (Haimann and Hilgert 1997: 276). Discipline "is the state of order in the organization where employees comply with the applicable standards and pursue the established objectives" (Schoen and Durand 1979: 213). Discipline "consists in regulating human behaviour with a view to achieving planned (and controlled) work results" (Torrington and Hall 1991: 538).

"Discipline may be perceived as something positive; it is not only a set of punishments, but first of all a method of educating employees and building proper intraorganizational relations. Discipline is "strengthening morale and self-control" (Boyd 1984: 202).

Disciplining also consists of providing employees with training bolstering their strengths. It is a process of recovering control over employee behaviour, also by means of forced obedience (Guffey and Helms 2011: 111–118).

The definition included in Webster's *New World College Dictionary* treats discipline as "training that develops self-control, character, or orderliness and efficiency" (as cited in Disciplining employee 2015) and as "training to fix incorrect behaviour or create better skills" (www1).

The aforementioned definitions of discipline belong to the trend in management connected with the supervision of employees. Developing the existing definitions, it is possible to state that discipline comprises all actions aimed at correcting the behaviour of all stakeholders of an organisation. In this approach, discipline applies not only to employees but also to customers, suppliers, owners and people hired to manage the organisation. Obviously, the scale of disciplinary actions depends on the possibilities of expressing authority. The scope of discipline in the case of customers will be different from that applicable to suppliers. In many sectors, e.g. the automotive sector, suppliers have to submit unconditionally to the standards followed by dominant organisations placing orders.

Disciplinary actions include not only punishments (which are always a failure and cause various economic and social costs), but also:

- training (including on-site instructions, mentoring, coaching, support for training processes);
- granting awards and motivating employees;
- social games whose objective is to achieve acceptance for standards or values;
- socio-technical methods of modifying behaviour (persuasion, threats, positive expression of emotions).

In discipline, an important role is played by people-management processes. Thanks to proper selection of employees, their adaptation, systems of assessment and remuneration, it is possible to cause required organisational behaviour.

Work discipline will be influenced enormously by the following:

- a diagnosis of employee behaviour;
- a constant analysis of social processes;
- an analysis of organisational values;
- communication (connected with both the identification of inappropriate behaviour and aimed at establishing standards of behaviour).

Most employees equate discipline with the applicable law and internal regulations. Work discipline is associated mainly with punishment. Legal regulations indicate what punishments should be imposed on employees who do not comply with the applicable rules and standards. Most superiors try to enforce discipline when it has already been breached and it becomes necessary to make a decision about punishment. Superiors frequently react emotionally, do not want or do not have time to think about the sources of non-compliance with the rules of discipline or about the consequences of punishment.

Discipline is connected not only with punishment but also with employee training, development and self-control. It includes a system of regulations recommending the required organisational behaviour.

Thus a small number of publications include definitions of discipline results, probably due to the fact that disciplining employees is provided for by the law (primarily by labour codes).

It is assumed that disciplining employees comprises punishments and sanctions, and is connected with attempts to enforce appropriate behaviour. The notion of "appropriate behaviour" may raise serious doubts. Such behaviour depends on how an organisation functions and what objectives and operational motives it has. For example, if an organisation has financial objectives only, the whole work discipline system is oriented towards achieving such objectives. The means of achieving these goals is usually of little importance, but they are not always ethical. Employees are punished for failing to achieve financial goals, but they are not punished for undertaking competitive and unethical actions aimed at obtaining better results than those of internal competitors, i.e. other employees.

The notion of discipline concerns the two supplementary approaches: the normative approach and the cultural approach.

The former approach assumes that employee behaviour should be influenced by means of a system of punishments. The criteria of such disciplinary actions are included in the normative system (mainly in the labour code, work rules and an informal system).

The cultural approach also takes into consideration the applicable standards, but disciplining is regarded as a tool of education, shaping employee attitudes, behaviour and relations required in a given culture. It is believed that discipline, i.e. a particular way of behaviour, can be learned. In this context, discipline means a certain acceptable manner of conduct closely connected with an organisational culture.

It can be assumed that, on the one hand, discipline is a product of an organisational culture, i.e. the existing standards, values, models of behaviour and beliefs (cf. the table below), and on the other hand, disciplinary actions undertaken in an organisation are to ensure the shaping, maintenance and development of its organisational culture (Table 1.2).

There must be many other ways of defining discipline. It is also possible to refer to many other elements of organisational cultures, study relationships among particular elements, and provide many more examples of the influence of beliefs, standards and values on employee behaviour. But this does not change the fact that discipline is connected directly with a particular organisation's culture.

Table 1.2 The elements of an organisational culture and their significance for discipline

Organisational culture	Impact on discipline	Limitations—examples
Standards: international, obligatory, non-obligatory, internal, group, imposed by stakeholders, quality chain participants, others	Standards exert considerable influence on discipline because their application is connected with the implementation of procedures specifying precisely the methods and stages of conduct	It happens that standards contain mutually exclusive criteria. For example, internal standards are contradictory to international standards
Autotelic values (values constituting goals in themselves); instrumental values (e.g. self-control, self-reliance, and responsibility); individual, social and ethical values (good and evil)	All values play a considerable role in management. They indicate operational objectives and methods of their achievement, types of behaviour and attitudes towards work and other people	The shaping and maintenance of discipline can be hindered seriously by contradictions between the declared values and those pursued in everyday activities of an organisation
Models of behaviour (e.g. the conduct of other stakeholders)	Against appearances, behavioural models do not have to play the dominant role in employee conduct. Their adaptation and impact on behaviour depend on a large number of different factors (an employee's adjustment potential, possibilities of their manifestation, assessment of their usefulness, etc.)	The lack of accurate information and convictions about which models are important for the organisation and employees leads to the situation in which employees do not accept various manifestations of behaviour and refuse to regard them as their own and valuable
Beliefs (e.g. What contributes to success and by what means can success be achieved? What is the acceptable, safe and beneficial level of commitment?)	Beliefs exert influence on employee behaviour and the ways of pursuing objectives. Thus they are important for discipline. For example, if the owner believes that success is possible thanks to the strict treatment of the employees, then punishments are the most important element in the discipline system	Beliefs are changeable and are sometimes shattered by pathological behaviour of other members of an organisation

The normative approach and the cultural approach are differentiated by the following:

First of all, efforts made by managers and the complication degree of undertaken actions. The first normative dimension is usually connected with copying particular provisions from the labour code into organisational regulations. Organisations issue internal rules informing employees of sanctions that can be imposed on employees for non-compliance with work discipline (cf. the text below).

> "An academic teacher is subject to disciplinary liability for any conduct constituting a breach of duties or the dignity of the teaching profession.
>
> For lesser disciplinary offences, the Rector gives the teacher a caution after becoming familiar with the facts of the matter. The Rector can also refer the matter to the Academic Teacher's Disciplinary Officer, who will carry out an investigation procedure. If the charges against the teacher are confirmed, the Disciplinary Officer refers the matter to the Disciplinary Commission for Academic Teachers. The Commission conducts a disciplinary procedure. The Rector can suspend the teacher against whom a disciplinary or penal procedure has been initiated. Such suspension is also possible during the course of an investigation procedure if the seriousness and credibility of the presented charges indicate that suspending the teacher in their duties is appropriate. During the period of suspension the basic salary of the teacher can be lowered. In this period the teacher is not entitled to any bonuses or remuneration for overtime. An employee who is not an academic teacher can be punished by the Rector for non-compliance with the work rules, OHS or fire prevention regulations, as well as the methods of confirming arrival and presence at work or justifying absence from work with a caution or reprimand. For an employee's non-compliance with the OHS or fire prevention regulations, absence from work without justification, coming to work in the state of intoxication or consuming alcohol at work, the Rector can also impose a financial penalty".
>
> Source: (www2)

Secondly, in the normative approach, discipline is equated with actions undertaken periodically: punishments are administered in the event of breaching legal regulations, normative rules, customer requirements, etc. In the cultural approach, discipline is a continuous process. As already been mentioned in the introduction, it is some kind of interaction occurring among employees. Such interaction takes place only in particular organisations with specific organisational cultures and climates, where various formal and informal standards are in force.

Thirdly, the cultural approach requires that managers have greater awareness, responsibility and knowledge concerning the possibilities of influencing employee behaviour, leadership competences, abilities to motivate employees and to assess their work. But it should be remembered that, irrespective of the knowledge of different methods and techniques, employees establish a psychological contact and exchange various ideas or views within the scope of their interactions.

It is symptomatic that, in both the literature and the colloquial speech, people use such terms as a discipline model, a discipline system, employee discipline, work or workplace discipline (a separate subchapter is dedicated to the types of discipline). At this point, it is worth explaining the notions of a system of discipline and a model of discipline.

A system of discipline is a notion referring to the systems theory. It is assumed that a system of discipline comprises related and interdependent actions aimed at ensuring behaviour that is favourable for the performance of tasks and achievement of goals, as well as restoration of control over employee behaviour in the event of any non-compliance. Any discipline system includes various punishments or sanctions and, unfortunately rarely, rewards. Discipline systems are characterised by various degrees of complexity. Besides punishments, more complex discipline systems include training, continually undertaken corrective and preventive actions, motivation programmes and managerial support. Conscious discipline systems comprise required behaviour-shaping programmes, employee support programmes, behaviour modification training and employee opinion surveys.

The notion of model applies to not only the elements of discipline, i.e. administered corrective measures (mainly punishments) but also the sequences of punishments and rewards. It also concerns whether punishments are toughened, used alternately with other sanctions (e.g. suspension in employee duties, granting a non-voluntary leave of absence).

Therefore, we can distinguish between the models of positive discipline and progressive discipline (both models are described further on of the book).

1.4 Types of Discipline

The literature on this subject does not contain types of work discipline. Few authors attempted to classify various types of work discipline. For example, D. Torrington and L. Hall (Torrington and Hall 1991) distinguished between managerial discipline, group discipline and self-discipline. S.H. Schoen and D.E. Durand (Schoen and Durand 1979) divided discipline into strong, weak and group discipline.

It is assumed that disciplining is mainly the duty of management, while punishments themselves can be administered not only by immediate superiors but also by other employees who are authorised or coerced to do so. Therefore, various types of work discipline are worth considering. For example, it is possible to distinguish the following:

1. *Cost discipline*

In many organisations, cost discipline manifests itself in that employees not only comply with established cost limits but also are obliged to lower them or identify sources of wastage. Compliance with cost discipline results in bonuses or other financial awards, while breaching such discipline entails punishments (including financial ones).

2. *Budgetary discipline*

Budgetary discipline is important in every organisation, e.g. during the performance of projects or research. For example, in public administration, budgetary discipline means that people drawing up budgets or changing their elements must not exceed strictly determined amounts of subsidies. Breaching budgetary discipline may result in local government officials' being denied acceptance of the discharge of their duties.

3. *Conscious and unconscious discipline*

For various reasons (e.g. the lack of competences or information), some employees are not aware of what standards, rules or principles are in force in their organisations.

4. *Procedural discipline*

It is based on the assumption that employees have to act in accordance with existing procedures. However, for this type of discipline to be effective, employees have to be guaranteed participation in the development of procedures and their continuous improvement.

5. *Discipline resulting from non-compliance with social standards*

Social standards are determined by different regulations or orders, but they also result from unwritten rules embedded in the organisational cultures of formal or informal groups. Non-compliance with formalised social standards usually causes the initiation of progressive discipline mechanisms. On the other hand, non-compliance with standards in informal groups may lead to the intensification of various organisational games (e.g. personal attacks), humiliation or exclusion from a group.

6. *Discipline resulting from non-compliance with quality standards*

In this type of discipline, employees are punished for non-compliance with established quality standards. In this case, the issue of punishment is very controversial. What is assumed in quality management systems is not only the fact that self-control exists but also the possibility of undertaking corrective actions. Punishment should be administered as a last resort if an employee persistently fails to meet quality standards or if the collective labour agreement provides for penalties after two audits with negative results.

7. *Progressive discipline*

It is assumed that, for subsequent cases of negligence, an employee receives increasingly severe punishments.

8. *Positive discipline*

In the model of positive discipline, punishments, rewards and temporary suspensions from duties have a corrective and motivational character.

9. *Ethical and unethical discipline*

Punishments imposed on employees can have an ethical character (i.e. if they result from common findings and decisions made according to the rule that every employee can correct their mistakes) or an unethical character (if social norms or legal regulations are breached; if an employee's reputation or dignity is damaged.

10. *Motivating and demotivating discipline*

Not only punishments but also the methods of their administration can increase or decrease employee motivation. For example, a punished employee who is aware of the source of their inappropriate behaviour and achieves new jointly established objectives can experience a higher level of motivation. And vice versa: a punished employee who has no influence on established standards or objective will feel strongly demotivated.

11. *Discipline based on trust*

This is a type of discipline whose character is determined by the trust that particular employees have in one another. A high level of trust decreases the intensity of control and causes the rules and objectives of discipline to be understandable to both the punished and those who impose punishment.

12. *Discipline based on intimidation*

Discipline based on intimidation consists of administering various forms of punishments that do not result from the formal discipline system. Employees are intimidated, very often verbally, indirectly by other employees or directly by managers. Punishments imposed in this type of discipline are both unethical and severe (they cause demotivation).

13. *Indirect and direct discipline*

As its name indicates, in this type of discipline employees are punished directly by their superiors or indirectly, usually informally, by their co-workers. Discipline entailing organisational games is a variant of indirect discipline. People who attack and intimidate other employees are in league with formal superiors. A characteristic feature of this type of discipline is that punishments are handed out before any offence occurs.

14. *Discipline resulting from the particular types of organisational cultures.*
In this group, it is possible to distinguish the following[2]:

Family discipline
In this case, work discipline results not from intimidation, but from closeness between people. Punishments are usually harsh because they result in exclusion from the organisation (disinheritance, deprivation of work and/or the closeness of co-workers).
Hard discipline
This type of discipline rewards initiative, achievement of goals and success at work, but all failures are stigmatsed painfully.
Work-hard-and-play discipline
What is welcomed in this type of discipline is giving up holidays or taking up additional work, e.g. at weekends. The maintenance of discipline is strengthened by means of various celebrations or rewards. There are more rewards than punishments.
"Smooth operation" discipline
This type of discipline stresses the importance of reasonable and long-term decisions. Analysis of the environment is important. Punishments result from employees' non-compliance with the established rules and methods of achieving objectives.
Discipline of lasting
Discipline results from established procedural rules. Mistakes are frowned upon and all deviations are punished harshly. What dominates is mistrust of employees (which is the source of suspicion and the administration of unjustified punishments). The system of punishments is not susceptible to change.

---

[2] An idea taken from the types of culture proposed by T. B. Deal and H.A. Kennedy. A description is included in: (Grudzewski et al. 2011: 218–220).

15. *Punitive and corrective discipline*

Punitive discipline is based on the assumption that disobedient employees can be given punishments only. They are to fulfil both the punitive and deterring functions.

Corrective discipline consists of undertaking actions that will cause changes in inappropriate behaviour (besides punishments, it provides for the use of training, organisational games, discussion of event scenarios; employees receive relevant support, e.g. psychological support).

16. *Strong and weak discipline*

Discipline can be strong when superiors are convinced that all applicable standards and objectives have been established correctly. And thus employees should follow them. They have to be controlled and forced to work. Weak discipline can result from superiors' convictions that nothing can be done because objectives and standards are not realistic enough. This can also result from the conviction that some employees (e.g. those working in research and development departments) work better when they are given complete freedom. Thus employees do not require constant control. Of course, weak discipline depends frequently on work organisation and the other two factors, i.e. management styles and reality of objectives (Schoen and Durand 1979).

17. *Team discipline*

Team discipline is "the supplement of self-discipline and strengthens it" (Schoen and Durand 1979: 214). Team discipline results from the simple fact that people performing particular tasks depend on one another; the results of their work depend on the conduct and behaviour of their co-workers. A failure of one worker very often means a failure of the whole team. Team discipline consists, on the one hand, of following standards applicable to the team and accepting its culture and, on the other hand, in taking into consideration the superior objectives and standards applicable to the whole organisation.

18. *Technological and pro-environmental discipline*

As mentioned above, discipline is connected directly with the existence of quality standards. But we must not forget about technological standards (related to the maintenance of quality standards and production process management principles). In some sectors (e.g. in coke and electrode plants, in the chemical sector), technological discipline consists of compliance with the principles, rules and requirements established by employees themselves. For example, technological discipline consists in ensuring that graphitisation furnaces are opened at precisely set times, furnace covers are positioned correctly, stronger ventilation is switched on, etc. Technological discipline frequently has a pro-environmental character because maintaining the technological regime reduces negative impact on the environment. For this very reason, companies implement EMAS systems as well as environmental management systems based on the ISO 14001 standards.

Besides workplace discipline, it is possible to distinguish employee discipline outside the workplace. This is not a new problem; it was discussed in the literature in the 1960s (Leonard 1968: 5). However, there are no unambiguous legal regulations or sociological analyses explaining how employees should behave in order to minimise the risk of losing their valuable knowledge, what relationship they should avoid, where the border lies between privacy and the sphere of occupational duties.

The above classification of the various types of discipline has an orientational character. In reality, the particular types of discipline are mixed and influence one another. For example, family discipline can have the form of either conscious or unconscious discipline, either formal or informal discipline.

It is necessary to clearly separate workplace discipline from employee discipline. Many occupations and fulfilled functions require that discipline also be maintained outside the workplace (e.g. members of management boards must not establish close or risky contacts with strangers).

Even such a simplified division of discipline shows that its particular types differ from one another with respect to the following:

- consequences for the person breaching discipline (dismissal, exclusion, ordinary penalties);
- sources of occurring irregularities (errors result from systemic conditions, bad management, lack of employee competences, etc.);
- possibilities of influencing compliance with discipline rules (e.g. cost-reduction programmes result from decisions made by management and employees cannot influence such decisions; employees have different scopes of participation in procedure development);
- methods of punishing (cf. the positive model, the progressive model);
- the time when punishments are imposed (before or after an offence);
- the ethical sphere (punishments can be ethical or unethical, i.e. humiliating employees or hurting their sense of pride).

1.4.1   Towards Relational Discipline

It has already been mentioned that discipline can be analysed from the perspectives of the normative and cultural approaches, which complement each other.

However, work discipline is a certain process that takes place in a particular environment. Behaviour is determined by not only culture and a system of sanctions but also everyday relations with other people, situational factors, motivation, experience and many other factors.

Our presence in an organisation can be compared to the presence of a ball in a pinball machine. When we come to work, our contacts, relations and interactions with other people are of considerable importance for us because, with other factors, they determine our behaviour (e.g. whether we avoid work, whether we have to be punctual, what scope of freedom we can enjoy).

Besides personality traits, motives, attitudes, role models or upbringing factors, whether somebody is disciplined or undisciplined depends on the following three mutually complementary areas: the process area connected with the development of social ties; the systemic area comprising, among other things, an individual's functioning within a team or group; and the strategic area which determines an organisation's key operational objectives.

1.4.1.1   The Process Area

Describing the process of the shaping of social ties, the outstanding Polish sociologist J. Szczepański observed that some people were connected by spatial closeness, while others established social contact and relations that led to the development of social ties. Also in organisations, we have closer relations with some people than with others; we meet some people on a daily basis, while others once a week or once a month. Such differences in relations have an effect on how we behave. What is important in this context is a person's position in the organisational structure, the range of their control and the current stage in the development of social ties.

> **Example**
>
> Andrew is a promotion specialist in the marketing department. His work is supervised by the department manager, whom he meets every day. In the morning the team discusses their tasks, goals and scope of work for the day. At the end of the work day, the manager checks what has been done and what still remains to be done. Andrew rarely sees the company's president. However, his tendency to comply with the work-time rules and perform his duties successfully is determined strongly by the president's periodic visits in the marketing department. There are strong emotional ties between him and the department manager, which is very important for discipline; even when Andrew fails to follow the boss's instructions, the boss does not punish or admonish him.

Whether there are social and material ties between an individual and an organisation is of fundamental importance for the following:

- performing duties properly ("I care about my salary and good relations at work", "this is a good place to work");
- administering punishments (it is difficult to punish somebody with whom we have close relations);
- determining tasks to be carried out by an employee (it happens that managers avoid allocating difficult tasks to employees with whom they have strong personal ties);
- making decisions about employee dismissal.

The problem is that even a small number of contacts and interactions can influence employee behaviour either positively or negatively. The factors influencing employee behaviour include the scope of control, the strength of relations (connected in this case with personality traits) and the factual range of authority. This means that we can have only occasional contacts with a particular person, but the very appearance of such a person can have a disciplining effect on us, especially if we know that they have real authority.

Employee behaviour is also influenced by the scope and strength of the psychological contract (a unique arrangement among employees) and the quality of relations.

1.4.1.2   The Systemic Area

Employee conduct also depends to a considerable degree on systemic factors. Within the social sub-system, it is possible to distinguish the scope of control exercised by co-workers, work organisation forms, points of reference, and what happens in employee groups.

The scope of control depends on many factors such as:

- existing infrastructure (e.g. so-called open space allows employees to control each other; common databases facilitate control activities);
- existing managerial solutions (sometimes employees receive instructions concerning the control of their co-workers; holacracy is characterised by transparency and social control exercised by everybody);
- previous experiences connected with control activities (negative results strengthen control behaviour);
- attitudes, habits and motives of particular co-workers.

The form of work organisation itself influences relational discipline. For example, it is common knowledge that work organisation based on groups causes the time and volume of work as well as workers' efforts to be the subject of arrangements among group members. However, it is necessary to remember two disturbing factors, namely the attitudes of management and disturbances accompanying group work. Firstly, after the restructuring of an organisation, its former functional managers do not always become experts. Sometimes the loss of formal authority causes an increase, not a decrease, in the scope of control. Secondly, organisational order, connected in this case with the allocation of responsibility, authority, duties, etc. depends on types of tasks (e.g. additive tasks need not favour group work organisation). When decisions are made about the division of tasks in groups, what happens frequently is the polarisation of decisions.

The theory of reference explains how mutual comparisons (e.g. comparisons concerning the volume, time and quality of work) influence employees to make conservative decisions. If others make less effort and supervisors treat them the same, doubt develops as to whether citizenship behaviour is worth manifesting (whether it is a good idea to work more, behave better or come to work on time). Mutual comparisons can result in perceived justice or injustice.

In employee groups, it is possible to distinguish various leaders as well as formal or informal superiors. Their management styles and relations with employees also influence the degree of compliance with work discipline. All such leaders determine group standards, ensure that they are followed and influence group structures (e.g. the positions of individuals within a group). Another important thing is relations connecting top-level managers with employees who are formally subordinate to lower-level supervisors. The very fact of maintaining relations between top management and regular workers influences the level of discipline among all employees. Such relations can raise suspicions and undermine trust among employees working in one department. As a whole, a group exerts considerable impact on its individual members; they can be cherished or isolated, favoured or destroyed emotionally.

1.4.1.3   The Strategic Area

In the strategic area, work discipline is influenced strongly by the establishment of objectives, the analysis of data and the adopted business perspective.

Another important factor regarding the methods of conducting control procedures and mutual relations is what strategic objectives there are, how they are formulated and divided into operational goals. For example, establishing financial objectives only in connection with remuneration for management causes the appearance and maintenance of "strong" discipline. If managers' salaries depend on how their subordinates work and it is only financial objectives that count, there is strong pressure for them to achieve.

Another problem is data analysis. In practice, there are two types of problems: either data are insufficient (e.g. there is no data or process indexes collection system) or there are too many data. The lack of data makes it impossible to assess results reliably and causes not only many misunderstandings but also the unjust treatment of employees. Employees do not know what is good or wrong; they receive no reliable feedback and consequently make many mistakes.

Too many provided data cause their recipients to disregard them (e.g. this is what happens in six sigma programmes).

A business perspective is a frequently disregarded factor influencing the methods of management and objective establishment, as well as employee training and motivating. Simplifying, we can divide organisations into those with a long-term perspective and those with a short-term perspective. Companies either want and have to function for a long time or are established only for the purpose of achieving some short-term objective (e.g. to sell a particular number of dietary supplements). To a considerable extent, such a perspective influences an organisational culture as well as management and motivation styles.

In organisations with long-term perspectives, employees constitute factual capital and undergo various types of training (but not in order to use manipulative methods of increasing sales). In such organisations, positive discipline can appear as most of them do not punish their employees and follow positive discipline models. In organisations with a short-term perspective, relations between superiors and subordinates are full of tension; exercised supervision is oriented not towards pursuing results but results themselves and consequently the principle of "the end justifies the means" prevails. Competing for the highest positions in rank, employees frequently allow themselves to behave unethically.

1.5   The Functions and Principles of Discipline

When we talk about discipline, what we have in mind is usually the fact of the existence of some clues concerning appropriate conduct, quantity or quality standards, recorded rules or traditions as well as the fact that failure to follow such standards can result in the administration of punishments.

We know little about the true impact of discipline on employee behaviour or the correction of such behaviour. This is probably because changes in behaviour depend on many personality, situational, structural and other factors. One of the studies conducted in the 1980s showed that discipline itself had a small but visible impact on employee efficiency (Beyer and Trice 1984: 743–764).

Discipline fulfils the following functions: deterring, motivational, insuring, educational, corrective, integrating, internalising and socialising functions, while badly exercised discipline can fulfil the destructive function.

a. *Deterring function*

Various rules, regulations or codes specify punishments that employees can face if they fail to follow the existing standards, principles and rules of behaviour.

Disciplining employees is unpleasant for either those who are disciplined or those who discipline, or both.

b. *Motivational function*

It is assumed that discipline should fulfil the motivational function. However, in order to achieve this result, many different conditions have to be met; for example, a high level of trust, an objective assessment of inappropriate behaviour, punished employees' awareness of the positive consequences of corrected behaviour. Furthermore, employees have to be able to exert influence on the performance of their duties and the pursuit of established objectives.

When individual motivation exhausts itself, discipline makes it possible to achieve a higher level of competence.

c. *Insuring function*

Work discipline fulfils also the insuring function. It secures organisations and their stakeholders against the consequences of inappropriate behaviour with a negative impact on organisations. Work safety discipline is an example of this type of discipline.

d. *Educational function*

Work discipline shapes the characters of employees. It influences their behaviour even after they have left an organisation.

> P. Ducker started to work for the newspaper *Frankfurter General-Anzeiger*, whose editor-in-chief was E. Dombrowski, known for being a very demanding boss. He made sure that the newspaper was always available on time, at six o'clock sharp. Work discipline maintained in the editorial office influenced the whole subsequent professional life of the future guru of management.

e. *Corrective function*

Discipline corrects people's behaviour and ensures that the proper quality of interpersonal relations is maintained.

f. *Integrating function.*

Discipline also performs an integrating function. On the one hand, the correction of behaviour should, at least theoretically, influence the integration of organisations and social groups. On the other hand, integration may concern such people or groups that express solidarity in the face of unjust punishment. It is assumed that work discipline is indispensable for the maintenance of organisational order. Without work discipline, the proper quality of interpersonal relations or cooperation among individual people or whole organisations is impossible.

g. *Internalising and socialising function*

Taking care of a common system of standards manifests itself in the process of internalisation.

Internalisation means "*regarding values, standards, views, etc. originally imposed from the outside as one's own*" (www3).

Maintaining discipline should foster the process of socialisation. Based on the sociological notion of occupational socialisation (Marshall ed. 2004), it is possible to state that socialisation should consist of assimilating such standards, attitudes and behaviour that are necessary for achieving a permanent level of organisational competence.

h. *Destructive function*

The wrong discipline system destroys mutual respect among employees, changes their status, undermines their independence, restricts their personal freedom and damages their dignity.

Discipline should be based on the following principles: the principles of correct information, the inevitability and immediacy of punishments, justice, and universality and transparency.

a. *Principle one—correct information*

Employees have to know the rules of discipline and be aware of what is expected from them. Work discipline is connected with the occurrence of employee expectations. Employees expect that, in return for good work, they will receive remuneration as well as employment security, respect and recognition. They express what they expect from their managers. Disciplining employees can arouse or destroy such expectations. The lack of correct information concerning expectations and work results introduces confusion and does not foster appropriate behaviour.

b. *Principle two—inevitability and immediacy of punishments*

Punishments are always a last resort and constitute evidence that management badly manages its human resources. However, employees who continually and consciously cheat their organisations have to be punished in ways generally known and commensurate with committed offences. Punishments have to be inevitable and immediate (punishments can be postponed or suspended only when applicable procedures provide for undertaking corrective measures).

c. *Principle three—justice*

It is one of the principles that is difficult to implement. Punishments should be just in the procedural sense and the distributive sense.

d. *Principle four—universality*

In accordance with this principle, punishments are universal, which means that their administration cannot be restricted to some selected social groups or individuals. Favouring or omitting particular groups or individuals is prohibited because it violates the principle of the equal treatment of employees.

e. *Principle five—transparency*

A punished employee has to be informed for what offences or events they have been punished, what appeal procedures are available to them and what punishments are provided for in the work discipline system functioning in a given organisation. Transparency does not mean that employees can be punished or stigmatised publically.

1.6   Discipline Versus Freedom

The notion of discipline is connected with the notion of freedom.

The notion of freedom has been studied by many philosophers (e.g. B. Russell, G.E. Moore, M. Merleau-Ponty, J.P. Sartre). However, one of the more interesting interpretations of freedom was proposed by I. Berlin (Dupre 2008: 204–205), who distinguished between negative freedom and positive freedom. He said that people frequently regarded freedom as situations in which no external restrictions existed. We are not free when we have no choice. Freedom has to be connected with self-control and independence. *"Nobody can enjoy unlimited freedom without violating the freedom of others, therefore, in the case of people living in society, some form of compromise is necessary"* (Dupre 2008: 205).

This quote perfectly conveys the character of people's functioning in organisations. Some people's failure to follow with established standards entails the violation of other people's freedom. If nobody manages employee behaviour and no restrictions are in force, conflicts arise. According to Berlin, freedom requires compromise. Therefore, the shaping of a work discipline system has to involve compromise, employee participation and, wherever possible, the joint establishment of objectives.

> *While negative freedom is freedom from external restrictions, positive freedom is usually defined as freedom to achieve particular goals, as a form of support allowing the individual to realize their potential, to fill in some forms of self-fulfilment, to achieve the state of personal independence and self-control.* (Dupre 2008: 206)

Thus work discipline should be connected with self-discipline and self-control.

A very important issue is freedom to pursue objectives. It manifests itself in the idea of self-governing teams. Employees have to be not only assigned individual objectives related to particular ranks and functions but also guaranteed opportunities to participate in making decisions about the methods of their achievement.

Work discipline is based on the conviction that other people must not be harmed. All behaviour is allowed that ensures that other people—members of the same organisation—are not harmed. However, if this is not so, responsible employees have to face sanctions. Thus all punishments have to be the means of ensuring other people's freedom.

We should pay attention to the fact that freedom determines the methods of disciplining employees. If we accept that work discipline depends to a considerable extent on management, then it should be noted that management itself is not "free".

Organisations are characterised by positive freedom because it is connected with external restrictions, but also with the existence of certain competence limitations. Management changes its behaviour depending on what knowledge it has, whether it depends on other people and within what structures it functions. These factors shape work discipline systems. Thus, the resources of possessed knowledge influence how other people are treated and how superiors behave. A low level of knowledge causes a superior to be dependent on other people who are more competent. A lack of knowledge can cause a manager to adopt compensatory behaviour (i.e. they will try to mark their presence in another activity), but it can also be the reason for excessive interference in what their subordinates do.

Dependence on somebody or something seriously restricts the possibility of undertaking disciplinary action. The employee on whom the professional career of their superior depends is frequently given complete freedom from any control. What is more, such an employee can select other people and add them to their "free circle".

Management's dependence on other stakeholders is particularly noticeable in the case of relations between managers and owners, but also where the fate of managers depends on people from the outside (e.g. in local governments where it is voters who decide the future of their mayors or councillors). Sometimes such dependence influences work discipline (which is frequently misunderstood, see the example below).

In a small town there was a change in the post of mayor after the local government election. The elected official did not have much in common with the employees of the town office, who had been frequently criticised in the past. The new mayor decided to maintain direct relations with his voters (after all, his next term of office would depend on their decisions). Town inhabitants came to the mayor with their problems, complained about dirty streets or bad services provided by the town office. During one such visit, a citizen told the mayor that somebody in their district had organised an illegal rubbish dump. The mayor was of the opinion that the matter was within the responsibility of the head of the environmental protection division and immediately, not waiting for any explanations, issued the department head with a reprimand. Intimidating the town office employees, he wanted to show the inhabitants that he cared about their interests. Unfortunately, the atmosphere of intimidation did not cause the office employees to work better.

Source: the authors' own work

Another factor that influences discipline is the level of superiors' commitment. If this level is low, managers undertake short-lived, spontaneous and emotional disciplinary measures. The lack of complete commitment causes the failure of even optimally designed pro-quality processes. This results from the simple fact that superiors not only fail to motivate employees but also lose contact with reality, do not supervise changes in processes and cause chaos which, in this case, is the derivative of the appearance of new decision-making centres.

The type of organisational structure also influences discipline. Besides many formal structures, there are also informal ones; this division constitutes the basis for the majority of studies into organisational behaviour. It should be noted, however, that within one organisation there may exist one formal structure and another one resulting from tradition or the held professional titles (higher education and military organisations are cases in point). If a superior has a lower professional title than their subordinate, they tend to refrain from any disciplinary action.

1.7   Factors Influencing Work Discipline

This subchapter is dedicated to the characterisation of factors influencing discipline maintenance and punishment administration. The literature on this subject has not presented any studies focusing on factors influencing behaviour favourable for work discipline. This is the same situation as in the case of research into the effectiveness of employee training. It is difficult to indicate which concrete factors have the largest impact on behaviour. And there are very many such factors. They are connected with personality traits, existing discipline systems, particular situations, etc. However, it is worth focusing on at least a few of the most important factors.[3]

1.7.1   External Factors

Discipline systems are influenced the most by legal regulations. In the vast majority of cases, they provide clues about the application of

---

[3] A considerable part of such factors has already been described in the subchapter "Towards relational discipline".

progressive discipline. Punishments include cautions, reprimands and disciplinary dismissals. The methods of punishment depend also on legal regulations aimed at preventing discrimination, nepotism, etc. Such regulations shape managers' behaviour and determine the manners of their conduct. For example, it has been demonstrated that, for fear of being accused of religious or racial discrimination, superiors are unwilling to use disciplinary measures (cf. e.g. Plotkin 2015: 7–8).

It should be assumed that the situation in the labour market influences employee behaviour. A high rate of unemployment and intense competition for jobs can have either motivating or destructive influence on employees. Some employees concentrate on keeping their jobs, but this approach can turn into conformist behaviour that does not favour creativity. Other employees do not worry about losing their jobs, irrespective of a high rate of unemployment.

A major impact on the behaviour of employees, in particular on their attitudes towards work discipline systems, is exerted by a high level of wage differentiation. When employees earn well in comparison to other companies and the situation in the labour market is difficult, their acceptance of work discipline systems increases. It can be expected that in such circumstances, even unethical behaviour of superiors will not be reported. Employees will not file complaints for fear of losing their jobs (see the example below).

> In our company, people earn much more than in other businesses located in the area. For a few years now no employee has been given any punishment. I think that, on the one hand, the employees value their jobs and good wages but, on the other hand, the management is not aware of various negative events taking place in our departments. Therefore, for a year we have been conducting employee satisfaction surveys and introducing various procedures, for example, an anti-mobbing procedure. We have noticed that when our employees decide not to tolerate mobbing, we have no complaints. Therefore, for some time, conflict situations have been reviewed by a team consisting of external experts. The result is that now the employees have more courage to report situations that they regard as mobbing.
> (a department director in a state-owned company employing over 30,000 people)

Another factor influencing work discipline and employee punishment is social pressure (see the example below).

For a few years I have been running a small education and training firm in a small town. Some time ago I employed an English language teacher, even though I had known previously that she could be trouble. She does not perform her duties properly. She is an employee who should be fired immediately. But I'm not going to do it. In such a small community, you can lose your reputation easily. I have to put up with it.
(the owner of a training firm employing five people)

Employee behaviour is influenced considerably by the educational system, family and environment in which certain personality traits develop.

1.7.2 Personality Traits of Employees

It has been shown that such traits as aggression (Michel and Bowling 2013), neuroticism (Scott and Judge 2013) and low level of self-assessment (Wei and Si 2013) favour non-compliance with work discipline. People of various personality types differ with respect to skills, motivation to act in particular conditions or situations, and social aspects of functioning in organisations (they have different moods, temperament, resistance to stress) (Argyle 1989: 52). What is very important from this point of view is the choice of appropriate people for particular tasks, employee groups, structures, etc.

Personality traits can have an indirect influence on disciplined behaviour because they play a prominent role in the manifestation of creative behaviour and productivity (Shalley et al. 2004: 933–958) as well as citizenship behaviour (e.g. Nafei 2012: 1–78; Li et al. 2014: 347–395).

The role of personality traits in undertaking organisational changes is also significant (Rogozińska-Pawełczyk 2013: 95–106).

1.7.3 Cultural Factors

The notion of culture has been defined in thousands of different ways. It can be accepted that an organisational culture "is a set of important notions such as standards, values, attitudes and convictions" (Stoner et al. 2001: 615).

Standards influence how people perform work, how long it takes them to carry out tasks and what actions they undertake to meet standards.

All autotelic, instrumental, individual, social and ethical (good and evil) values play a very important role in management. They indicate operational objectives and methods of their achievement, types of behaviour and attitudes towards work and other people.

Employee's attitudes determine their "mindset towards people and social phenomena" (Marshall 2004: 245). Attitudes are connected with conducted assessments. They can either facilitate or hinder the pursuit of established objectives.

Convictions concern how people should perform work, how much time they should spend at work, what is important and what is unimportant. Obviously, all elements of culture are connected with one another. Values determine convictions. Standards can become values.

An organisational culture can have an enormous influence on discipline. It determines which types of behaviour are desirable. If employees do not adjust to the standards, values and convictions of their company, they are subject to applicable sanctions. Some organisations have cultural standards that provide employees with clues about how to behave. In other organisations employees have to guess which types of behaviour are expected and which are frowned upon.

In the startup company HubSpot, cultural standards are oriented towards teamwork. The management is of the opinion that work should be associated with entertainment rather than with effort. Accordingly, a well-equipped workplace should be associated with comfort and well-being (the employer provides a beer shelf and a hammock to lie in). The company claims that it not only sells its products but also carries out an important mission of changing the world and helping others. When an employee is dismissed from the organisation,, the word dismissal is not used; instead it is replaced by the term graduation (www4).

Cultural factors can be closely connected with religious factors. More and more often, work discipline depends on what religious values employees hold, how strongly they emphasise such values and demand respect for their religious identity (see the example below).

> In a certain company, an employee of the personnel department responsible for IT affairs demanded the introduction of another work break. He wanted to devote it to prayer. Additionally, he asked the employer to build a small altar. Because the company president denied his requests, he would stop work and pray ostentatiously when other people kept working. After some time this peculiar dispute was settled amicably. The employee was granted the right to work flexitime.
> (a former employee of the personnel and training department in an industrial company employing 2000 people)

Quite often, forcing employees to adopt a particular style of conduct characteristic of a given religion causes numerous conflicts and breaches of work discipline. Religious factors also generate legal problems connected with determining the rules of work discipline. Labour codes guarantee employees the right to have their religious, political and sexual diversity respected. But employers often do not know how such rights can be reconciled with internal or customer requirements (see the example below).

> Samira Achbita, a Muslim, was employed in a Belgian company providing security and monitoring services. After more than three years' employment, she started to demand the right to wear a Muslim headscarf at work. The employer gave her a notice terminating her employment, referring to the internal company rules prohibiting employees from wearing any political or religious marks. The dispute was brought to the European Court of Justice, which found that in this case there had been no direct discrimination and the dismissal resulted not from religious prejudice but from the established internal rules of the company. Source: (Guza 2016)

1.7.4 Organisational Structures

Organisational structures determine scopes of control, methods of cooperation among people and methods of conducting processes. Within an organisational structure, it is possible to distinguish the following: the division of individual tasks and responsibilities, the specialisation of work, the levels of authority, and the combination of employees into groups (e.g. sections, departments, divisions). Organisational structures have an indirect influence on behaviour that favours discipline. They determine scopes of control related to information acquired by superiors. In strongly hierarchised structures, contacts among employees exist only between particular rungs of the hierarchical ladder. Preferring the autocratic style, such structures ensure discipline, the speed of instructions and the efficiency of group management. However, decentralisation does not have to entail improvement in interpersonal relations. The lack of promotion opportunities can result in conflicts, while the delegation of power and authority causes superiors to establish their own separate control systems. In weakly hierarchised structures, relations between employees and the group are poor, frequently mechanical and deprived of depth. Such structures may foster disorganisation, divergence of interests and break up of interpersonal ties. Organisational structures determine functional relationships; research indicates that the weaker the functional relationship in an employee group, the greater the probability of the occurrence of counterproductive attitudes and behaviour (Priesemuth et al. 2013).

1.7.5   Styles of Management and Leadership

Work discipline is influenced directly by leadership styles. Research indicates that managers' inappropriate behaviour (e.g. a humiliating and insulting supervision style) is the reason for breaches of work discipline rules (Wei and Si 2013). When managers introduce unclear and unfair rules concerning competition among employees, this can also develop into unethical behaviour (Flaherty and Moss 2007; Enns and Rotundo 2012). The autocratic management style increases the probability of the occurrence of mobbing because it is connected with the use of strong, sometimes unethical, discipline (cf. Ertureten et al. 2013: 205–216). B.J. Tepper introduced the notion of "abusive supervision", i.e. supervision that can cause unethical behaviour (Tepper 2000: 178–190).

It is accepted conventionally that there is a style oriented towards tasks and a style oriented towards employees. But such a division is not completely justified. In some situations of emergency, managers, who normally motivate their subordinates and treat them with respect, have to adopt the style oriented towards the performance of tasks, they have to supervise them closely, give quick orders and strictly control how they are being executed.

There are a large number of researches into the phenomenon of leadership. There is no doubt that leaders shape organisational cultures and to a considerable degree influence employee behaviour. For the behaviour of employees, it is important whether their leader is emotional, narcissistic, charismatic, participatory, sagacious, supportive or possessive. Managers use various forms of work discipline depending on their preferences, the strength of evidence for non-compliance with work discipline rules and many other factors (cf. Fandt et al. 1990: 253–265).

> I worked in a good company. The work atmosphere was perfect. Nevertheless, the company was too big. In my technical division, the boss was a true egoist. He was interested in nothing but his personal career. He wanted at any cost to show the other members of the board that he was the best. He had previously lost the competition for the position of company president. He controlled us the whole time and it was impossible to oppose even the most stupid of his ideas. We lived in constant fear. Nobody had enough courage to voice their own opinion.
>
> In my company, where I worked for more than a dozen years, everybody was afraid of the technical director. I remember that he always came to work wearing a hat, which he later hung outside his office. Hedwig, his secretary, was extremely scared of him. One day the director went home after work, but his hat still hung on the stand outside his office. The secretary was too scared to check whether her boss was still in his office and stayed at her desk the whole night. In the morning she discovered with surprise that her boss had gone home for the night. The director was very interested to know what she had been doing in the office at night.
>
> (The personnel director in an industrial company employing 2000 people)

1.7.6   A Technical System of Organisation

Machines, technical equipment and infrastructure also exert influence on work discipline. As mentioned earlier in the chapter, Ford's production line required employees to be strongly disciplined (they had no choice as they had to work at the pace dictated by the technical equipment). On the other hand, however, the production line favoured organisational games. Employees became customers for one another in a simple relationship.

The lack of opportunities for fulfilling other needs made them undertake various games and practical jokes. For example, they glued cardboard boxes to production lines or changed particular functions in cars, such as pressing the gas pedal started the windscreen wipers or sounded the horn (Argyle 1989: 204).

The first robots to appear in industrial plants were kept in cages. The primary purpose was to ensure employees' safety. However, this form of cooperation between people and machines had an enormous effect on discipline. The rules of work discipline applied to the forms of cooperation among people; they required that robots not be used in particular situations and that their operation be supervised. Nowadays a new generation of robots is becoming more and more popular. They are called cooperating robots because they help people to perform particular tasks. The German automotive manufacturer Daimler has introduced a new form of work which it calls "robot farming". In robot farming, employees supervise robots similarly to shepherds tending sheep. The goal is to make robots cooperate with people and interact with them. According to specialists, this is the only way to ensure productivity improvement (Our Friends Electric 2013: 18–19). Technical equipment makes it possible to control employees tightly. Almost every transport company provides its vehicles with GPS systems. They make it possible to determine the position and speed of a vehicle, whether the driver has bought petrol, closed the door or stopped at a car park. But technical equipment does not always contribute to higher work effectiveness.

In my company, which produces heat exchangers, the boss has implemented a computer system that checks precisely the duration of tasks performed by employees. For example, an employee is given seven minutes to process an invoice. When we are late, usually through no fault of our own, the boss makes a scene. Her lack of flexibility and refusal to take into consideration the differences between particular tasks has caused us to work less well.
(a worker in a manufacturing company employing 50 people)
For a few years, workers providing maintenance services for gas equipment have had company mobile phones. Every action (e.g. arriving at a customer's address, finishing work) is documented. By means of text messages, duty officers are informed of what is being done at a particular moment. This method of supervision forces our service technicians to spend a lot of time texting.
(A worker in a manufacturing company employing 80 people)

1.7.7 Types of Employment

It should be noted that disciplinary methods depend also on the type of employment contract. For example, people working under civil agreements do not undergo assessment procedures (some organisations try to assess such workers in the same way as service providers). They are being remunerated on the basis of performed tasks or work time. Commercial agents are also treated differently. They are not company employees, and therefore, their disciplining comprises indirect punishments, particularly financial ones (lower volumes of goods allocated for sale, lower commissions, smaller sales markets, shorter terms of agency agreements).

1.7.8 Knowledge of Offences

Research shows that supervisors used discipline primarily as a response to certain behaviors and when the work context was supportive of its use (Beyer and Trice 1984: 743–764). Knowledge of offences is of key importance for making decisions about punishing employees. But it is not always possible to acquire such knowledge because superiors do not always observe employee behaviour. Some negative events are covered up or masked by employees and employers.

1.7.9 Social Categories and Stereotypes

In the majority of organisations, the enforcement of discipline rules is influenced by such factors as age, gender, closeness of relations, physical features, and knowledge of an employee's potentially positive impact on the functioning of the organisation.

It can be assumed that the stereotypical perception of employees has a considerable impact on the administration of punishments. Research shows that employee assessment is influenced greatly by the following:

- physical attractiveness (Doliński 2005);
- particular physical features, including obesity (Ashrafian et al. 2004: 1641–1647);

- gender (Fischer et al. 1997: 361–382; Zinkhan and Stoiadin 1984: 691–693);
- nationality (Hill and Tombs 2011: 649–666).

For example, people who are physically attractive receive more lenient sentences and are listened to more carefully. It is possible that the same applies to punishing employees for labour-related offences.

1.7.10 Management Concepts

Work discipline is influenced significantly by applied management concepts. There are differences between disciplining employees in companies that have implemented the lean or TQM management concepts and those which follow traditional management methods (e.g. the carrot-and-stick method). For example, in quality management, it is necessary to remember that a discipline system should take into account the possibilities of using employees' competences. What is important is the autonomy of decision making, the improvement of competences by ensuring the appropriate work environment and the participation of employees in projects (Kaushik 2015: 10–11). In quality-oriented organisations, employees have to make a greater effort to fulfil the criteria of quality standards and/or quality management principles. What they usually expect in return for their greater efforts is guaranteed safety of employment (organisational changes will not threaten the level of their salaries or their professional status). Quality management specialists are of the opinion that an important role in discipline is played by superiors; in managing teams of employees, they have to take into consideration such values as justice and objectivity in work assessment procedures (cf. Lindborg 2015: 56–57).

1.7.11 Types of Organisations

The type of organisation strongly influences its work discipline. It is important whether an organisation belongs to the public or private sector.

Example 1

The organisation X was the manufacturer of carbon and graphite products. Almost 80 per cent of its output was sold abroad (Sweden, the Czech Republic, Hungary, the US, Canada, Germany, Austria). the number of people it employed varied from 1200 to 2500 people. The organisation used professional recruitment methods (including psychological tests) and adaptation programmes (including their assessment and pedagogical training for tutors), assessed employees based on the 360 degrees method, trained employees and supported them in this process (it covered all costs of studies and courses, including the costs of tuition, travel, books, research, accommodation, etc.), motivated employees (using various methods, not only material ones), maintained direct contacts with former employees (every retired employee could use the company canteen free of charge and received periodic benefits). The organisation was a joint-stock company listed on the stock exchange.

Originally, the company had an ordinary functional organisational structure. The structure comprised the sections of economics, production and accounting, each of them headed by a deputy of the general manager. The technical section was divided into departments. Each department was divided further into smaller units called divisions. The remaining sections consisted of divisions only. The level of work discipline was high with respect to both formal discipline resulting from the labour code and informal discipline. There were considerable differences in the administration of punishment in particular organisational units. All employees, with the exception of the members of the management board, had to record their work time. An employee could leave the company premises only with the consent of their boss. There were differences in the treatment of the employees of the particular divisions; for example, those working in the research and development division had the most freedom, the technical personnel had limited possibilities of leaving their workstations, and productions workers had to carry out particular tasks for six or eight hours with a few short breaks. Work discipline depended on whether supervision over employees was exercised on a continuous or ad hoc basis. It also depended on the frequency of visits of members of the management board. The organisation used various informal punishments. For example, employees who decreased work output had to buy other team members rounds of beer. People coming late to meetings had to pay a small amount to the common fund for each minute of delay. A worker who failed to follow the foremen's instructions had to do sit-ups or run around the shop floor with a bucket of water. More informal punishments were used among production and technical workers (whose level of education was generally lower).

Work discipline depends on management styles. In the organisation X there were both liberal and authoritarian managers, those exercising ostensible power and those exercising absolute power. The intensity of discipline is low where liberal management styles dominate, but it does not mean that employees work less effectively (self-discipline prevails and a lot depends on whether employees find their work interesting and whether they can pursue their own ideas). Discipline is also influenced by established quality standards. Turners working in the production division exercised self-control. The organisation X had about a dozen obligatory procedures in place (related to the supervision of records and document circulation, commercial agreements, audits, non-compliant products, corrective or preventive actions). Work discipline depended also on the organisation's financial position. In period of crisis, solidarity among employees was very easy to notice. Even office workers undertook additional tasks in the production section. After the devastating flood in 1997 when the company's machinery stock and work-in-progress were completely destroyed, all employees participated in the reconstruction of the firm, not counting on any overtime pay or not even being sure of continued employment. Work discipline depended also on the style of management in a given section. The economics section was managed rather liberally. The technical director tried to maintain discipline, but at the same time he did not mind being the butt of ridicule and numerous jokes. People performed their duties, aware of the threat of potential punishments.

Example 2

The organisation Y belongs to the public sector. It employs approximately 150 people. The organisation does not follow the rules of competition because it provides public administration services consisting of issuing administrative decisions and orders. Appointed employees supervise the work of administrative units, mainly secondary schools.

There are two forms of authority in the organisation. Direct supervision of employees is exercised by the heads of the departments and the secretary. Elected in local government elections, the board determines the organisation's lines of action, manages its internal relations, and communicates with councillors and the directors of the subordinate units. Formal work discipline is consistent with the provisions of the labour code. Employees can be punished with a caution, reprimand or disciplinary dismissal. For a few years there have been no cases of disciplinary dismissal, although a few employees have resigned voluntarily. Informal punishments are not used. Managers have special talks with employees experiencing difficulties with the performance of their duties. Every second year every employee undergoes an assessment procedure (the company has a formal internal assessment system in place). Two negative assessments may result in dismissal. However, all employees are assessed positively. The work of the majority of employees does not require self-control (with the exception of control over the preparation of proposed decisions). Work time is recorded; employees sign attendance lists. The required level of self-discipline is not high. Employees mainly perform tasks provided for in administrative procedures.

1.7.12 Forms of Ownership

Another factor influencing work discipline is an organisation's legal form. Research has shown that there are differences between reasons for punishing employees in the private and public sectors. For example, public sector employees are more frequently punished for sexual harassment and non-performance of professional duties. In the public sector, labour disputes are more often settled in arbitration procedures (Cooper 2012: 195–210). It is generally believed that public sector employees, particularly those working in public administration, enjoy a wider scope of protection—they are more difficult to punish or dismiss. For example, people working in the civil service may have an opportunity to acquire the status of a civil servant. This status "is characterized by a more stable form of employment relationship than in the case of a regular employee of the civil service (a limited statutory catalogue of possibilities for terminating employment relationship), additional benefits (e.g. the civil service allowance, the extra holiday leave" (www5). Such a situation is not a Polish exception. In the US, for example, dismissing a public officer is often possible only after a long process and as the consequence of very serious negligence or crime.

Family businesses and firms with dispersed ownership also use different forms of disciplining and punishing employees. According to various researches, the majority of family businesses fall apart because of family conflicts. Disputes and conflicts often occur in relations between a father and a son as well as between siblings (Cieśla 2016: 39–40). In Saudi Arabia, some large and rich firms have problems with succession, which leads to the division of powers or businesses. Sometimes intervention from the outside is necessary to settle numerous disputes concerning the division of assets or the management of a business (Schumpeter 2016: 58).

In large companies with dispersed ownership, work discipline depends on managers, who are very often hired to make profit. The way in which employees are treated depends on the strength of leadership and the methods followed by mid-level managers.

The division of factors influencing work discipline presented here is not complete, fully exhausting the issues under discussion. Disciplining is a process of interaction taking place between different people; it can also result from playing social games or from unethical or even criminal behaviour. Which disciplinary measures are taken by particular employees depends on their behaviour within an organisation. It is generally believed that disciplining is the prerogative of management. But this is not quite true. Every employee can undertake disciplinary actions, not necessarily formal ones. Work discipline results not only from legal regulations or organisational rules. Its scope and strength are dictated by numerous environmental, structural and situational factors.

1.8   Further Research

From the research conducted so far, we know that work discipline consists, among other things, of assigning responsibility and authority. And in this context, many new research issues appear.

We do not know to what extent assigning decision-making authority strengthens work discipline. Does the possession of authority to make decisions increase the level of responsibility? If the theory of ownership is taken into consideration (every process needs to have its owner), then we conclude that such a relation exists. However, a wider scope of authority means more power and this, in turn, can be the reason for the manifestation of counterproductive behaviour and pursuit of personal goals.

Another interesting research issue is procedural discipline, in particular its influence on product quality and reasons for its maintenance.

In some organisations, work discipline and related employee assessment depend on procedures that are developed by people from outside the organisation. For example, petrol station employees have to strictly follow all customer service procedures. Such procedures specify successive stages of providing a service (from a welcome through an offer of additional products to a thank-you and a goodbye). Compliance with the procedures is controlled by mystery shoppers. All this causes a situation in which employees are not able to act flexibly and adjust to a customer's individual needs. What is more, customer service does not take into account the basic quality assessment criterion, namely time (strict compliance with successive instructions lengthens customer queues). Hence the question arises: why does it happen like that? Maybe the reason is management remuneration systems that are based exclusively on quantitative, and not qualitative, criteria. If a business model allows for the necessity of remunerating employees based on revenues from the sale of additional products, this only intensifies the problem of the low quality of services.

The introduced notion of relational discipline definitely requires further research and theoretical analysis. Despite a considerable body of knowledge concerning the functioning of social systems, we still do not know how, when and to what extent it exerts influence on work discipline. From the sociological point of view, what is important is the balance of a system and centres of control. But we do not know anything about how discipline is influenced by the level of group integration or the quality of interpersonal relations.

Also very little research is conducted into the notion of discipline outside the workplace. Is it possible that this type of discipline is the cause of the lower quality of work or resignations from employment?

H. Arendt introduced the notion of "nobody's responsibility, which is the consequence of 'wandering responsibility'". When work discipline is breached, a question arises of who is responsible for this. Is it employees? What are the true reasons for failures in this respect?

Is it not possible that the victim of unethical behaviour is also partially to blame?

Further research should focus first of all on the notion of spontaneous discipline and antinomy as formulated by H. Dubreuil.

Some contemporary organisations follow double standards of discipline. Talented employees of research and development departments and employees who establish the first contact with customers are treated differently from other employees. Such a method of double supervision of employees is destructive for organisational justice. But is the joint establishment of standards, objectives and tasks enough for free discipline to appear in an organisation? Certainly not always. So how does the restriction of such freedom (in consequence of identifying breaches of work discipline) influence the morale of organisation members?

The fragment about the cultural dimension of discipline stresses that, "against appearances, behavioural models do not have to play the dominant role in employee conduct. Their adaptation and impact on behaviour depend on a large number of different factors (an employee's adjustment potential, possibilities of their manifestation, assessment of their usefulness, etc.)". However, the question arises whether strong cultural models can perform the dominant function. They certainly can. But, on the other hand, there may appear justified doubts about how such models can be shaped in practice. Formally, it seems to be an easy task. We have regulations and ethical codes; we train employees and assess their competences. However, an assessment of models depends on the quality of interpersonal relations and interactions, and they are sometimes changeable.

Another question arises: which elements of organisational cultures, and in which environments, play the superior role in the process of maintaining work discipline?

It has been stated above that work discipline fulfils many functions (deterring, motivational, insuring, educational, corrective, integrating, internalising, socialising and destructive functions). These functions require further research. So far only relations between discipline and work efficiency have been established (Beyer and Trice 1984). There has been very little or no research into discipline under the influence of such factors as rates of unemployment, social pressure, ownership forms of organisations, types of organisation, technical equipment and infrastructure. Against expectations, we know rather little about cultural and religious factors. There is extensive pedagogical literature indicating that teaching methods influence students' discipline. But we know little about what changes occur in "disciplined" graduates and future employees in different types of organisational cultures and to what extent they change their systems of value and convictions. Can business objectives and related remuneration change employees completely and turn them into individuals insensitive to the suffering of other people? The situational theory does not provide explanations for the motives and behaviour of such people.

Furthermore, doesn't this discipline restrict creativity? Isn't it the reason for conformist behaviour being harmful to organisations? What is the difference between submissive discipline and the conscious performance of allocated tasks?

We have some knowledge about the stereotypical perception of employees and their unjust assessment, but we do not know whether such assessments translate into work discipline. Therefore, the last sub-chapter concerning factors influencing discipline is just an introduction to further classifications and research.

References

Argyle, Michael. 1989. *The Social Psychology of Work*. London: Penguin.

Ashrafian, Hutan, Tania Toma, Leanne Harling, Karen Kerr, Thanos Athanasiou, and Ara Darzi. 2004. Improving Care and Health. Social Networking Strategies That Aim To Reduce Obesity Have Achieved Significant Although Modest Results. *Health Affairs* 33 (9): 1641–1647.

Beyer, Janice M., and Harrison M. Trice. 1984. A Field Study of the Use and Perceived Effects of Discipline in Controlling Work Performance. *Academy of Management Journal* 27 (4): 743–764.

Boyd, Brandford B. 1984. *Management-Minded Supervision*. New York: Gregg Division McGraw-Hill Book Company.

Catt, Stephen E., and Donald S. Mille. 1985. *Supervisory Management and Communication*. Ithaca, NY: University Cornell.

Cieśla, Jan. 2016. Rodzina na swoim. *Polityka*, nr 9(3046) z 24.02.2016.

Cooper, Laura J. 2012. Discipline and Discharge of Public-Sector Employees: An Empirical Study of Arbitration Awards. *ABA Journal of Labor & Employment Law, Winter* 27 (2): 195–210.

Disciplining Employees: Myths and Realities. 2015. *Periodical Managing People at Work*, 12/15/ 2 (24).

Doliński, Dariusz. 2005. *Techniki wpływu społecznego*. Warszawa: Scholar.

Dupre, Ben. 2008. *50 teorii filozofii*. Warszawa: PWN.

Enns, Janelle R., and Maria Rotundo. 2012. When Competition Turns Ugly: Collective Injustice, Workgroup Identification, and Counterproductive Work Behavior. *Human Performance* 25 (1): 26–51.

Ertureten, Aysegul, Zeynep Cemalcilar, and Zeynep Aycan. 2013. The Relationship of Downward Mobbing with Leadership Style and Organizational Attitudes. *Journal of Business Ethics* 116 (1): 205–216.

Fandt, Patricia M., Chalmer E. Labig Jr., and Andrew L. Urich. 1990. Evidence and the Liking Bias: Effects on Managers' Disciplinary Actions. *Employee Responsibilities & Rights Journal* 3 (4): 253–265.

Fischer, Eileen, Brenda Gainer, and Julia Bristor. 1997. The Sex of the Service Provider: Does It Influence Perceptions of Service Quality? *Journal of Retailing* 73 (3): 361–382.

Flaherty, Shane, and Simon A. Moss. 2007. The Impact of Personality and Team Context on the Relationship Between Workplace Injustice and Counterproductive Work Behavior. *Journal of Applied Social Psychology* 37 (11): 2549–2575.

Grudzewski, Wiesław M., Irena K. Hejduk, Anna Sankowska, and Monika Wańtuchowicz. 2011. *Sustainability w biznesie czyli przedsiębiorstwo przyszłości. Zmiany paradygmatów i koncepcji zarządzania*. Warszawa: Wyd. Poltex.

Guffey, Cynthia J., and Marilyn M. Helms Dr. 2011. Effective Employee Discipline: A Case of the Internal Revenue Service. *Public Personnel Management* 30 (1): 111–127.

Guza, Łukasz. 2016. Zdejmij burkę przed klientem. *Dziennik-Gazeta Prawna*, A 10–11, 9–11 September.

Haimann, Theo, and Raymond L. Hilgert. 1997. *Supervision. Concepts and Practice of Management*. Chicago: South-Western Publishing.

Hill, Sally Rao, and Alastair Tombs. 2011. The Effect of Accent of Service Employee on Customer Service Evaluation. *Managing Service Quality* 21 (6): 649–666.

Kaushik, Sunil. 2015. Beyond the Carrot and Stick. *Quality Progress* 48 (12): 10.

Leonard, John W. 1968. Discipline for Off-the-Job Activities. *Monthly Labor Review* 91 (10): 5–11.

Li, Ning, Murray R. Barrick, Ryan D. Zimmerman, and Dan S. Chiaburu. 2014. Retaining the Productive Employee: The Role of Personality. *Academy of Management Annals* 8 (1): 347–395.

Lindborg, Henry J. 2015. Management vs. Punishment. *Quality Progress* 48 (10): 56–57.

Marshall, Gordon, ed. 2004. *Słownik socjologii i nauk społecznych*. Warszawa: PWN.

Martyniak, Zbigniew. 2002. *Historia myśli organizatorskiej. Wybitni autorzy z zakresu organizacji i zarządzania w pierwszej połowie XX wieku*. Kraków: Wyd. UE.

Michel, Jesse S., and Nathan A. Bowling. 2013. Does Dispositional Aggression Feed the Narcissistic Response? The Role of Narcissism and Aggression in the Prediction of Job Attitudes and Counterproductive Work Behaviors. *Journal of Business & Psychology* 28 (1): 93–105.

Morgan, Gareth. 1999. *Obrazy organizacji*. Warszawa: PWN.

Nafei, Wageeh A. 2012. The Impact of Organizational Justice and the Personal Characteristics on the Organizational Citizenship Behavior: An Applied Study on the Saudi banks at Al-Taif Governorate. *Journal of King Abdulaziz University: Economics & Administration* 26 (2): 1–78.

Our Friends Electric. 2013. *The Economist*, 7 August.

Plotkin, Thomas I. 2015. Legally Safe Discipline and Discharge: The 4 Key Do's and Don'ts. *HR Specialist: Employment Law*, 45 (7): 7–7.

Priesemuth, Manuela, Anke Arnaud, and Marshall Schminke. 2013. Bad Behavior in Groups: The Impact of Overall Justice Climate and Functional Dependence on Counterproductive Work Behavior in Work. *Units Group & Organization Management* 38 (2): 230–257.

Rogozińska-Pawełczyk, Anna. 2013. Osobowościowe uwarunkowania gotowości pracowników do zmian organizacyjnych. *Zarządzanie Zasobami Ludzkimi* 2 (91): 95–106.

Schoen, Sterling H., and Douglas E. Durand. 1979. *Supervision. The Management of Organizational Resources*. New York: Prentice-Hall.

Schumpeter. 2016. Succession Failure. *The Economist*, 6.02.2016.

Scott, Brent A., and Timothy A. Judge. 2013. Beauty, Personality, and Affect as Antecedents of Counterproductive Work Behavior Receipt. *Human Performance* 26 (2): 93–113.

Shalley, Christina E., Jing Zhou, and Greg R. Oldham. 2004. The Effects of Personal and Contextual Characteristics on Creativity: Where Should We Go from Here? *Journal of Management* 30 (6): 933–958.

Stoner, James A.F., R. Edward Freeman, Daniel R. Gilbert, and Jr. 2001. *Kierowanie*. Warszawa: PWE.

Tepper, Bennett J. 2000. Consequences of abusive supervision. *Academy of Management Journal* 43 (2).

Torrington, Derek, and Laura Hall. 1991. *Personnel Management. A New Approach*. New York: Prentice Hall.

Wei, Feng, and Steven Si. 2013. Tit for Tat? Abusive Supervision and Counterproductive Work Behaviors: The Moderating Effects of Locus of Control and Perceived Mobility. *Asia Pacific Journal of Management* 30 (1): 281–296.

Zinkhan, George M., and Lydia F. Stoiadin. 1984. Impact of Sex Role Stereotypes on Service Priority in Department Stores. *Journal of Applied Psychology* 69 (4): 691.

[www1]. http://www.yourdictionary.com/discipline. Accessed 6 Jan 2016.

[www2]. http://www.dso.uj.edu.pl/akty-prawne/sprawy-dyscyplinarne. Accessed 12 Feb 2016.

[www3]. http://sjp.pwn.pl/sjp/internalizacja;2561811.html. Accessed 12 Mar 2016.

[www4]. http://fortune.com/disrupted-excerpt-hubspot-startup-dan-lyons/. Accessed 26 Mar 2016.

[www5]. https://dsc.kprm.gov.pl/mianowanie. Accessed 31 Dec 2015.

2

Models of Discipline: Self-Discipline and Organisations Without Bosses

2.1 Introduction

There are various models of work discipline; beside the progressive model, in which the strength of punishments is increased gradually, positive discipline models are being introduced with varying degrees of effectiveness. They have been developed and described by many researchers and management practitioners (Osigweh and Hutchison 1989; King and Wilcox 2003; Grote 2001; Grote 2006). Self-discipline is an interesting manifestation of discipline. It is based on the conviction that employees want to work well and share their knowledge with others, and fully accept standards and rules in place in their organisations. Previous publications on this subject indicate that self-discipline plays the key role in implementing and maintaining quality programmes such as lean or six sigma (e.g. Jaca et al. 2014; Cox and Ulmer 2015). It is not only one of the elements of the 5S programme but is also regarded as a crucial factor in the processes of acquiring new knowledge (Duckworth and Seligman 2005) and influencing economic behaviour (Tang et al. 2015). Self-discipline is indispensable in situations of uncertainty (Dongsoo and Starbird 2009)

© The Author(s) 2018
M. Bugdol, *A Different Approach to Work Discipline*,
https://doi.org/10.1007/978-3-319-74008-9_2

and even in the shaping of an organisational culture (Kachoui 2014). A relatively large number of publications have been dedicated to the possibilities of shaping self-discipline (Pepper and Henry 1985; Wayson 1985; Jaca et al. 2014).

Work discipline is the most often studied from the perspective of relations between superiors and subordinates. Thus, does it mean that there is no discipline in organisations without bosses? An answer to this question is given in the last subchapter, which presents characteristic features of organisations without bosses (Southerst 1992; Shawn 2007; Ewalt 2012; Budman 2013; Silverman 2015b).

2.2 The Progressive Discipline Model

According to some sources, the progressive discipline model was developed in the 1930s (Osigweh 1987: 3–40). It is believed that progressive discipline was to be a response to the increasing demands of trade unions. Employers were supposed to impose increasingly severe punishments for subsequent repeatable mistakes, events of offences or unacceptable behaviour.

In the US, the progressive discipline model was described in a statutory document, The National Labor Relations Act (NLRA), and provide for the following four types of punishment to be administered successively: an oral caution, a written caution, suspension and dismissal (King and Wilcox 2003: 197). One of the reasons for following the progressive discipline model is that employers secure themselves against possible legal disputes. If an employee is being dismissed without any previous punishments (cautions, reprimands), labour courts tend to question such decisions (unless dismissal is caused by a serious violation of work discipline rules). In order to avoid legal disputes or internal conflicts, organisations formalise employee-disciplining processes.

In the middle of the 1980s, 90 per cent of British businesses employing more than twenty-five people had formal disciplinary procedures in place. One-third of smaller companies also had such procedures (Edwards 1989).

2.2.1 Progressive Discipline: Not Only Punishments

Although the progressive discipline model provides for a gradual increase in punishments, in practice it is not only punishments that fulfil the deterring function. Some organisations develop recovery plans in which disciplinary talks play the corrective and educational role.

Affirmative discipline is a type of progressive discipline. Although its name implies that employees have their rights and needs, its character is truly progressive. This type of discipline provides for the development of a recovery plan which provides information on further consequences (punishments) for employees, as well as tasks to be carried out by employees in order to eliminate inappropriate behaviour. It focuses on improving employee efficiency and commitment (Human Resource Management in Local Government: An Essential Guide 1999).

As has been mentioned before, the majority of disciplinary programmes have a progressive character, i.e. the severity of punishments has to be increased gradually. Simultaneously, progressive discipline models assume that punished employees (4 Principles for Creating a Progressive Discipline System That Works 2015: 4–5):

- should be afforded opportunity for improvement;
- should be informed clearly about which rules or standards they have breached;
- should be informed in advance about the consequences of inappropriate behaviour.

The great majority of published manuals on disciplining employees are based on the assumption that employees have to be informed accurately about the reasons for their boss's dissatisfaction (particular behaviour, situations or even competences) and have to be provided with an opportunity to correct their mistakes.

When an employee breaches discipline rules, they are first invited to a disciplinary talk, they are then sent a written caution describing the occurring irregularities. The next stage is suspension from duties, followed by the final measure, i.e. dismissal (including disciplinary dismissal).

In the progressive discipline model, a very important role is played by a disciplinary talk which, according to the assumption, should fulfil both the educational and informative functions.

A disciplinary talk with an employee can be conducted by a direct superior; in some organisations, this is the responsibility of the personnel/human resources (HR) department; in others, such talks are attended by trade union representatives or managers from other departments.

"A shop steward is a person representing employees before the employer in matters related to the work environment. A shop steward should care about the interests of all employees in matters important for the work environment". (§6–2(1) The Norwegian labour code (www1)".

Such talks have to be conducted in an atmosphere of trust without any outsiders present. According to existing manuals, an employee should be invited to a disciplinary talk during the course of a work day, but the talk itself should take place after work is finished for the day.

Providing advice on disciplinary talks, specialists claim that (Macdonald and Russell 2015: 20–21):

- the accused employee should be notified in advance (at least two days) of the date of the talk,
- the accused employee should be notified of the objective of the talk (it has to be directly connected to what has been previously written in the procedure),
- the employee has to be ensured the right to demand the presence of other people (e.g. trade union representatives) during the talk,
- if necessary, the employee can receive an internal memorandum (with a detailed justification for the intended punishment, information about which rules have been breached, and on the basis of what data the punishment has been required).

2.2.1.1   Criticism of the Progressive Discipline Model

Practitioners' opinions on progressive discipline are not always positive. It is believed that this model was developed at the time when work processes were dominated by production lines.

This model does not take into account that:

- coming to work, employees do not want to make mistakes,
- employees should be given a chance to learn from mistakes (if each successive punishment is more severe, there is no opportunity for learning).

The majority of publications on this subject emphasise that, in this model, employees are treated like children who do not have their own strong will to change their behaviour. The model is based on the optimistic assumption that the administration of increasingly repressive punishments will cause employees to change their behaviour, while punishments themselves will fulfil the deterring function with respect to other employees. Thus, on the basis of some unknown premises, it is believed that other employees will know about the administration of particular punishments.

In the progressive discipline model, punishments:

A. are to prevent other employees from behaving inappropriately.

There is a serious error in this logic. Punishments are imposed after some negligence has already occurred and been disclosed. We do not know anything about the duration of inappropriate behaviour or costs incurred in connection with it. This model is based not on trust, but on control, which can destroy trust if there is any trust left at all.

B. do not encourage employees to increase their commitment.

In the progressive discipline model, punishments fulfil the moderating function; they are to deter other employees and show them possible consequences of inappropriate behaviour. Imposing subsequent punishments constitutes a serious barrier in the process of getting people involved, getting them to present and pursue their own ideas.

C. do not favour the quality of interpersonal relations.

In the progressive discipline model, superiors do not fulfil the participatory function, do not participate in the whole process of occupational development and frequently limit their own actions to performing the supervisory function.

Specialists in work discipline are of the opinion that discipline that consists of the administration of increasingly harsh punishments can have negative consequences. Firstly, employees can oppose any change (punishments have consequences opposite to those intended); secondly, progressive discipline increases employees' inclination to terminate their employment (King and Wilcox 2003: 197).

The progressive discipline model assumes optimistically that every employee has to be treated the same, irrespective of the held position, occupation, role, function, gender, etc., but practice shows that this is not so simple. The work environment is not deprived of connections, cliques, biases or discrimination.

Conducting a disciplinary talk itself is difficult because it depends on many factors, e.g. relations between the employee being disciplined and the disciplining manager. Another important role during a disciplinary talk is played by the quality of interactions between the participants. The paradox is that punishing destroys the quality of such interactions.

Contrary to appearances, too high a level of social ties does not always increase the effectiveness of disciplinary actions. Too close ties at the workplace hinder an objective and just assessment of behaviour. The research conducted by Rasmusen Report indicates that one-third of employees (present managers and former co-workers) witnessed unethical behaviour, but only half of them reported the manifestations of unethical behaviour to their bosses (Gustaw 2013: 42). Employees do not report the manifestations of unethical behaviour, even if they are obvious, because:

- they are afraid of a possible confrontation;
- they are afraid of their bosses;
- they do not want to be perceived as difficult employees and colleagues (troublemakers).

If there is good communication among employees (mainly between management and regular workers), i.e. bosses provide regular feedback and are able to control their subordinates on an ongoing basis, then a disciplinary punishment is an absolute failure (nobody has reacted early enough). Employees often do not know their bosses' opinions on performed tasks; they are not aware which types of behaviour are acceptable or not. Applied work discipline systems usually provide for punishment for poor work results. However, the problem is that work results do not necessarily depend on employees themselves. E. Deming claimed that 94 per cent of problems with quality resulted from poor management. The literature on the subject emphasises that the lack of information on the factual sources of non-compliance with discipline rules results in a situation where, when punishing employees, they are all treated the same; but we do not know what their individual levels of commitment were, how much effort they devoted to perform their duties, how their work was organised.

Consequently, punishing can cause employees' disbelief in the reality of objectives, the destruction of morale, and forming the impression that some forms of behaviour could be accepted (Bellizzi and Hasty 2000: 154–159).

Developing their work discipline procedures, many organisations supplement the provisions concerning punishments with information about the possibility of appealing against them. However, what remains neglected is the stage of determining the reasons for non-compliance with discipline. When somebody breaches discipline rules, they are usually punished, but for various reasons, the factual causes of inappropriate behaviour are disregarded (see the example below).

Example 1

The company Y punished its marketing department employee, who, as it turned out, had prepared a faulty report on the development of the sales market for products K. Preparing a sales forecast, the employee was using many sources, including commercial reports provided by sales agents. The motivational system for agents provided for an increase in jobs necessary to acquire new customers. But, in order to acquire new customers, agents needed to have larger sales amounts (greater volumes of products) at their disposal. Thus, they informed the company in advance about potential, but not reliably verified sales opportunities.

Example 2

Quality data analysed by the quality assurance department indicated that one of the turners improperly machined a piece of material entrusted to him.

The company had already implemented self-control principles. But it was the final quality inspection that revealed a serious decrease in quality. The employee was deprived of the bonus which depended on the maintenance of the quality standard.

After some time the employee's own investigation revealed that a mistake had been made at one of the earlier stages of production (the material had been removed too early from a furnace). Thus, the lower quality of the final product had been caused not by the turner, but by his colleagues from the same department.

Going through the particular stages of the progressive discipline model, we have to remember a few barriers (Haimann and Hilgert 1997). Firstly, disciplinary talks do not always result in changes in employee behaviour. This is so not only because superiors are not always able to conduct such talks but also for other reasons—inappropriate behaviour is not connected with the employee's ill will (but has other causes that need to be diagnosed earlier).

Secondly, if formal punishments such as cautions or reprimands do not entail any other consequences (e.g. financial ones), they may fail to fulfil the preventive function.

Thirdly, a change of a position within an organisation (e.g. to a position which pays less) is painful because it causes loss of job satisfaction, but simultaneously there may occur a decrease in motivation. What is more, punishments of this type can have a destructive impact on other employees' behaviour (cf. Haimann and Hilgert 1997).

Disciplining employees, especially in its formal variety, is a manifestation of inappropriate employee management. In practice, disciplining is a continuous process; employees who know established standards and work rules function in a particular organisational environment; they know their place in the organisation and know which types of behaviour are desired and which are not.

2.3   The Positive Discipline Model

2.3.1   Genesis

The first models of positive discipline were developed in the 1980s (King and Wilcox 2003: 197). Unlike the case of progressive discipline, they were based on the assumption that employees should be accountable for their actions (they have the will to improve their behaviour). These models have to contain an unambiguous list of expectations established for employees. When a problem appears, employees are not punished, but together with their bosses, they look for ways to avoid such problems in the future. Thus correcting and corrective actions are undertaken jointly.

Correcting actions are taken when both the sources and negative consequences of somebody's behaviour are known. Corrective actions are taken when the causes of inappropriate behaviour remain unknown and only its consequences can be observed. Similarly to quality systems, also in the case of work discipline systems, it is possible to talk about significant irregularities, i.e. ones which are repeatable and cause serious risks, and insignificant irregularities, i.e. ones which are not repeatable and do not cause a high risk of further complications. Thus, it can be stated that the disclosure of a significant irregularity can result from malfunctions in the monitoring system (to some extent, it is a failure of superiors). Within a work discipline system, it is also necessary to calculate the risk of inappropriate behaviour and, if necessary, establish thresholds for allowable concessions.

One of the first positive discipline models was developed for the company Union Carbide.

> The company's management concluded that the traditional work discipline system did not positively influence changes in employee behaviour. The process of implementing a positive model was initiated in 1997, in one of the company's factories without trade unions, located in Brownsville, Texas. The company introduced the following three rules originally called the positive discipline structure. Firstly, relations among employees (including those between superiors and subordinates) have to be based on formal and informal communication.
>
> Secondly, when a problem arises, it has to be solved jointly (two methods were used: coaching and consultations). Thirdly, if consultations, negotiations and the employee support system fail, then three levels of punishment (equivalent to progressive discipline) are used, i.e. an oral warning, a written warning and dismissal.
>
> However, these three successive punishments had a character different to that in progressive discipline. All communications, both oral and written, take into account employees' accountability and their further commitment (e.g. to achieving set objectives).

Formal talks are conducted when previous informal talks and discussions have failed to cause changes in behaviour. Such talks focus on problems concerning behaviour and work standards as well as on expectations related to employee behaviour. Sometimes a memorandum is drawn up at the end of a formal talk; it contains information on what the parties have agreed and further actions to be taken. Before a written warning, an employee is always invited to a talk with an HR employee in order to explain the causes and consequences of inappropriate behaviour. However, a written warning is already a formal document, which is attached to an employee's file. In every case, the company tries to keep the employee's promise that their non-compliant behaviour will be changed. It is important for two reasons. Firstly, if subsequent breaches of discipline occur, the disciplinary talk not only focuses on what has been done wrong but also on previously made promises. Secondly, the employee's failure to keep the promise makes them feel ashamed. If disciplinary talks and written warnings fail, the employee is given a day off with pay (which, in fact, is suspension of duties). After such a break, the employee does not return to work automatically. First, they meet their superior in order to discuss the problem (is the employee able to change their behaviour?)

Source: (Osigweh and Hutchison 1989)

The author of the most popular positive discipline model is D. Grote (2006). According to him, employees have to be guaranteed the opportunity to change their behaviour. In the positive discipline model, superiors fulfil the functions of mentors and coaches. Their role consists of teaching employees appropriate behaviour and the methods of recognising reasons for inappropriate behaviour. During talks, employees should receive information on work standards and what they should do to receive remuneration for work. If such talks are ineffective, they can be conducted in the presence of other people enjoying public trust. The second stage can consist of a written notification in which the essence of the problem is highlighted. A talk is also necessary in this case. The third stage is a day off during which the employee should consider their behaviour. The last stage is a disciplinary and very serious talk called a talk of the last chance or D. Corleone's talk. If the employee continues to make mistakes, it means that they lack particular skills and should be sent for training. According to Grote, informal measures (discussions, instructions) should be taken first. Only when they fail is it possible to use an oral warning, followed by a written warning and eventually to dismiss the troublesome employee. The advocates of positive discipline are of the opinion that punishments should be a last resort.

Today, positive discipline models comprise various forms for disciplining employees, for example, suspension in duties, supervision for a definite period of time or reflective time off. Some companies offer their non-compliant employees last-chance agreements. Others try to use disciplinary measures proposed by employees themselves (King and Wilcox 2003: 197).

2.3.2 Positive Discipline: The Assumptions of the Model

The positive discipline model is based on the assumptions that:

- the traditional, i.e. progressive, disciplining system discourages employees from assuming responsibility for undertaken actions (punishments discourage employees and cause them to be less active and more conservative);

- the models of progressive discipline ignore employees who behave in accordance with the standards and rules in place in organisations;
- precisely defined types of desired behaviour have to supported effectively in discipline systems;
- methods of disciplining should take into account the quality of occurring interactions (important factors include communicative skills, interpersonal trust);
- a disciplining system should provide for the possibility of self-control and re-commitment of employees (Osigweh and Hutchison 1989: 367–383).

Furthermore, it is assumed that: (Grote 2001: 52):

- the positive discipline model is the manifestation of faith in employees (e.g. when the employee receives a day off with pay to analyse their behaviour; it is an expression of the organisation's belief that the employee's behaviour can change);
- some forms of disciplining such as a day off or suspension of duties change anger into guilt or shame;
- positive discipline (also called discipline without punishment) is more acceptable for managers (some of them do not like to punish employees and feel uncomfortable when punishments have to be intensified);
- this form of discipline is adequate for every job (which cannot be said about progressive discipline, e.g. it does not work in the case of managing a research and development department or outstanding specialists demanding autonomy or in the case of following unconventional management methods);
- positive discipline reduces aggressive attitudes oriented towards annoying an organisation (e.g. in the progressive discipline model acts of violence or sabotage occur) and strengthens organisational values.

2.3.2.1   Criticism of the Positive Discipline Model

An analysis of positive discipline models can give rise to a few doubts.

Firstly, following the assumptions concerning the positive discipline model, we must not forget that, despite organisations' faith in employees, some of them cheat, steal, spread rumours, resort to mobbing, etc. With respect to such employees, it is necessary to use the methods of progressive discipline models.

Secondly, there is no evidence that positive discipline models contribute to the improvement of organisational values. Values such as commitment, trust, justice and solidarity depend on many factors (management methods, justice of human resource management procedures, an organisational climate and culture, personnel policy, etc.). It is easy to upset a value system by using double standards in the treatment of employees, which is highly probable (e.g. in multicultural organisations). Employees are not treated the same.

Thirdly, positive sanctions (disciplinary talks, days off, supervision for a definite period of time, suspension) used in the positive discipline model can appear to be more severe for particular employees than a caution or reprimand.

Supervision of employees may cause them to make even more mistakes (they will not have an opportunity to learn from their own mistakes).

Fourthly, it cannot be assumed that positive discipline is more acceptable for managers. The application of sanctions can be as difficult as the administration of punishments (the stages of positive discipline are, in their own right, punishments). Some managers do not impose punishments provided for in progressive discipline systems.

For many years I've been the director of a printing company. I don't use any punishments; I just talk to people and try to have influence on their recruitment in the first place. I think that punishing people is pointless. Why should you punish someone? Punishment means that we don't understand each other and can't cooperate. Punishing people results in bad interpersonal relations.

I follow an open-door policy. After all, people bring different experiences from their previous jobs and this influences their behaviour. Once a new employee didn't receive her salary on time and only after a few days did she report having financial problems. It turned out that our payroll department had forgotten to enter her in the system. We corrected the error quickly.

> The employee came to my office and thanked me for taking care of her problem immediately. I couldn't believe that. It was me who should be apologising to her. Now she's one of the best employees in the company (managing director in a printing company employing 250 employees).

Fifthly, there is no evidence that positive discipline sanctions encourage employees to assume responsibility for actions undertaken or increase their commitment (commitment depends directly on organisational trust).

2.4   Self-Discipline

S.H. Schoen and D.E. Durand (Schoen and Durand 1979) claim that people are predisposed to act in accordance with social standards. This is determined by their upbringing system. People are afraid that disregard for applicable standards will be frowned upon. Behaviour that is oriented towards cooperation is connected with rewards, even if the award is the absence of punishment or fear. By participating in various social groups, people learn to cooperate, become aware that behaving in accordance with standards is to a certain extent a limitation of their freedom, but that cooperation with other group members can be profitable. Breaking the rules and standards in place in a social group causes misunderstandings, disputes and conflicts. It usually results in various punishments imposed by the whole group (e.g. social isolation) or particular individuals (not necessarily by group leaders).

Therefore, employees realise that all manifestations of insubordination can lead to punishment, but punishment itself is not the most important factor in shaping appropriate attitudes; what counts is a system of education, employees' convictions and needs. Self-discipline is based on the conviction that employees want to work well and share their knowledge with others, and accept standards and rules in place in their organisations. But self-discipline is something that employees need to be taught. For example, in quality management, considerable time is spent on maintaining order at the workplace, controlling quality individually and helping those who have problems with complying with quality standards. When work instructions or procedures are changed, it is the responsibility of superiors, first, to establish new requirements with employees and, second, to convince employees that the introduced changes are justified. Self-discipline also results from the fact that employees are aware of the negative consequences that they may face if intra-organisational regulations are ignored; maintaining health and safety at work (OHS) discipline is a case in point.

Although known and dominant in some tools used in Total Quality Management (e.g. in 5S), the problem of self-discipline is a rarely approached research topic.

The research conducted so far indicates that self-discipline is very important where some changes have already been introduced and have to be maintained, e.g. in the process of implementing lean tools (Jaca et al. 2014; Cox and Ulmer 2015). Self-discipline is one of the factors important for the knowledge assimilation process (Duckworth and Seligman 2005) and influences economic behaviour (Tang et al. 2015). It is a tool allowing its user to cope in situations of uncertainty (Dongsoo and Starbird 2009) as well as a crucial factor in shaping organisational cultures (Kachoui 2014). A relatively large number of researchers and consultants demonstrate the possibilities of shaping self-discipline (Pepper and Henry 1985; Wayson 1985; Jaca et al. 2014). However, we know that such possibilities are limited because they result from the type of work, personality traits, as well as situational, structural and other factors.

2.4.1 Definitions of Self-Discipline. Related Notions

Self-discipline is defined in different ways. It is believed that self-discipline is:

- an internal process aimed at correcting one's own behaviour in order to improve operational effectiveness (Pepper and Henry 1985: 264);
- an ability and will to undertake actions resulting from the existence of particular needs (such actions are being performed until the needs have been fulfilled) (Rogus 1985);
- the most effective form of discipline (Rogus 1985: 271);

- a process in which the internalisation of the rules in place in a given organisation takes place (individuals accept such rules when they have become familiar with them and when they know the organisation's objectives (Curtin 1996: 51–52).

The notion of self-discipline appears in the positive discipline model. It is absurd to assume that every employee requires supervision, punishing or corrections in their work. The positive discipline model assumes that there are employees who are responsible for their actions; their characteristic feature is self-discipline (Osigweh and Hutchison 1989: 367–383).

The notion of self-discipline is related to other notions such as self-control, self-assessment (a sense of self-worth), self-certainty and self-regulation.

Self-control is the ability to control one's emotions and to regulate one's impulses and desires in relations with others (Baumeister 2015: 60–65). But there is no general agreement on whether self-control can be regarded as typical control because it is not related, at least directly, with exerting influence on other people (Das and Teng 1998: 491–512).

Self-control is only one of the elements of self-discipline. In some business enterprises, self-control results from the character of work and is secured (e.g. by means of check sheets where employees enter results of self-control).

Self-discipline depends on an employee's sense of self-worth and dignity. A high level of dignity is connected with feeling good in an organisation, but excessive self-assessment can be related to aggressive behaviour and biases (Vaughan et al. 2014: 299–310). A sense of well-performed self-control can strengthen an individual's self-assessment.

Self-discipline is related to the phenomenon of self-certainty.

The research conducted so far indicates that self-certainty influences the process of self-assessment, the pursuit of objectives and a sense of satisfaction. People with great self-certainty can adjust better to changing conditions in the environment (Wu and Yao 2007). Self-certainty, or a sense of certainty, has a considerable influence on the rationality of control. Somebody who is certain of their conduct and the decisions they have made is convinced that they know how to behave in particular situations (Baumgardner 1990: 1062–1072).

Self-discipline also requires self-regulation, i.e. the ability to assimilate socially acceptable behaviour, despite the absence of external monitoring (Maxwell 1989: 149–155).

2.4.1.1   Self-Discipline as an Element of the 5S Method

In quality management, the term self-discipline appears in the context of applying the 5S method. The 5S system comprises sorting, setting in order, shining, standardising and self-discipline. The Japanese word *Shitsuke* means building and maintaining self-discipline.

The term self-discipline, which appears in the description of the 5S method, is translated into English as "sustain" and means that what has been done or established will be maintained (e.g. Cox and Ulmer 2015: 70–77). The 5S method includes the notions of discipline and self-discipline. Self-discipline, or rather its shaping, consists of developing the skills necessary to do what should be done or what is expected. On the other hand, according to Hirano, discipline is developing habits of maintaining procedures (Jaca et al. 2014: 4574–4586). According to C. Wiśniewski, self-discipline means "complying with understanding with all rules in place in the company". It can also be referred to as using appropriate procedures in a routine manner (Wiśniewski 2010: 41).

The literature emphasises that the 5S method has to take into consideration cultural factors and organisational values such as trust, increasing autonomy, participation and commitment. Among the 5S, it is self-discipline, related to the ability to maintain positive changes, which is the most difficult to achieve. It requires perseverance and self-motivation. The effectiveness of applying the 5S method depends on good communication, employee attitudes and generally on the organisational culture (O'hEocha 2000: 321–330).

2.4.1.2   The Significance of Self-Discipline

There is little detailed research into the importance of self-discipline in the area of management sciences. This problem is relatively well described in the pedagogical literature (the first articles on self-discipline started to be published in the 1950s). Self-discipline is one of the factors differentiating students' ability to learn (Duckworth and Seligman 2005: 939–944). The research on such differentiation takes into account intellectual qualities, including long-term memory and the ability to think abstractly. Meanwhile, self-discipline belongs to extra-intellectual qualities (besides motivation). The aforementioned qualities are of key importance in the process of learning.

Thus, it can be assumed that the same importance can be attached to self-discipline in the process of assimilating knowledge by employees.

Research confirms that people who have the ability to discipline themselves are more responsible in financial behaviour (Tang et al. 2015: 376–406).

Self-discipline is a tool allowing the user to cope in situations of uncertainty and is therefore the subject of research taking into account the principal-agent problem (Dongsoo and Starbird 2009: 289–304). Self-disciplined people cope better at school and at work, are healthier, have better intimate relations and are even less exposed to criminal behaviour (Baumeister 2015: 60–65).

Some practitioners emphasise that self-discipline, like self-education or self-initiative, is an important factor in the shaping of the quality culture (e.g. Kachoui 2014: 10–11).

2.4.2 Possibilities of Developing Self-Discipline

One of the techniques of developing self-discipline is "assuming responsibility for one's actions". Developing self-discipline (understood as increasing responsibility for one's actions) requires that encouraging actions be undertaken (e.g. training activities, getting employees involved in projects, etc.) (Pepper and Henry 1985: 264).

Developing self-discipline requires the commitment of the whole personnel (Wayson 1985: 227). Self-discipline requires internal determination and the conviction that it is worth being self-disciplined, but in the work environment, it is important for employees working on their self-discipline to receive support from others. It is important to lead from the front and provide evidence that bosses are also self-disciplined.

The elements of developing self-discipline include assessing the effects of undertaken actions and drawing conclusions for the future (Rogus 1985). It is important for employees to be convinced that self-discipline makes work easier (e.g. there is less work to do) and to reward themselves for work performed well. And in the event of any obstacles, barriers or mistakes, they should be able to carry out a thorough analysis of the sources of the problems with maintaining self-discipline.

Research also indicates that self-discipline has to be promoted; it requires an environment favourable for learning processes (Rogus 1985: 271).

An assessment of self-discipline development takes into consideration the progress made so far. Progress can be described by means of self-reports or reports prepared by other people (e.g. superiors), but such assessments are a difficult task.

One of the methods of developing self-discipline is working in one particular area of specialisation. Self-discipline in one area should lead to its development in other areas (Trunk 2009).

Organisations following the lean or TQM principles shape their employees' habits in various ways: they train them or allow them to perform tasks on their own (learning from one's own mistakes); during training activities, they have members of management perform operations that are the responsibility of regular workers (Jaca et al. 2014: 4574–4586).

Implementing self-discipline, the organisation motivates employees "to try to improve their workplace continuously, without their superiors' instructions" (Wiśniewski 2010: 41). In the 5S method, self-discipline consists of following procedures, but, according to some authors, it is important that employees "take active part in the establishment of standards and their further development" (Staniewska and Pałęga 2012: 586). In Japan, the 5S method is some kind of philosophy of action (similarly to TQM). It is a holistic concept requiring that employees be trained and encouraged to participate in order to increase their autonomy and commitment (Gapp et al. 2008: 565–579).

Talking about the possibilities of developing self-discipline, we have to remember that:

- self-discipline should be taught, but this requires special competences and knowledge of processes (e.g. all key processes and their particular stages);

- people behave differently in different situations (e.g. a given employee may need to be reprimanded at work, but outside their organisation, they behave appropriately);
- people learn appropriate behaviour under the influence of standards in place in the environment and therefore, learning how to behave appropriately consists, among other things, of shaping the normative environment.

Self-discipline depends not only on individual personality traits, management styles or standards concerning effort made at work. It can be assumed that employees' experiences influence their self-discipline. According to some authors, the level of self-discipline among Polish workers is lower than that of their Japanese counterparts (Krasiński 2013: 145–153). Some research has shown that self-discipline can be influenced by gender. Women display a higher level of self-discipline (Duckworth and Seligman 2006: 198–208).

To sum up, self-discipline is the highest form of discipline. For self-discipline to appear, many conditions have to be met. The basic conditions are as follows:

- employees' participation in establishing objectives (despite numerous limitations such as mutually exclusive expectations);
- clearly defined cooperation rules and principles;
- a self-regulation system (a group tries to correct all deviations from the social standards itself);
- awareness that cooperation is profitable (it is connected with rewards and not with punishments).

Most employees know that they can count on their superiors' support as long as they fulfil their expectations (i.e. they act in accordance with the social standards). Self-discipline is possible only when it is demonstrated by the superiors themselves (cf. Haimann and Hilgert 1997: 278). These two conditions have to be kept in mind at the beginning of the process of developing a discipline system.

2.5   Organisations Without Bosses

Traditional organisations dominated mainly by mid-level managers are increasingly replaced by a new organisational model referred to as holacracy, or organisations without bosses. Holacracy destroys the traditional model of supervision in which superiors supervise their subordinates. In the years 2005–2015, more than 300 American organisations, including those from the public sector (the Washington State government) and various consulting firms (e.g. David Allen Co), implemented this management model (Silverman 2015b). Thus, the following question arises: what kind of discipline are they characterised by? There is no systematic research into this subject, but descriptions of organisations without bosses are available (Southerst 1992; Shawn 2007; Ewalt 2012; Budman 2013); what is also known to some extent are the conditions of implementing this new organisational form, as well as the obstacles encountered by employees in this process (e.g. Silverman 2015b).

The case of the company Valve:
  In 1996 Gabe Newell, a former Microsoft employee, established the company Valve. His firm was to function without managers and thus without top–bottom management. Valve operates according to the following rules (Guza: 18–19):

- when an employee has an idea for a project, they report it to the other employees and try to persuade them to accept it;
- tasks are carried out within teams which determine division of work and objectives;
- employees have considerable freedom in the performance of their duties (e.g. they can work from home).

  According to *Forbes*, the value of Valve was estimated at 2 billion US dollars in 2016. Other specialists think it could be worth as much as 3 billion US dollars.

Gabe Newell has a majority stake in Valve. The company quite carefully launches new products in the market, just a few games each year. In 2011 Portal 2 was generally regarded as one of the best games of the year (Ewalt 2012: 77–78). Gabe Newell is also cautious about outsourcing. He admits that success in business must depend not just on employing the cheapest labour, but on searching for the best specialists. According to "the Valve philosophy", the recruitment process is the most important. This approach is connected with risk management in the company (many outsourced projects end up in failure). Cooperation with customers, listening to their opinions and ideas are very important tasks (Shawn 2007: 40–41).

Company employees decide about their salaries and can work wherever they want (there are no desks allocated to particular employees). Once a year the staff go on a holiday together. The company has a flat organisational structure. Thus, there is no reason to introduce a formal reporting system (www2).

The case of Ciba-Geigy Canada Ltd.:

The chemical company Ciba-Geigy Canada Ltd. increased its productivity by 20 per cent by introducing a work organisation system without bosses. The employees were entrusted with the tasks that previously had been the domain of the management. The employees plan their work themselves, manage costs, determine scopes of work, make decisions concerning personnel matters, and participate in making both strategic and everyday decisions. The company dismissed half of its managers and the employees themselves decide about any further dismissals. The roles of the remaining managers changed. For example, the production manager became a consultant (Southerst 1992: 46).

The case of the company Semco:

Semco is one of the most famous companies using the management system without bosses.

After taking the company over from his father, R. Samler dismissed 60% of the management.

In Semco, it is the employees who decide about production volumes or what hotels to book during business trips. The company functions very wel,l even when Semler is away (The Case for a 'Bossless' Organisation 2015: 94–97). When Semler is on holiday, he does not check what his employees are doing. It is surprising that Semco has increased its efficiency and profits significantly.

The company's basic management principle are as follows:

- information transparency and accessibility;
- all employees' participation in profit sharing;
- democracy.

Semco does not have any procedures or dress codes. In 2012 the company increased its profits by 40 per cent.

There are not inspections or audits; the owner claims that it is a bad idea to humiliate the majority of the employees in order to identify a few dishonest ones (e.g. opportunist thieves). Semco has replaced specialist departments with simple organisational units. Semler believes that one such unit should have no more than 150 employees (in order to ensure ties among them). Semco has only three levels in its organisational structure: consultant, partner and co-worker. Consultants (there are six of them) provide other employees with general lines of action. Partners are heads of organisational units. Some co-workers are team leaders; then they are called coordinators. Nobody is hired or promoted without the acceptance of co-workers.

Every year all employees provide feedback on the reliability of their leaders and the company itself. Decisions, especially important ones, are made by voting (sometimes even Semler's proposals are voted down). Twice a year, 23 per cent of profit (after tax) is allocated to organisational units. Three elects decide about the distribution of profits. In the majority of units (all of which have profit distribution plans), all employees have the same share in profits (Budman 2013: 1–1).

2.5.1   Self-Managed Teams

Self-managed teams were a substitute for organisations without bosses. A self-managed team usually consists of 5–30 employees who are authorised to manufacture a product or provide a service and are not subject to direct supervision, or supervision is limited to the minimum. A team free from strict supervision learns from its own mistakes. From a long-term perspective, such a process of acquiring knowledge strengthens one's confidence in oneself and one's abilities. Self-managed teams are used in such corporations as Digital, FMC, Frito-Lay, GE, General Foods, GM, Hewlett-Packard, Honeywell, and Pepsi-Cola (Barry 1991: 31–47).

It has been observed that work effectiveness depends on team members' communication skills and whether individual employees are able to focus entirely on pursuing and achieving objectives (Barry 1991: 31–47).

Self-managed teams are not deprived of leadership. What is more, some researchers (e.g. Barry 1991) only confirm the generally known presumptions, claiming that leadership is difficult. It requires the knowledge of not only the traditional management techniques (e.g. preparing schedules, supervising employees, planning activities, allocating resources) but also communication techniques, group coherence and information sharing. Some organisations maintain the function of an external leader of self-managed employee teams. An external leader is a typical manager. Research shows (e.g. Druskat and Wheeler 2001: F1–F6) that the role of an external leader is to support the idea of self-management, coordinate, support teams, build appropriate relations, provide necessary information and empower other employees (Greenfield 2015).

Without leadership, self-managed teams are troubled by unnecessary tensions and conflicts over the division of power (Barry 1991). The dynamics of self-managed teams are much more complicated than in traditional teams. It is even believed that previous leadership theories (e.g. the style-based theory, the situational theory or the functionalist theory) are no longer valid.

In some organisations, self-management occurs only in employee teams dealing with one particular matter, e.g. quality improvement. This form of work teaches self-discipline, but it can also create a conflict of roles.

Janusz was a specialist in product research and development. He reported directly to the head of his organisational unit. In March 1999 he was appointed a member of the team responsible for developing a new strategy for the company. The team was supervised by the deputy president responsible for production. After some time Janusz and the vice president became friends. Their families started to visit one another. His work in the team responsible for strategy was assessed very highly, but his work in his organisational unit very negatively. A conflict developed between the head of a functional unit and the vice president of the company.

2.5.2   Conditions for the Existence of Organisations Without Bosses: Difficulties With Implementation

Holacracy is successful where employees are independent, responsible and simultaneously willing to cooperate. In holacracy, employees do not have professional titles, but it is important to determine their roles precisely and make them fully responsible for undertaken actions, including promises that they give themselves.

It is believed that the whole process of implementing holacracy can take up to a few years. Before the implementation of a new form of work organisation, it is necessary to assess employees' competences and to develop their soft competences, i.e. ones related to cooperation, communication, expressing trust or self-disciplining. Holacracy does not mean anarchy; before it is implemented, meetings are organised in order to determine organisational order (who does what? who is responsible for what?). Holacracy requires a long period of adjustment, a series of training courses and sessions.

In some companies, the initial stage of introducing holacracy resulted in some confusion (Silverman 2015b). On the one hand, organisations without bosses pursue the empowerment of their employees and want them to focus on changes; on the other hand, there is a lot of talk about the lack of power. Employees, especially those accustomed to the traditional management methods, find it difficult to perform autonomous work. Therefore, some employees resign. Since 2015 the company Zappos has not had any managers. Since the implementation of holacracy, fourteen per cent of the staff have resigned (Silverman 2015a: A1–A10).

2.5.2.1 Discipline in Organisations Without Bosses

When asked how they imagine organisations without bosses, students who work for various companies answer that such work organisation is impossible in this country (Poland) and would result in the destruction of any business. Without bosses, people would most probably do very little, smoke cigarettes or play cards. Although quite widespread, this opinion is wrong.

Firstly, there are various forms of leadership in organisations without bosses (coordinators, shift leaders, informal leaders). Work is coordinated by co-workers and leaders. Discipline results from the fact that every employee knows their tasks and duties.

Secondly, organisations without bosses are characterised by a slightly different type of discipline which can be referred to as friendly discipline or team discipline. Results depend on cooperation and the extent to which particular employees can adjust to overall requirements (this does not apply to all positions). Employee behaviour is observed and frequently corrected by employees themselves. Many decisions are made in a team and employees have to establish objectives and tasks together. Work control consists of self-control, but it is secured by social control (all decisions, even financial ones, are transparent).

Thirdly, new employees have to pass an examination on the rules of the new form of work. They are being disciplined already at this stage. For example, they are required to be punctual (if they are not, they are dismissed).

Fourthly, holacracy demands enormous self-discipline (money is often the driving force, e.g. in the Semco company, employees are guaranteed a considerable share in profits).

2.6   Further Research

The progressive discipline model is a model in which the severity of successive punishments increases gradually. The problem is whether such punishments are effective and whether they are perceived to be in the category of punishment at all. A written caution entered in personnel files is not always followed by subsequent financial penalties. A caution may make an employee feel shame, but it is not a real or heavy punishment. It does not fulfil the educational function and does not restore justice (if justice has been breached). Both work discipline models have been reviewed critically. Neither of them is perfect. For example, the positive discipline model does not take into consideration the input data of an educational process.

There is much advice about conducting disciplinary talks. According to the literature on the subject, the effectiveness of such talks depends on the following factors:

- the knowledge of the true reasons for breaches of discipline;
- the skills of superiors.

However, there is no research referring to the third factor, namely, the competences, attitudes and motives of the accused person.

We also do not know how effective last-chance agreements are. In the case of such agreements, a lot depends on the level of superiors' intervention. Most probably if this level is very high, deprived of their freedom, employees tend to make subsequent or new mistakes.

There is no research into the consequences of the diversified disciplining of employees (both within large organisations and in external relations, e.g. contractors and subcontractors). It is difficult to assume that the models of positive and progressive discipline are generally known and used. There are many ways of punishing and educating employees. A lot depends on such factors as age, gender, contacts, biases and experiences. While research in the field of pedagogy has shown that self-discipline is of considerable importance in the process of assimilating knowledge, the management sciences accept silently the same relations. One of the elements of self-discipline is self-assessment. It should be remembered that excessive self-assessment can entail aggressive behaviour and biases. Hence, establishing what role is played by self-discipline in the knowledge management system could be an interesting research topic. It is also difficult to talk about self-discipline in various concepts of quality-oriented management where "self-discipline" is connected with compliance with applicable procedures. It can happen that a proposal to change a procedure will be regarded as a breach of discipline, even if it is objectively correct but uncomfortable for other employees. Therefore, whether self-discipline should be an element of 5S programmes deserves further research.

Organisations without bosses constitute an extremely interesting testing ground for researchers specialising in sociology, psychology or management sciences because there is no research identifying and hierarchising factors influencing friendly discipline.

References

4 Principles for Creating a Progressive Discipline System That Works. 2015. *HR Specialist: New York Employment Law* 10(2).

Barry, David. 1991. Managing the Bossless Team: Lessons in Distributed Leadership. *Organizational Dynamics* 20 (1, Summer): 31–47.

Baumeister, Roy F. 2015. Conquer Yourself, Conquer the World. *Scientific American* 312 (4): 60–65.

Baumgardner, Ann H. 1990. To Know Oneself is to Like Oneself: Self-Certainty and Self-Affect. *Journal of Personality and Social Psychology* 58 (6): 1062.

Bellizzi, Joseph A., and Ronald W. Hasty. 2000. The Effects of Hiring Decisions on the Level of Discipline Used in Response to Poor Performance. *Management Decision* 38 (3): 154–159.

Budman, Matthew. 2013. Openers. *Conference Board Review* 50 (4, Fall).

Cox, Cody R., and Jeffrey M. Ulmer. 2015. Lean Manufacturing: An Analysis of Process Improvement Techniques. *Franklin Business & Law Journal* 2015 (2): 70–77.

Curtin, Leah L. 1996. Ethics, Discipline and Discharge. *Nursing Management* 27 (3): 51.

Das, T.K., and Bing-Sheng Teng. 1998. Between Trust and Control: Developing Confidence in Partner Cooperation in Alliances. *Academy of Management Review, nr* 23 (3): 491–512.

Dongsoo, Shin, and S. Andrew Starbird. 2009. Risk Taking as Self Discipline in Contractual Relationships. *International Journal of the Economics of Business* 16 (3): 289–304.

Druskat, Vanessa Urch, and Jane V. Wheeler. 2001. Managing from the Boundary: The Effective Leadership of Self-Managing Work Teams. *Academy of Management Proceedings & Membership Directory* 46 (4): 435–457.

Duckworth, Angela L., and Martin E.P. Seligman. 2006. Self-Discipline Gives Girls the Edge:Gender in Self-Discipline, Grades, and Achievement Test Scores. *Journal of Educational Psychology* 98 (1): 198.

———. 2005. Self-Discipline Outdoes IQ in Predicting Academic Performance of Adolescents. *Psychological Science (Wiley-Blackwell)* 16 (12): 939–944.

Edwards, Paul K. 1989. The Three Faces of Discipline. In *Personnel Management in Britain*, ed. Keith Sissons. Oxford: Basil Blackwell.

Ewalt, David M. 2012. Valve's Gabe Newell Is The Newest Video Game Billionaire. Forbes.com. 3/7/.

Gapp, Rod, R. Ron Fisher, and Kaoru Kobayashi. 2008. Implementing 5S Within a Japanese Context: An Integrated Management System. *Management Decision* 46 (4): 565–579.

Greenfield, Rebecca. 2015. THE FUTURE IS BOSSLESS. *Business Week*, 7/13/, Issue 4434.

Grote, Dick. 2001. Discipline Without Punishment. *Across the Board* 38 (5): 52–57.

————. 2006. *Discipline Without Punishment*. New York: AMACOM.

Gustaw, Grzegorz. 2013. Prawdziwych przyjaciół poznajesz w pracy. *Poradnik Psychologiczny Polityki*, tom 11, nr 2.

Guza, Łukasz. Pracownik bez żadnych ograniczeń. *Gazeta Prawna*, nr 54 (4201).

Haimann, Theo, and Raymond L. Hilgert. 1997. *Supervision. Concepts and Practice of Management*. Chicago: South-Western Publishing.

Human Resource Management in Local Government: An Essential Guide. 1999. *International City/County Management Association*. Washington, DC: International City/Council Management Association.

Jaca, Carmen, Elisabeth Viles, Luis Paipa-Galeano, Javier Santos, and Ricardo Mateo. 2014. Learning 5S Principles from Japanese Best Practitioners: Case Studies of Five Manufacturing Companies. *International Journal of Production Research* 52 (15): 4574–4586.

Kachoui, David. 2014. Restaurant Day. *Quality Progress* 47(8).

King, Karen N., and Denise E. Wilcox. 2003. Employee-Proposed Discipline: How Well is it Working? *Public Personnel Management* 32 (2, Summer): 197–209.

Krasiński, Marek. 2013. Ewolucja form pracy zespołowej w wybranych japońskich przedsiębiorstwach w Polsce. *Acta Universitatis Lodziensis. Folia Oeconomica* 283, 2013.

Macdonald, Lynda, and Tim Russell. 2015. *Dealing With Discipline*. Employers Law, November.

Maxwell, Jennifer P. 1989. Mediation in the Schools: Self-Regulation, Self-Esteem, and Self-Discipline. *Mediation Quarterly* 7 (2, Winter): 149–155.

O'hEocha, Mary. 2000. A Study of the Influence of Company Culture, Communications and Employee Attitudes on the Use of 5Ss for Environmental Management at Cooke Brothers Ltd. *The TQM Magazine* 12 (5): 321–330.

Osigweh, Chimezie A.B. Yg. 1987. Communication, Responsibilities and Pro-Rights Revolution in the Industrial Workplace. In *Communicating Employee Responsibilities and Rights: A Modern Management Mandate*, ed. Chimezie A.B.Yg. Osigweh. New York: Quorum Books.

Osigweh, Chimezie A.B. Yg, and William R. Hutchison. 1989. Positive Discipline. *Human Resource Management* 28 (3, Fall): 387.

Pepper, Floy C., and Steven L. Henry. 1985. Using Developmental and Democratic Practices to Teach Self-Discipline. *Theory Into Practice* 24 (4, Autumn): 264–270.

Rogus, Joseph F. 1985. Promoting Self-Discipline: A Comprehensive Approach. *Theory Into Practice* 24 (4, Autumn): 271–276.

Schoen, Sterling H., and Douglas E. Durand. 1979. *Supervision. The Management of Organizational Resources*. New York: Prentice-Hall.

Shawn, Elliott. 2007. Quickfire Interview. *Games for Windows* (2), January.

Silverman, Rachel Emma. 2015a. Going Bossless Backfires at Zappos (Cover Story). *Wall Street Journal—Eastern Edition*, 5/21/, 265(118), A1–A10. 2p. 3.

———. 2015b. At Zappos, Banishing the Bosses Brings Confusion. *Wall Street Journal* (Online). 5/21/.

Southerst, John. 1992. First, We Dump the Bosses. *Canadian Business* 65 (4): 46–51.

Staniewska, Ewa, and Michał Pałęga. 2012. Możliwe obszary doskonalenia procesów logistycznych z wykorzystaniem rozwiązań Kaizen. *Logistyka*, nr 6.

Tang, Ning, Andrew Baker, and Paula C. Peter. 2015. Investigating the Disconnect between Financial Knowledge and Behavior: The Role of Parental Influence and Psychological Characteristics in Responsible Financial Behaviors among Young Adults. *Journal of Consumer Affairs* 49 (2, Summer): 376–406.

The Case for a 'Bossless' Organisation. 2015. *Business Today*, 7/5/, 24 (13).

Trunk, Penelope. 2009. How to Have More Self-Discipline. http://blog.penelopetrunk.com/2009/07/08/how-to-have-more-self-discipline. Accessed 30 Mar 2016.

Vaughan, Jessica, Virgil Zeigler-Hill, and Randolph C. Arnau. 2014. Self-Esteem Instability and Humor Styles: Does the Stability of Self-Esteem Influence How People Use Humor? *Journal of Social Psychology* 154 (4): 299–310.

Wayson, William W. 1985. Opening Windows to Teaching: Empowering Educators to Teach Self-Discipline. *Theory Into Practice* 24 (4, Autumn): 227–232.

Wiśniewski, Cezary. 2010. Wpływ wdrożenia zasad Lean Manufacturing na efektywność i jakość produkcji. *Problemy Eksploatacji*, nr 2.

Wu, Chia-huei, and Grace Yao. 2007. Relations Among Self-Certainty, Sense of Control and Quality of Life. *International Journal of Psychology* 42 (5): 342–352.

[www1]. http://www.arbeidstilsynet.no/binfil/download2.php?tid=226656. Accessed 13 Nov 2015.

[www2]. http://www.bbc.com/news/technology-24205497.

3

The Control and Punishment of Employees

3.1 Introduction

In the past, various forms of punishment, including corporal punishment, were used. Describing the role of punishment in the maintenance of quality, H. Drummond gives an example of punishment from 1382: "Then five burghers came to the mayor. They were shown two pieces of rotten and smelly fish, which they had bought that same day. The fishmonger was punished severely for the bad quality of the fish. He was pilloried for one hour, was obliged to return 6 pence to the aggrieved customers, and the fish—in accordance with the verdict of the elders—was burnt in the presence of the dishonest seller" (Drummond 1998: 15).

Punishments fulfilled various functions; they not only resulted from concern for the assurance of quality but also were supposed to maintain trust within social networks. For example, Jewish merchants used multilateral punishments. When somebody cheated one of a group of businesspeople, all other partners refused to cooperate with such a crook. Fraudsters were put on special lists containing names of people with whom it was forbidden to trade.

© The Author(s) 2018
M. Bugdol, *A Different Approach to Work Discipline*,
https://doi.org/10.1007/978-3-319-74008-9_3

In various organisations different forms of punishment took place and continue to do so. For example, in military organisations, discipline has always been of primary importance. In communist Poland, informal punishment imposed by older soldiers on "cats" (a slang expression for newly drafted conscripts) frequently replaced formal forms of maintaining discipline. Young recruits were victims of elaborately cruel forms of punishment. They were frequently not so much punishment as acts of revenge for having been treated with equal cruelty by older recruits a year before. Even worse forms of punishment were administered in the past. For example, the ancient Macedonian army used gang rape as punishment (a known victim of such punishment was Pausanias, a soldier in the army of Philip, the father of Alexander the Great).

With time, various countries codified their methods of imposing punishment on employees in legal acts. For example, until 1875 the English law had allowed employers to punish their employees if they failed to comply with their employment agreements. According to the provisions of the Master&Servant Law, an employee could be subjected to punishment meted out by the court. Between 1858 and 1875, British courts received over 10,000 petitions for the punishment of employees (e.g. for demanding higher wages by organising strikes, abandoning work, etc.) (Woś 2016: A32).

This chapter discusses reasons for the use of punishment. The various researches conducted so far indicate the importance of the following factors: employees' personality traits and previous experiences (Bellizzi and Hasty 2000), poor results (Podsakoff 1982), employers' relationships with employees (Fandt et al. 1990) and personal complexes (Kohn 1993). The use of punishment has various consequences, which will be described in the next subchapter. Researchers differ in their opinions on the results of punishment (O'Reilly and Weitz 1980; Smith et al. 1967). Although punishment causes changes in behaviour, these are usually short-lived (Connellan 1978). Greater changes in behaviour are achieved by means of rewards, which are a neglected element in discipline maintenance. Research on the role of rewards in the shaping of discipline has been conducted, for example, by Deci and Ryan (1980), Podsakoff et al. (1981), Strid and Andréasson (2007). The models of progressive discipline and positive discipline provide for the use of various formal punishments.

But in practice, many informal punishments are administered. On the basis of his own research, the author describes the most frequent informal punishments (including those imposed on managers). The part devoted to the punishment of employees has been supplemented with a description of the conditions in which punishments are meted out, as well as the problems related to their administration.

The punishment of employees is connected with their control. The chapter describes the development of the control functions, the types of control (budgetary, strategic, documentary, functional, process-based, preliminary, ex-post, comprehensive, fragmentary, and control within the quality chain). The classification of the control functions is based not only on the author's own ideas but also on earlier research (e.g. Stoner et al. 2001; Szczepankowski 2007; Stępak-Miczek 2015; Samani et al. 2015).

The subchapter on the influence of control upon behaviour discusses various approaches to control, such as the humanist approach, the accidentality approach, the rational approach, the normative approach, and the approach based on interpersonal relations (Ramaswami 1996; Bacharach et al. 2002). Research conducted so far indicates the following:

- strict control undermines the level of safety at work and may be the cause of perceived danger (Vander Elst et al. 2014);
- detecting control does not have to cause a decrease in productivity if employees receive relevant feedback (Christ et al. 2012);
- preventive control does not have to improve productivity and, if exercised improperly, may have a negative impact on internal motivation (Christ et al. 2012);
- control over the work environment influences the level of satisfaction (Samani et al. 2015).

The ways of exercising control depend on many factors such as whether employees are shareholders in the organisation (Chan and Tan 2015), salary levels (Chen and Sandino 2012), the type of performed work (Allen et al. 2015), the level of formalism (Rodrigues et al. 2015), and the behaviour of managers (Hall and Atkinson 2006).

Close relationships exist between control and trust (Şngün and Nazli Wasti 2007; Neves and Caetano 2006; Atuahene-Gima and Li 2006; Inkpen and Currall 2004; Yang and Farn 2009; Kusari et al. 2005). These relationships are described in the next subchapter entitled "Connections between control and trust".

Organisations more and more frequently decide to use various tools of technical control. They install cameras, follow activities on websites, eavesdrop on telephone conversations, etc. There are various reasons for applying this type of solution, and opinions on their effectiveness are often very negative (Rosner 1999; Ball 2010; Chory et al. 2016). The problem of control that is exercised by using technical devices is discussed in the last subchapter.

3.2   The Punishment of Employees

3.2.1   The Causes of Punishment

There are certainly very many reasons for punishing employees. Punishment is connected with people's failure to comply with different standards or occupational health and safety regulations, but it cannot be ruled out that punishment is also handed out for fun, to derive some deviated pleasure, etc. For example, J.A. Bellizzi and R. W. Hasty (2000) found that the administration of punishment was influenced by managers' previous experiences, character traits and the personality features of employees themselves. The severity of punishment is influenced by employees' physical characteristics, gender or belonging to a particular racial or ethnic group. P.M. Podsakoff found that the most frequent reasons for punishment were poor results achieved by employees, while the very manner of its administration depended on superiors' previous experiences (Podsakoff 1982: 58–83). The problem of sanctions aimed at decreasing the scale of deviant behaviour was examined the most often with respect to contextual variables, the personality traits of the supervising personnel as well as the forms of behaviour displayed by people breaching work discipline. Superiors use different forms of punishment depending on their relationships with employees (e.g. Fandt et al. 1990: 253–265).

Cooper (2012) conducted research on the use of punishment in the public sector and established that the most frequently given reasons were as follows: the unsatisfactory quality of work (18.64%), insubordination (15.68%), failure to follow instructions resulting from the existing policies (9.69%), absenteeism (7.72%); verbal or physical humiliation of students, patients or co-workers (7.22%), sexual harassment (7.14%), the neglect of duties (6.49%), offences committed off duty (6.08%), lies (4.68%), data forgery (4.60%).

Punishment is administered not only when employees violate rules, standards or principles effective in the workplace. For example, punishment can be meted out to employees who, for instance, have offended their boss at a corporate team-building event ("Punishment and rewards are two sides of the same coin. Rewards have a punitive effect because they, like outright punishment, are manipulative. 'Do this and you'll get that' is not really very different from 'Do this or here's what will happen to you'" (Kohn 1993: 58, 54–63).

Discipline results from a number of factors. However, sometimes an employee is punished as a consequence of pressure exerted by a customer (cf. the example below).

A company producing promotional materials was commissioned to print out images of characters from fairy tales which were to be added to packages with chips. This was to encourage children to buy this particular brand of chips. The images could be collected or used in various games. The customer demanded that the information on what was to be printed out be confidential. During one of school visits the customer's representative wanted to show the children the new characters. He announced them as a "true hit". However, one of the children said that she knew what the novelty was. It turned out that her mother worked in the aforementioned company. She had wanted to give her daughter a surprise and had taken the newly printed images of the new characters from the production line. The representative was outraged, knowing that the new characters constituted proprietary material which could not be disclosed without the customer's knowledge and consent. He exerted pressure on the company director and had the responsible employee fired. The director knew that the employee had never been punished for anything before and had always conscientiously fulfilled her duties. But he had no option but to fire her when the customer threatened to withdraw the order.

Source: the author's own work

Punishment is also imposed because the existing customer service procedures disregard customers' expectations and requirements, emphasising compliance with legal regulations only (cf. the example below).

In a certain office, a clerk received documents from a client, but was not entitled to initiate the service provision procedure because he had not yet received relevant documentation from an institution where the client had acquired the right to drive motor vehicles. It seems that such behaviour on the part of the office worker anticipating the client's expectations and needs would deserve praise. After all, quality can be understood as a degree to which such needs and expectation are met. Unfortunately, what happened was a breach of the office's procedure according to which the performance of a service may be initiated only when the office has received all documents from an institution granting particular rights or qualifications. The employee was punished.

Source: the author's own work

It happens, unfortunately, that employees are punished for quality-related mistakes (although most of these mistakes have a systemic character, which was proved by E. Deming). Punishing employees for quality mistakes disregards the fact that quality depends on a number of events taking place along the quality chain. Quality mistakes occur frequently when an organisation cannot cope with the balancing of its production operations. Consequently, in periods when it becomes necessary to increase the production output quickly, employees are burdened with an excessive workload (cf. the example below).

I work for a printing company. Sometimes our workload is rather light, but sometimes we have to work overtime (and nobody likes that). The other day I received a financial punishment for having incorrectly printed a few rolls of material. Generally, if you make a mistake, you have to take into account the possibility of punishment. But the problem was that we were truly tired then. A man is not a machine, and when we get tired, we get confused and lose our focus. For me, the punishment was rather unpleasant and unfair.

(an employee of a printing company, a student)

When reasons for the use of punishment are considered, alleged mistakes made by employees are given the most frequently. What is missing is a thorough analysis of the root causes of undesirable situations. And the primary reasons for punishment can be factors connected with the behaviour of superiors, embedded in their attitudes, personality traits and motives. Punishment is also administered for various other reasons; for example, because of pursuing one's own interests or in retaliation for having one's pride wounded (cf. the example below).

> I work for a company manufacturing aircraft parts. According to the regulations, before a part is sent to the customer, we have to sign a checklist. It is me and my boss who are authorised to sign checklists. The other day my friend, the manager of another department, came to me and demanded that I sign his checklist. I knew that he had made some arrangements with the customer. There were some shady connections between them. When I refused, he started to threaten me with punishment. If he wanted to, he could ask my boss to punish me with an official reprimand entered in my personal employee file.
>
> (a student, an employee of a design and production company employing 300 people)
>
> I worked in a bar. One day the owner asked me for a cup of coffee. When I was handing the cup over to him, my hand suddenly jerked and I poured the coffee on his shirt. For this, I was punished with an official reprimand. But the result was that after the punishment I made even more mistakes.
>
> (a student, a corporate employee of a small catering firm employing five people).

Punishment is also connected with teasing an employee; there is a wide range of reasons and motives for such behaviour. For example, punishment takes place because bosses want to stay longer with people who, for various reasons, are important to them (cf. the example below).

> I worked in a large corporation as an assistant to the general manager. I don't know why, but my boss often insisted on my staying late at work. So I worked for ten to twelve hours a day. Usually at the end of the shift, the boss called me to his office and stated that some letter or agreement needed to be prepared. It was always a lie. After talking to the other employees, I would always find out that the letter or whatever he wanted

> had been already prepared and I had to sit politely behind my desk with nothing to do. I considered such situations as punishment. After some time I realised that the boss was punishing me for not giving him coffee on time or just because he was in a bad mood.
>   (a student, an employee of a large production company employing over 2000 people)

The existing reasons for imposing punishment can be divided as follows:

- rational and justified reasons (e.g. evident and persistent neglect of duties, deliberate counterproductive behaviour);
- irrational and unjustified reasons (e.g. punishing for quality mistakes without regard for the process theory; sometimes the blame should not be put on the employee, but on a particular series of events);
- reasons resulting from personal intentions to tease somebody or to pursue one's personal interests (against the interests of the whole organisation).

3.2.2   The Consequences of Punishment

The first attempts to study the influence of punishment and financial incentives on employees' productivity were made in the 1960s (Smith et al. 1967: 411–417).

Opinions on the impact of punishment on employee behaviour are divided. This is because the very analysis of the process of punishment is insufficient. What is important is the context in which punishment is imposed and whether any other measures have been taken earlier. It is necessary to establish what relationships exist between the punishing and the punished and, obviously, to what extent punishment is perceived as fair.

Many research studies prove that punishment is less effective for causing changes in behaviour than rewards (e.g. Tremblay et al. 2013: 233–249). It was demonstrated that changes in employee behaviour resulting from the administration of punishment were immediate but short-lived. Furthermore, the scope of such changes is limited because of the occurrence of various side-effects such as the emotional relationships of people receiving punishment (Connellan 1978). Punishment is not supposed to function only as a disciplinary tool or deterrent. The existence of punishment in work discipline systems proves that organisations uphold their values and want to be perceived as just and fair. This may be the reason why some research shows a positive impact of punishment on employee productivity (O'Reilly and Weitz 1980: 467–84). On the other hand, however, it is common knowledge that the fear of punishment increases work discipline. Such an approach is (deplorably) effective in manufacturing organisations where employees have no freedom in the performance of tasks, have to cooperate with machines, and are dependent on the performance of other people at the production line.

Fortunately, many sectors found out a long time ago that employee punishment systems did not generate the expected results. For example, the retail sector is troubled by frequent petty thefts committed by both employees and customers. It is believed that in order to limit such thefts, retailers should implement dedicated theft prevention systems (product tagging, protective labels, monitoring) and mutual discipline principles (employees supervise one another). Such solutions are better than the traditional punishment of employees provided that employees are not punished for what other people, including customers, do.

Unfortunately, in many Polish retail establishments it is the employees who receive financial punishments for theft. In one shop, the owner told the workers to "pitch in and buy a spy camera". It was demonstrated that improper punishment was the reason for employees' disbelief in the reality of objectives, the destruction of morale, the occurrence of the impression that some forms of behaviour could be accepted (Bellizzi and Hasty 2000: 154–159).

In some cases, the unfair punishment of employees is the cause of serious economic problems (cf. the example below).

I used to work in a company producing electric wire harnesses for the automotive industry. I was responsible for training new employees. Training programmes always lasted a few months because the objective was to reduce the number of potential mistakes. The company received a huge

> order and it became necessary to recruit new employees quickly. The boss told me to reduce the training programme to two weeks. I told him it was impossible and would result in a dramatic fall in quality. When I refused to shorten the training programme, I was punished with an official reprimand. I perceived it as exceptionally unfair. I decided to quit my job. It turned out that the person who replaced me agreed to cut down the duration of training. After a couple of weeks there were so many mistakes on the production line that the company lost subsequent potential contracts.
>
> (an employee, a team leader in a manufacturing company employing about 150 people).

Punishment regarded as unfair has the following consequences:

- Social capital becomes undermined and subsequently so does employees' motivation, trust and satisfaction (this is so because justice is the foundation of trust, which, in turn, constitutes one of the elements of social capital).
- Employees may display unethical and counterproductive behaviour (upon deciding to quit the organisation, the employee who feels dissatisfied and treated unfairly may undertake actions aimed at decreasing the employer's value or destroying its property).
- New groups or alliances are formed in order to establish a friendly working environment or to harass people.
- Employees keep to themselves and do not want to cooperate (frequently because of a sense of shame or low self-esteem).
- They believe less and less that it is worth improving one's work and learning.

3.2.3   Punishment or Rewards?

Many studies have shown that punishment is not as effective as rewards in attempts to change employee attitudes (Podsakoff et al. 1981: 151–155). Both conditional and unconditional rewards exert a positive impact on employee satisfaction and productivity; they are something attractive for employees. At the same time the positive influence of conditional rewards is much stronger in the case of employees performing their work well (high performers) (Podsakoff et al. 1981: 151–152).

The effectiveness of punishment and rewards is related to the extent to which they are perceived as fair (e.g. Podsakoff et al. 2006: 113–142). Rewards, particularly those based on objective criteria, strengthen organisational values and develop trust if they are connected with fair treatment from superiors. In an environment where productivity depends strongly on rewards (where employees value rewards highly), the use of rewards may lead to increased productivity (Podsakoff et al. 1981).

It is generally believed that when we want to change somebody's behaviour, a good idea is to use conditional rewards (good behaviour is rewarded). However, according to some researchers, rewards may destroy the sense of self-determination and self-competence (Deci and Ryan 1980: 39–80). Some authors claim that rewarding and punishing employees increases the distance between superiors and subordinates. Rewards act for a short period of time and are of little significance where creativity counts (Strid and Andréasson 2007: 127–129).

The influence of rewards on work discipline is not a popular subject of research. However, observations conducted so far indicate that, paradoxically, rewards may be a cause of breaches of work discipline, particularly if employees receive financial awards. In some organisations, employees receive various amounts for offering ideas aimed at work improvement or for factual effects of the implementation of such ideas. But sometimes employees put forward various fictitious ideas, which, nevertheless, receive the approval of their bosses. This happens in the following places:

- in the service sector, where the assessment of effects is very difficult and requires a longer period of time;
- in organisations fraught with corruption (employees share their rewards with their bosses);
- in organisations where managers' remuneration depends to a considerable extent on their employees' work assessment (various forms of pressure are exercised and distorted calculation data are provided);
- in manufacturing companies which do not use proper tools for the evaluation of quality assurance programmes (at the beginning, improvement ideas are effective; however, with time they continue to be submitted but are no longer implemented).

Among many conditions for the use of rewards, the most important one seems to be the guarantee of universal application. If financial rewards are granted to one selected group of people (e.g. executive employees only), they do not contribute to changes in employees' attitudes. This is so because, firstly, rewards are perceived as unfair and, secondly, there is no motivation for the organisation to maintain a rewards system (cf. the example below).

> As a consultant, I developed a rewards system for the employees. It provided for the granting of annual awards to those employees who fulfilled their duties the best (entered correct data, complied with the working time regulations, didn't make mistakes influencing the further stages of the service provision process). The management team was excluded from the awards system. I wanted to avoid situations in which managers grant financial rewards to one another only. After one year the award system was given up. The management was not interested in the further maintenance of the system.
>
> (a commercial proxy—consultant, a production company employing about 300 people)

3.2.4   The Types of Punishment

The punishment of employees may adopt the following two forms:

- imposing punishment on employees;
- depriving employees of pleasant things they are entitled to.

Punishment consists not only of the imposition of sanctions, or the entry of reprimands or cautions in personnel records. Punishment may also take the form of a change in somebody's behaviour. The table below presents selected types of punishment (Table 3.1).

Punishment may be divided into intentional or unintentional, direct or indirect. For example, intentional punishment is imposed on employees in order to change their behaviour, to penalise them for committed offences, but also to humiliate them or force to behave in a particular way. Unintentional punishment results from the decision maker's lack of knowledge or confusion, as well as from various circumstances.

Table 3.1 Types of punishment

Punishment	Types of punishment	Comments
Formal punishment	Financial punishment	Administered the most frequently for failure to comply with OHS regulations (but also for thefts committed by customers)
Formal punishment	Caution	A caution is issued in writing, subject to the deadlines provided for in the Labour Code. It is entered in personnel records
Formal punishment	Reprimand	According to the Labour Code, a reprimand is more a caution. A reprimand does not have to be preceded by a caution
Formal punishment	Disciplinary dismissal	This punishment is administered for serious violations of regulations, e.g. leaving one's workplace without authorisation, working under the influence of alcohol, theft, wilful sabotage
Informal corporal punishment	Beating (e.g. with a ruler, rod)	Illegal punishment. Used in some employee groups and relationships (e.g. in the past by trade instructors)
Informal corporal punishment	Physical exercise	Such punishment is imposed not only in uniformed services (e.g. for a minor offence, the employee has to do ten knee bends).
Informal corporal punishment	"Stillness" punishment	Punishment consisting in restricting the employee's freedom of movement (e.g. the necessity to remain within the limits of a circle or square drawn on the floor)
Informal punishment	Financial punishment	Employees who violate group regulations receive financial penalty (e.g. in a certain company, employees had to pay 5 zlotys for every minute of being late for work)
Informal punishment	Behaviour-related punishment	The intentional or unintentional manifestation of changeable behaviour, hostile attitudes or participation in various organisational games.
Informal punishment	Other informal punishment	Shortening work time, increasing work quotas, transferring employees to other "worse" positions or shifts, decreasing wages or refusing a holiday leave
Informal punishment	Group network punishment	Humiliating or intimidating employees (e.g. by publishing hateful remarks online)

Source: the author's own work

As its name implies, direct punishment is imposed directly on those guilty of an offence. However, employees may sometimes be punished for their boss's inept management or the boss is penalised for their subordinates' offences. When employees, for various reasons, decrease their work productivity, punishment may be imposed on their supervisors.

There are two varieties of financial punishment: punishment meted out to managers or to employees. Research on the acceptance of punishment showed that employees were more willing to accept financial punishment if it is targeted at managers (Siang 2012: 86–97). Financial punishment tends to be optional rather than obligatory. This means that, for the same offences, it is possible to administer non-financial punishment (Herbert 1997).

> In Poland, employers started to impose financial punishment on industrial workers in the first half of the nineteenth century. When the country regained independence in 1918, the financial forms of punishment were entered in work regulations and employment contracts pursuant to the order of the President of the Republic of Poland ,16 March 1928 (Herbert 1997: 41–42).

Employees may be penalised in many different ways. The selection of a particular form of punishment is influenced not only by the legal system, the normative system or the ingenuity of those imposing punishment; it is also determined by the political system of a particular country where business activities are conducted. For example, in socialist countries, punishing employees consisted of their exclusion from the political party, which usually prevented them from holding any managerial positions (promoting employees to higher positions was the prerogative of party committees functioning in particular enterprises). Exclusion from the party continues to be practised, for example, in China (cf. the example below).

> In 2015, fourteen employees of the Industrial and Commercial Bank of China were excluded from the party. The conducted investigation had demonstrated that the dismissed managers had been accepting bribes from employees working at lower positions.
> Source: (Cendrowski 2015)

3.2.4.1   The Most Frequent Forms of Informal Punishment

The literature on this subject focuses mostly on the administration of formal punishment. However, organisations use many different forms of informal penalties. Their scope of application and their types depend on a number of factors such as, for example, the ingenuity of either managers or employees, the traditions and character of a particular organisation or group, or organisational customs. Informal punishment consists, among other things, of the following:

a. shortening the amount of time available for work or increasing work quotas;
b. transferring employees to other positions;
c. transferring employees to "worse" work shifts;
d. decreasing wages;
e. refusing a holiday leave;
f. humiliating employees in front of other people.

What follows below are examples of the use of informal punishment.

In my company, managers used many forms of informal punishment. For example, people who were coming to work to earn as much as possible (and wages depended on the number of working hours) were punished by having their working time reduced to thirty hours. If you wanted to earn well, you had to work at least fifty-five hours. A slightly different approach was used in the case of those employees whose wages depended on meeting particular thresholds. They, in turn, had to work for as long as fourteen hours. But nobody paid them for exceeding the thresholds.
 (a student at WSB Opole)
 If an employee was late after a lunch break (irrespective of who was to blame), as punishment they were not allowed to work overtime (which was the only way of increasing the meagre basic wages). Another type of informal punishment was to change an employee's workplace. For example, if you worked in a group, suddenly you were transferred to a position where you worked alone, or the other way round.
 (a student at WSB Opole)

> If an employee refused to follow the shift manager's instructions, as punishment they were transferred to another, much worse, shift. Such refusals resulted from the fact that what employees were told to do was outside their scope of duties. Sometimes it happened that employees were deprived of the possibility of taking holiday at the requested time.
>
> (a student at WSB Opole)
>
> If an employee had a doctor's note, their discretionary bonus was reduced. If your sick leave lasted up to three days, your bonus was 5% lower; from 4 to 7 days—10% lower, more than 10 days—15% lower. This punishment was implemented in order to reduce short one-day or two-day sick leaves. Now those who are truly ill suffer the most.
>
> (a student at WSB Opole)
>
> In our company, informal punishment has the form of repairing a production mistake. An employee has to stay at work longer in order to correct what has been done wrong during the shift. But it is not always the punished employee who is responsible for a quality mistake. Other employees know about it and frequently accompany the victim and help them to right what has gone wrong (hoping for the return of the favour should they happen to be punished in the future). On the shop floor, everybody can see the board with the "Today's Top Reject" banner. It gives information about which shift produced that reject and at what time. So it's not difficult to identify the worker responsible for the mistake. Besides such information, there are also data concerning financial losses. But nobody worries about it. Mistakes happen not only because of oversight or tiredness (working in three shifts) but because sometimes we receive faulty components.
>
> (a student at WSB Opole)

3.2.4.2   Contractual Penalties

Contractual penalties constitute a separate category of punishment. For example, for each product that does not comply with the specification, the employee is fined in proportion to the value of a relevant complaint. In some of the researched organisations, such penalties are provided for in-work regulations. It happens, however, that such penalties have an informal character and their amounts are determined unilaterally by the management. Contractual penalties may be imposed for smoking cigarettes on the shop floor or for coming to work under the influence of alcohol. Such employees are not dismissed disciplinarily, but are given a day's leave; subsequently, the relevant amount of money is deducted from their wages.

3.2.4.3   Punishment Imposed by Subordinates on Their Superiors

The administration of punishment is not the sole prerogative of managers. Employees have no possibility of inflicting any form of formal punishment on their bosses. But in practice, if an employee wants to punish their superior, they can undertake various efforts to achieve their goal. Such punishment usually consists of the following:

- taking a day off on demand (during a very busy period);
- deliberately tarnishing the image of the manager by posting malicious comments online;
- filing complaints with competent controlling authorities;
- performing acts of sabotage (see examples below).

> In a certain organisation, during an audit of the environmental system, employees deliberately scattered pieces of cloth saturated with oil around in order to create the impression that the company was badly prepared for the audit (the application of a penalty for non-compliance was connected with the annulment of a bonus for the company's president).
> (a director in a public sector institution employing 150 people)
> In a certain construction company, during a private meeting, a few employees seduced the manager's wife in order to "mete out punishment to him" for his aggressive and unfair management style.
> (a president of a construction sector company employing 150 people)
> In November 2016, knowing that the management board was planning a downsizing campaign, the employees of one of the German airlines decided that they would all go to the doctor's and paralyse their company's operations (www1).

Attempts to punish managers do not always end well for the employees themselves. And sabotage is not only punishment but a deliberate action resulting from various motives.

3.2.4.4   Disciplinary Dismissal as a Special Type of Punishment

Disciplinary dismissal is a special type of punishment indicating that both the punishment administered so far and other preventive actions have been ineffective. Disciplinary dismissal may also result from a superior's wish to get rid of a troublesome employee. "The reasons for this form of terminating the employment relationship may be the following:

- a grave violation of basic employee duties (e.g. consumption of alcohol, absenteeism, coming to work under the influence of alcohol, theft, destruction of property, obvious and proven actions to the detriment of the employer);
- an offence committed during the term of the employment relationship which makes it impossible for the employee to continue holding a particular position (if an offence is obvious or has been confirmed by a final and binding sentence), or
- the employee's losing their qualifications necessary for the performance of work at a particular position" (www2).

A proper assessment of actions performed by employees is very important in the administration of this type of punishment. It is generally accepted that the neglect of employee duties does not constitute a basis for disciplinary dismissal. People dismissed as a result of disciplinary action have problems finding a new job (disciplinary dismissal is the so-called "negative reason for losing a job"). They cannot count on unemployment benefit, either. In such circumstances, both parties very frequently arrange to terminate the employment relationship by mutual agreement. In this way, the employee gets a chance to find a new place of employment.

3.2.5   The Conditions of Administering Punishment

The punishment of employees indicates the employer's failure, but, in various circumstances, it is unavoidable. If, for various reasons, punishment is eventually imposed, employers need to keep in mind the following conditions:

3.2.5.1   The Existence of Legal Grounds

One of the necessary conditions for the administration of punishment is its establishment in the legal system. There is research confirming the thesis that procedural justice has a considerable influence on the perception of punishment (e.g. Zoghbi-Manrique-de-Lara 2011: 272–282).

There are very many different studies of court or arbitration disputes. The majority of legal publications emphasise that the administration of punishment should be strongly documented. Many disputes take place concerning the interpretation of the law. For example, in one article, the author considers whether employees sleeping at work should be punished. But there are doubts whether employees sleep or just doze.

3.2.5.2   The Factual Influence on Work Results

Various work discipline systems allow punishment for poor work results. However, the problem is that work results do not necessarily depend on employees themselves. E. Deming claimed that ninety-four per cent of problems with quality resulted from poor management; thus it is managers and improper work organisation that bear responsibility for such problems. It makes no sense to punish employees if their influence on work results is insignificant.

3.2.5.3   Reliable Information

The knowledge of committed offences and their context influences the choice of punishment to be imposed on employees (Beyer and Trice 1984: 743–764). The lack of information about the true sources of breaches of discipline causes a situation in which all employees are punished the same. Employers frequently do not know their individual employees' level of commitment or effort put into their execution of duties or how their work is organised. Penalties, but also rewards, are effective only when decision makers possess reliable information (evidence for breaches of work discipline). If such information is not available, the use of either punishment or rewards is pointless. It has been demonstrated that superiors punish and reward those who do not deserve it. Furthermore, punishment can be imposed on those who work better than others (e.g. Podsakoff et al. 2010: 291–303).

3.2.5.4   Impartiality and Non-Favouritism

Punishment has to be universal, even if the person who is to be punished is our relative or friend. The selective application of punishment, which unfortunately happens sometimes, destroys the sense of fairness, increases the social distance among employees, introduces chaos into the organisation, and makes it difficult for people to cooperate or undertake change.

3.2.5.5   Previous Training

Punishing an employee who has not undergone proper training is a frequent mistake. Such an employee not only lacks the competence to fulfil their duties properly but also feels disillusioned and unfairly treated. After the administration of punishment, some employees continue to make the same mistakes (cf. the example below).

A certain district office was to hold a ceremony of signing a cooperation agreement between the F. district and its partner from Germany. The mayoress of the town of F. was one of the representatives of the Polish hosts. In the afternoon the German guests were invited to dinner. One of the waiters in the restaurant was a novice employed just a few days before. The guests ordered beers. The waiter was very nervous because he wanted his service to be perfect. But his nervousness resulted in the dropping of a tray with five mugs full of beer on the head of the mayoress. Soaked with beer, the woman went to the hotel to change her clothes. When she returned to the restaurant, she ordered a beer. Serving her, the same waiter dropped his tray on the mayoress's dress. He was punished by the restaurant owner and obliged to apologise to the mayoress by giving her a bunch of flowers.

3.2.5.6 Problems with the Administration of Punishment

Advice given to managers on how to administer punishment can be frequently reduced to punishing for unethical behaviour and rewarding for ethical behaviour.

However, employees behave unethically for many different reasons. The literature on unethical behaviour indicates that such behaviour occurs within the context of an organisational culture, organisational climate or a rewarding system; however, there are people who are unethical by nature (Baucus and Beck-Dudley 2005: 355–370).

There are many problems connected with the application of punishment. The most serious problems occur when a superior has to decide whether evidence presented for an employee's inappropriate behaviour is objective and convincing enough for punishment to be meted out. The problem is that various forms of punishment are used for the same offence. Superiors try to explain such situations, claiming that some forms of behaviour are documented better than others. In other words, more severe punishment is imposed on those whose inappropriate behaviour has been described in more detail by other employees. But if no objective evidence is available, no punishment should be administered (an ordinary explanatory talk should suffice).

> In my previous workplace, financial punishment was used quite often. It consisted of depriving those employees who were responsible for the rejects of bonuses. After some time, it turned out that as much as twenty per cent of all products were being returned to the plant with various complaints. We weren't able to figure out why, despite inter-operational control and self-control, there were so many faulty products. It turned out that the employees were hiding their mistakes for fear of financial punishment. They had arranged not to report mistakes, hoping that financial punishment would omit them. As a result of the conspiracy between the production workers and the packers, the latter didn't hesitate to pack products that were obvious rejects. Nowadays my company follows another principle—no more financial punishment. When a quality mistake occurs, the responsible employee notifies me of such an event, which has no impact on their wages. We try to talk to the employees and deal with quality problems together.
>
> (a production manager in a printing company employing 250 people)

With respect to punishment, it is necessary to take many factors into consideration; for example, the issue of honesty and commitment of employees.

> The F hotel employed two people. Both of them had been working there for three years. After some time they both started to be taken ill quite often. Employee K was afraid of losing his job and cared about his reputation very much. Employee J was sure that within a few months' time he would be looking for a new job. When K fell ill (and his illness was real), he didn't notify his manager of his condition until the end of the shift. He hoped that he would be somehow able to overcome his weakness. But he wasn't able to – the disease developed quickly and it was only the following morning that he informed the kitchen manager of his condition. Such an attitude caused the disorganisation of work in the kitchen. As a consequence, K was punished with a reprimand. Employee J informed his manager a day in advance of his forthcoming absence. No punishment was imposed on him (there were no grounds for it).
>
> (a director in a hotel employing ten people)

Various situational factors such as circumstances in which offences are committed influence the type of punishment and even withdrawal from its administration. When an employee evidently violates OHS regulations, punishment should be adjusted to the seriousness of the offence. If an offence is committed for the first time, a disciplinary talk is usually enough. Nevertheless, situations occurring at work may be surprising (cf. the example below). Managers have many problems deciding whether punishment should be exercised and if so, in what manner. Should employees be punished for offences committed outside their workplace?

> An employee of the electrical division knew that his boss, whom he liked very much, was celebrating his birthday. But he hadn't prepared a present for his boss. During the lunch break he jumped over the fence, went to the housing estate nearby and stole a bunch of flowers from a garden. The owner of the garden witnessed the whole situation and called the police immediately. When the employee was handing the flowers to the boss, two policemen were entering the shop floor.
>
> (an electrician in a metallurgical company employing 2000 people)

3.3 Control Over Employees

Control is regarded as one of the functions of management. When we speak about control, we usually mean the process of confirming whether undertaken actions and pursued objectives are consistent with what has been agreed before. Control results from standards, rules or arrangements among the members of an organisation. But control over employees may be also a tool used to influence their behaviour, to play organisational games or to intimidate employees. Control is related directly to disciplinary activities. It allows supervisors to correct mistakes and constitutes a regular process thanks to which elements of a system become predictable in their pursuit of required objectives (Leifer and Mills 1996; Robbins and Decenzo 2002). When a mistake is identified, both corrective and disciplinary activities are frequently undertaken.

In practice, the identification of irregularities (failures to comply with legal, normative, customer and intra-organisational requirements) does not lead to any disciplinary action. If anything, employees' improper behaviour is corrected by means of training or simple instructions. Sometimes, however, control is aimed directly at imposing punishment. In the latter case, control is deprived of any sense (unless there is sense in the self-destruction of an organisation). This is so because punished employees do not undertake any preventive or corrective action and, taking care of their own employment, they initiate competitive behaviour.

The relationships between control and discipline are not the subject of research. It is assumed that the goal of control is to collect information on irregularities that need to be eliminated and for which employees may be punished.

Nevertheless, some authors claim that control should influence behavioural strategies (Arvey and Jones 1985: 367). It was H. Mintzberg who said that control was necessary for the coordination of various actions. There are many sources of behaviours that hinder such coordination. For example, improper work organisation, technology or work environment, but it should be noted that they result from intentionally unethical behaviour or non-conscious deviant behaviour.

3.3.1 The Development of the Control Function

Building their huge tombs, the Chinese developed a triple system of controlling the quality of work performance. The bottom of the workers' hierarchy was occupied by slaves, who were usually unskilled workers. Their work was supervised by tradesmen. Tradesmen's work was controlled by the emperor's official, while all operations were the responsibility of the highest state officer. Bad workmanship was punished with fines (if a worker was not able to pay a fine, they had to work overtime for free). Very cruel forms of punishment such as the cutting of hands were sometimes applied.

According to R. Edwards (1979), in the past, control appeared in three forms. Starting from 1880, control was based on hierarchical divisions (supervisor–employee). At the beginning of the twentieth century, technical control appeared (thanks to more and more popular technological lines and the development of Taylorism). The period after World War II witnessed the development of procedural control based on prearranged rules and procedures. More and more bureaucratic control procedures started to appear (Edwards 1979). Along with developments of the knowledge of management, changes simultaneously appeared in the approach towards the role and importance of control. Control has always comprised people, their products and behaviour. But the character of control does not have to be restrictive. In well-functioning organisations, control is oriented towards collecting information related to strategic management, organisational learning and quality improvement.

3.3.2 The Types of Control

There are various types of control. For example, it is possible to distinguish budgetary control, strategic control, documentary control, functional control and process control, control of procedural compliance, preliminary control and expost control, comprehensive control and fragmentary control.

3.3.2.1   Budgetary Control

The control of financial resources included in financial plans or preliminary estimates is one of the methods of checking whether such resources are being spent correctly. But a budget itself is a tool of control. The existing control systems take into consideration functions and intentions. The control of a function (e.g. a sales function) is to guarantee that a company's particular function is performed correctly (Stoner et al. 2001: 549). The control of plans is much more complicated. The planning of an undertaking requires the preparation of a preliminary financial estimate to guarantee that the costs of planned actions will not exceed a particular threshold amount and that it will be possible to carry out the particular stages of a project within established financial limits.

3.3.2.2   Strategic Control

Strategic control provides managers supervising strategy implementation processes with information on completed stages, strategic objectives, incurred costs, etc.

3.3.2.3   Documentary Control

Documentary control is limited to examining whether required documents are available in a given organisation, organisational unit or workplace; whether such documents are correctly supervised, approved, archived and protected against any improper use. Such control may apply to a particular selected management system or activity (e.g. control comprises OHS documentation or personnel files).

3.3.2.4   Process Control

Unlike functional control which comprises various functions (e.g. production or sales functions), process control applies to particular stages and operations carried out within the scope of one process (sometimes one process runs across many functional cells). Relationships among processes are rarely the subject of control activities, although, according to the ISO standards and the Lean principles, it is necessary to establish connections among processes. In practice, very few organisations are able to identify such connections correctly.

Process control does not fulfil any penal or disciplinary function. Its objective is to optimise a process or to confirm that applicable time-related quality standards are met or that a process's preliminary round has been carried out in accordance with predetermined requirements.

In practice, process control applies to the following:

- process inputs and outputs;
- a whole process (all its stages and operations);
- critical points (i.e. those with the largest influence on the final quality);
- a whole quality chain.

The effectiveness of the control of quality chains depends on whether an organisation:

- has the possibility to audit its suppliers and distribution network;
- applies horizontal integration.

The scope of control is usually broader if an organisation acquires a whole network of suppliers and distributors.

3.3.2.5   Procedural Compliance Control

Control not only concerns manufacturing processes but also whether employees comply with procedures describing the course of processes. Some organisations in the service sector employ "auditors" who are, in fact, employees trained in the use of the mystery shopping method.

I work for a company providing telecommunication services. From time to time we're controlled by a mystery shopper. Last month they fired one of my employees, who'd had good results before. It turned out that she wasn't following the customer service procedure (and this procedure is tragic!). She was caught twice when she wasn't talking to a customer as the procedure describes it. I got an email telling me to fire her.

In my organisation, we have this procedure of talking to customers; in fact, it is a procedure oriented towards selling additional services. If you confuse the order in which you talk about things (a whole conversation is to last 40 minutes), you should expect a punishment.

(employees of a retail outlet, who are also university students)

3.3.2.6 Project Control

Project control comprises the particular stages of a project (initiating a project, planning a project, adding new elements to a project plan, developing control plans, determining a work analysis structure, developing project plan details, estimating project costs, creating a network of actions, performing work). During the implementation of a project, particular stages are verified and possible changes are controlled. Control plans concerning changes to a project, as well as the provision of supplies and the actual execution of a project, need to be developed.

Project control is exercised for various purposes. The most frequent goal is to obtain information about whether, from the methodological point of view, a project is being executed correctly (to ensure no stage has been omitted, whether costs and profits have been assessed correctly, whether people responsible for project implementation have been selected, etc.); sometimes, however, control is exercised in order to indicate the person responsible for the failure of a project (cf. the example below).

A certain state-owned company was executing a project that was to implement an electronic customer service system. During the execution process, it turned out that the system had some defects; there were irregularities in the transmission of data among the company's branches. The project was very expensive. A dozen million zlotys had already been spent. After talks with the contractors executing the project, the chief of the project team concluded that the identified problems were of a transitory character and that it would be possible to eliminate them when the system became fully operational. After many months it turned out that customers were not receiving invoices for received services. After parliamentary elections the management board was dismissed and the new management team reviewed all completed projects. The person responsible for the failure of the project was still employed as vice president. The new management wanted to get rid of the representative of the "old regime" as soon as possible. They decided to carry out a detailed inspection of the project in order to find an excuse for dismissing the vice president responsible.

3.3.2.7 Preliminary Control and Ex Post Control

Preliminary control has a preventive character and is oriented towards preventing possible inconsistencies. Final control aims to collect information on how particular planned activities have been performed. In well-managed organisations, knowledge of this type is used in subsequent projects or tasks (Szczepankowski 2007: 218–219).

3.3.2.8 Comprehensive Control and Fragmentary Control

Comprehensive control comprises the whole range of completed tasks and projects. Its character is both documentary and financial. Sometimes it is applied to a selected period of an organisation's operations (usually three years). It is undertaken ex post. Fragmentary control concerns only one selected section of works, a task or a project. Such control may be planned or unplanned.

Social control constitutes a specific type of control. It has two varieties. One of them is related to control exercised by employees themselves and applies equally to all employees. Such control requires the full transparency of decision-making processes (usually all decisions as well as expenditures are entered in the Intranet). The other variety consists of control exercised by people from the outside who decide indirectly about the continued employment of appointees (cf. the example below). This type of control occurs in local government organisations.

> When somewhere on the street doesn't say "Good morning" to me, I ask, "You're not from here, are you? We all know each other here. No regional accounting chamber or any other institution is able to control local decision makers better than their local opposition and websites focusing on local affairs" (The more the state has to say in local affairs 2016: 8).

It is also possible to distinguish substantive control, material control, formal control, and informal control (Szczepankowski 2007: 218–219). Besides the aforementioned type, it is possible to refer to employee control, working time control, and loyalty control.

Furthermore, lawyers talk about health control, sobriety control, or personal data control (Stępak-Miczek 2015).

There are also types of control that refer to the relationship between the supervisor and the employee as a supervised person. In practice, it is possible to observe various types of controlling behaviour from employees. Employees control their utterances, behaviour and relationships with various people. It is also possible to talk about the control of the personnel over the work environment (Samani et al. 2015: 28–35).

Because of the character of undertaken actions, control may be divided into ethical control and unethical control. For example, process control is ethical control. On the other hand, control exercised without any previously established standards or work limits may be unethical. Also, employee loyalty control tends to be unethical (cf. the example below).

> In my previous logistics firm, from time to time I received phone calls from an alleged representative of a headhunting firm. She offered to meet me to discuss new employment opportunities, of course much better than those in my previous job. In fact it wasn't a representative of any headhunting company but somebody hired by my boss who wanted to know how loyal I was to him.
> (a logistics specialist in an international organisation providing logistics and forwarding services; workforce—about 80 people)

With respect to the types of existing interpersonal relationships, it is possible to distinguish direct control (exercised directly by a manager or supervisor) and indirect control (exercised by colleagues and co-workers). The implementation of indirect control results from the lack of not only possibilities (e.g. the lack of time) but also knowledge or trust (cf. the example below).

> In my company, the boss told me to have a disciplinary talk with one of my colleagues. The boss believed that the colleague had made a mistake and failed to enter data in the computer system. But I already knew that he had done it, and the computer system is unreliable. Unfortunately, it's impossible to convince my boss that he may not always be right about something. He doesn't understand that mistakes result not from our behaviours but from defects in the hardware. I don't know what to do. I'm afraid that if I talk to my colleague about it, it may cause a permanent conflict between us (an employee in a computer company employing ten people).
>
> I've been working in this production firm for two years. I started as an ordinary production worker. After some time my boss decided to transfer me to administrative work. But I was also given a new duty—I was to function as a bridge between production and administration; in particular, I was to provide my boss with information about what was going on in the production department and what mistakes they tended to make. I don't want to do it because the foreman, with whom I worked in the past, is a very strict person. Any attempt to show him his mistakes can turn into a row. I find this type of work very uncomfortable.
>
> (a student, an employee in a production company)

Collaborative control is a variety of indirect control. It consists of initiating cooperation with the traitors of an organisation, i.e. people who want to harm somebody.

The exercise of control is increasingly supported by technology. Companies employing office workers control their computers, emails and working time. The use of the GPS system has become universal in transport enterprises. Manufacturing companies install large numbers of cameras in order to ensure the full monitoring of production processes.

3.3.3   Control and Employee Behaviour

At present researchers specialising in the impact of control on employee behaviour distinguish the following approaches to control: the humanist approach, the accidentality approach, the rational approach, the approach consistent with the trend of interpersonal relationships, and the normative approach. According to the humanist approach, control is a manifestation of the lack of trust in employees, which limits their autonomy. The accidentality approach assumes that the effectiveness of control depends on the context (on how employees perceive supervision and the principles of fairness). For example, the research conducted by S. Ramaswami (1996) distinguished the following three factors: employees' convictions concerning the level of participation, supervisors' knowledge of workmanship, and supervisors' tactfulness (Ramaswami 1996: 105–120). According to the rational approach, employees display counterproductive behaviour because the principles, roles and policies effective in their organisations are unclear to them. The approach consistent with the trend of interpersonal relationships assumes that employees may behave improperly because in their workplace various organisational conflicts and tensions exist. The normative approach assumes that employees sometimes behave improperly because the integration of standards does not take place or collective standards are not developed (cf. Bacharach et al. 2002: 637–658).

The control of employees exerts indirect influence on people's behaviour because the manner and kind of control influences the quality of relationships among people and control itself may cause unnecessary tensions and stress. Moreover, control, in particular strict control, undermines the level of work safety and may be the cause of perceived danger or the lack of safety (Vander Elst et al. 2014: 671–693).

It is generally believed that detecting control, i.e. control identifying mistakes, impacts negatively on employee behaviour. However, what is important is the character of such control and whether identified mistakes result from the employee's lack of knowledge, deliberate actions or from improper work organisation. It is obvious that detecting control which does not refer to proper work organisation is destructive and demotivating. It is a different situation when the employee is the source of mistakes and work organisation is correct. Contrary to expectations, detecting control does not have to cause lower productivity if employees receive relevant feedback. It does not have a negative impact on internal motivation, either. Preventive control does not have to improve productivity and, if exercised improperly, it limits autonomy and may also have a negative impact on internal motivation (Christ et al. 2012: 432–452).

It is also important to what degree employees may control their work environment. A lack of control over the work environment (e.g. in the case of open space offices) causes dissatisfaction (Samani et al. 2015: 28–35).

In studying the relationships between control and employee behaviour, we should pay attention to a number of factors influencing its level, scope, and methods of exercise. For example, the level of control itself depends on the type of organisation, the styles of management and even the legal form of an organisation. If, for example, employees are shareholders, it is assumed that the level of control should be lower (Chan and Tan 2015: 38–56).

Remuneration may be a factor influencing the strength and scope of control. It can be assumed that higher salaries contribute to a lower number of thefts (cf. Chen and Sandino 2012: 967–1000), but the question arises whether people who earn more (in comparison to the same positions and competences in other organisations) may be controlled less. Such a situation is dangerous because it differentiates employees and introduces a sense of unfairness that may decrease the motivation to work and job satisfaction. It is also accepted that control should take into consideration what employees do and what tasks they perform. An interesting issue is the control of employees working on new and innovative products. For example, it is believed that employees working on new and frequently innovative products need not be controlled because this limits their freedom and autonomy. However, various studies have shown that this problem is much more complicated. A lot depends on the type of knowledge possessed by employees. If their knowledge is incomplete or distributed, control may have a negative impact on their behaviour (Allen et al. 2015: 371–379).

Control may be dangerous for creative behaviour. Therefore, management practitioners have to confront the dilemma over whether creative employees should be controlled or not. They have to decide what can be done so that the different methods of control exercised over creative employees and regular employees do not destroy their sense of equality and fairness. It should be remembered that the application of different control methods is unavoidable in many cases. Control over research and development employees is different from control over customer service employees. In the former case, control is connected with the supervision of projects (an assessment of particular stages or the change supervision process); in the latter case, the results of control are based on the opinions of customers (also mystery shoppers) and on the effectiveness of activities related to service provision procedures.

In practice, however, controllers very rarely pay attention to factors influencing the particular forms of employee behaviour. The lack of knowledge about what causes improper behaviour may lead to the negative consequences of control procedures, i.e. lower motivation, satisfaction and, consequently, productivity.

If control constitutes a threat to proper, productive and cooperative behaviour, maybe the complete lack of control is a better solution? Unfortunately, the lack of control may be the source of dysfunctional behaviour and cause employees to be focused on their own duties, not on common goals and tasks. Therefore, even holacracies exercise social control and implement the principles of transparency and self-control. Control of behaviour is unavoidable. The presence of other people and work organisation itself create a situation in which people are always controlled.

However, control has different faces. It is not always traditional (inter-operational, quality, budgetary) control. Control is necessary where a process of change takes place; for example, a decision is made to empower employees. Such a process should not only be supported but also controlled. However, such control consisting of checking behaviour and the results of undertaken activities does not have to be destructive. Good control should reduce the power of stimuli for opportunistic behaviour. According to some researchers (Coletti et al. 2005: 477–500), control inclines people to cooperate, reduces relational risk, thus having a positive impact on trust. For this to take place, however, a proper environment is necessary. Employees have to have an opportunity of observing cooperative behaviour.

As mentioned before, we can distinguish between formal control and informal control. These two types of control appear side by side. Formal control is to have a corrective influence on employee behaviour because it is predetermined and results from established work standards. Informal control may also have a positive influence on employee behaviour (its force is often much greater than that of formal control). However, the lack of acceptance of informal control and its destructive character are the causes of various negative organisational conflicts and tensions. Various environments and cultures manifest preference for either formal or informal control. For example, research conducted in the service sector showed that informal control exerted a stronger influence on employee behaviour (Rodrigues et al. 2015: 350–371). Control is connected with the existence of formal tools (usually control procedures), but in many situations, it is the behaviour of managers themselves that exerts a greater impact than the formal methods of control (Hall and Atkinson 2006: 374–385). For example, in many organisations which had implemented the principles of reengineering or lean management, it was observed that reducing the number of levels in the organisational structure did not result in less control. Middle-level managers who fulfilled advisory functions during transition periods created their own control mechanisms which tended to be more rigorous than formal control mechanisms.

3.3.4   Relationships Between Control and Trust

Research into control and trust indicates the following:

- When there is a high level of trust and a low level of risk, then there is usually little control (Şngün and Nazli Wasti 2007: 430–464).
- A high level of trust increases employees' commitment when the level of control is low (Neves and Caetano 2006: 351–364).
- Process control may strengthen trust in people exercising supervision (Atuahene-Gima and Li 2006: 342–358),
- The mutual learning processes play the main role in the shaping of trust and proper control (Inkpen and Currall 2004: 586–599).
- The levels of control and trust influence the effectiveness of knowledge management (Yang and Farn 2009: 210–218).
- The alternate expression of trust and exercise of control may lead to the loss of loyalty (Kusari et al. 2005: D1–D6).
- People deciding to enter into a partnership are aware of the role of trust and the necessary level of control in such arrangements (cf. Gallivan and Depledge 2003: 159–190).

Improperly exercised control destroys trust and/or limits its development. This happens when control:

- is exercised selectively (only with respect to particular employees or groups of employees);
- is carried out suddenly and unexpectedly (e.g. for the single purpose of acquiring evidence necessary to dismiss an employee);
- turns into a critical assessment of an individual employee (e.g. of their traits of character);
- causes an unfavourable change in employees' status (Bugdol 2010).

3.3.5 Technical Control of Employees

The first research papers on the use of modern technologies in controlling employees were published in the 1980s (e.g. Garson 1988).

Studies published in 2000 indicated that as many as 27% of large American companies check their employees' emails, while fewer and fewer employers inform their employees about such practices (84% in 1999, 91% in 1998). The financial sector is the leader in the field of using various employee monitoring technologies (including the recording of private conversations) (after Fox 2000: 10–10). Research published in 2015 showed that as many as 24% of small enterprises used monitoring cameras (Gonzalez 2015). It is necessary to distinguish between employee monitoring and surveillance. The latter term means that employees are monitored secretly. Employees have to be familiar with the scope and goals of monitoring (therefore, it is not secret control). The problem with monitoring, which is too frequently used to control employees, is not new. It has often been analysed in the context of the existing legal solutions or ethical issues.

3.3.5.1 Reasons for the Use of Monitoring

Employee monitoring (e.g. recording) is increasingly often used. The following arguments are advanced:

- Monitoring prevents theft (not only theft of materials or tools but also theft of time).
- Operating systems are my property. Therefore I have the right to know what happens in them and what operations are conducted.
- I pay my employees for working time, and not for downtime.
- I have to know how my employees behave.

There are various reasons for the application of technical control. Cameras and mirrors are installed where theft is a problem. In this way, an organisation prevents theft committed by customers, but simultaneously it is able to observe the behaviour of its employees. In the retail sector, cash gets stolen from tills and goods get stolen from shelves (An Eye on Spyware 2014: 26.)

According to the US "Retail Fraud Survey" in 2015, the cost of thefts committed by employees is estimated at $23 billion (Retailers Fight Theft at Every Turn 2016: 88). Research conducted in Poland showed that employees do not always spend their working time properly. It was found that they paid bills or did shopping on the Internet (the most transactions are carried out between 10:00 am and 4:00 pm) or engaged in sex.

The strengthening of control takes place under the influence of various events; for example, after a leak of secret information. In 2014 the American administration strengthened its control over the employees of government agencies after Edward Snowden leaked a huge amount of secret information.

Many researchers specialising in law and ethics emphasise that employee monitoring can only be justified when employers aim at ensuring work safety (Miller and Weckert 2000: 255–265). Many countries have legal regulations concerning the application of technical control (e.g. in the United Kingdom, it is the Regulation of Investigatory Powers Act 2000 and the Data Protection Act 1988). These acts regulate the methods of performing monitoring activities, storing data and checking emails.

Specialists emphasise that the application of technical control requires not only legal regulations but also the proper training of employees. In reality, training in the use of technical equipment is not enough. What counts the most is the ability to analyse and interpret observed events.

3.3.5.2 Selected Technical Control Tools

There are many ways of exercising control over employees using technical equipment or even chemical agents. Employers may use video cameras, interception of communications and GPS systems. They control employees' Internet activities and email correspondence. Visited websites and phone-billing accounts are checked (Table 3.2).

Table 3.2 Selected technical control tools

Control tools	Function	Comments
GPS trackers	Used mainly in transport companies; they make it possible to locate a vehicle, its parking places and travelling routes; they protect vehicles against theft	Monitored employees need to be aware of the use of GPS trackers
Breathalysers	Employers can check whether the employee has consumed alcohol	A sobriety test has to be justified (e.g. incoherent speech, smell of alcohol)
TV monitoring systems	Used to monitor selected areas as well as employees' behaviour; they prevent theft, destruction of property, robberies, assaults	The monitoring of welfare facilities, toilets is forbidden
Lie detectors	Used to test truthfulness; they are used in selection processes and in the event of crime	The value of using lie detectors depends on the value of the applied diagnostic methodology. The problem with the use of lie detectors is legal restrictions—access to information
Crime prevention traps	Specially installed technical equipment or chemical agents (e.g. pastes, powders, fuel markers)	Such traps are used for a particular purpose, e.g. to identify thieves (they can be used by the police, the customs service)
Interception of communications and control of telephone connections	Used to monitor telephone connections as well as their content	Employers are not authorised to intercept or check telephone conversations. The exception is the protection of customer interests (hence the use of this type of monitoring in call centres)

Source: The author's own research and (Stępak-Miczek 2015; Góral ed. 2010)

3.3.5.3 The Consequences of Technical Control

By the 1990s some researchers were claiming that the use of monitoring systems might decrease employees' morale (Rosner 1999: 26). This is because there are many other more 'moral' methods of solving problems in the workplace. For example, it is possible to ask employees to propose ways of increasing productivity or preventing theft. The problem is that for cameras to prevent theft, they need to be hidden so that monitoring is conducted without employees' being aware of it.

> In one meat processing company, the owner installed cameras in women's toilets. He must have known that such monitoring is forbidden. It is against the law to monitor employees in any welfare facilities. The owner justified his action with alleged care for the women's welfare ("any of them may collapse; I have to know about it"). It turned out that the true reason for the owner's decision was thefts in the company. The women employees used the toilets to hide stolen meat and meat products.
> Source: the author's own work

Research shows that technical control changes employee behaviour because it prevents various manifestations of unethical behaviour. However, it should be remembered that good results achieved in one sector do not mean that other sectors will be equally successful. For example, positive changes in behaviour are observable in the retail sector and in restaurants.

The permanent monitoring of employee behaviour contributes to the better identification of potential accidents. Determining the causes of work-related accidents, OHS specialists do not have to rely on evidence collected during interviews because they have camera recordings at their disposal. Nowadays, analysis of the content of social media or sent emails is used more and more often in employee assessment, increases opportunities for the shaping of communication networks, and facilitates the creation of project teams relying on the means of distance communication.

Despite the obvious advantages resulting from the use of modern technologies, there also exists a serious risk of losing data or even financial resources. Employees have a justifiable concern about their privacy. The inappropriate use of modern technologies may be the reason for many misunderstandings, may result in financial claims or lead to court disputes. Excessive surveillance destroys trust in the management and reduces employees' commitment (Chory et al. 2016: 23–43).

When various forms of self-management are introduced, this may result in the loss of organisational values. On the one hand, the top management creates conditions for the development of self-control (through increased autonomy and participation), while, on the other hand, various, mainly technological, forms of surveillance are introduced. As a consequence, the organisation does not improve its results because civil behaviour is destroyed and counterproductive behaviour is fostered (cf. Jensen and Raver 2012: 308–346).

The use of modern technologies causes situations in which, despite the absence of direct social control, employees know that their actions are continuously observed and assessed. The total rejection of social control may hinder the development of social relationships. Organisations have the right to protect their tacit knowledge and reputation. However, the use of modern technologies constitutes an ethical problem, causing numerous questions. For example, how should employees' actions be observed? Does the permanent operation of monitoring equipment influence employees' motivation and commitment?

Besides using cameras and systems monitoring work on computers, some companies even record conversations between employees. Surveillance may destroy the organisational climate (employees' well-being), damage the existing organisational culture (transform it into a culture of distrust), kill creativity, and decrease motivation and productivity (Ball 2010: 87–106).

The use of control based on modern technologies involves considerable risk. Even monitoring may turn into surveillance. Very few applied technologies allow the user to assess the risk of lower productivity. Often the most that managers know is that something has been done wrong, some deadlines missed or somebody has left their workstation, but they do not know the reasons for this. It is not clear how modern technologies may support employees or react to their individual needs.

The implementation of even the simplest methods of technical control, for example, a working time recording system, without providing the controlled with necessary knowledge (What is the goal of control?) and without conducting process audits (What are employees' tasks? What is their workload? How long does it take them to perform particular tasks or operations?) may cause a decrease in trust and productivity (cf. the example below).

In a certain university, every employee received a magnetic card. It was to be used to open doors and to collect keys from the security room. In reality, however, collected data were used to control the employees' working time and to establish who stayed where and who communicated with whom.

A certain company manufacturing environmental protection equipment installed control gates on its premises. After leaving their workstations, the employees were obliged to record their times of departure and arrival. The personnel department ascertained that some employees spent too much time on consultations conducted in the other departments. The disciplined employees started to shorten their visits in the other organisational units. But as a result, it became impossible to arrange anything as the employees were unwilling to leave their offices.

Source: the author's own work

The worst solution is establishing a connection between a work monitoring system and an employee assessment system (cf. the example below).

A certain bank collects data concerning the following: how much time an employee spends talking to customers and to colleagues, how much time an employee spends at a computer keyboard, the number of telephone connections, the number of effective conversations and matters forwarded to colleagues, how much time an employee spends at work, etc. Such a strict monitoring system causes continuous and fierce rivalry. It is also the source of short-lasting solidarity among wronged employees.

Source: the author's own work

The problem of employee monitoring requires further research because it can be assumed that monitoring is a manifestation of mistrust in employees. In many cases, it restricts operational flexibility, causes employees to feel considerable mistrust, and prevents them from working efficiently and creatively.

3.3.5.4   The Future of Technical Control

As mentioned before, the monitoring of emails, records made by computer software or telephone conversations is gradually becoming a common practice in sectors such as finances or logistics. But soon, thanks to ideas put forward by IT and psycholinguistics specialists, managers will have even more powerful tools at their disposal for the monitoring (surveillance?) of employee behaviour. In his article published in *Fortune* magazine, R. Parloff (2016: 56–60) writes about projects aimed at developing better methods of associating words with emotions. Moreover, such statistics will make it possible to create rankings based on the following criteria: Who is the most dissatisfied with their work? Who treats customers improperly? Who speaks ill of the company? Who constitutes a threat to the company? Who is the most stressed employee?, etc.

It will suffice for employees' memos or emails to contain such words as "zero", "no", "nothing", "fire", "weary", "give up", "too many duties", "trash", "force" and dedicated software will associate the words with employees' dissatisfaction. It is assumed that such phrases as, for example, "too much" or "take advantage of" may signal the abuse of employees. Frequently written in quotation marks, words expressing negative emotions may indicate anger. Corporations are already in possession of such tools as SIEM, DLP, BA, AM (cf. the table below) (Table 3.3).

3.4   Further Research

Among other things, further research should focus on reasons for imposing punishment on employees. It is assumed that punishment is used when formal standards are not complied with. However, this is not necessarily true. Already, preliminary research indicates that punishment may be motivated by a desire for revenge or sadistic pleasure. We know equally little about rewards. Is it really true that their impact on changes in behaviour is greater than that of punishment? And what about the use of severe and heavy punishment?

The knowledge of the administration of informal punishment is rather limited. In casual conversations, employees give various examples of such

Table 3.3 Selected modern tools used to control data and behaviour

Security information and event management (SIEM)	Data loss prevention (DLP)	Behaviour analytics (BA)	Activity monitoring (AM)
A tool allowing, firstly, the gathering of all relevant data to be used in the future (it is the responsibility of the IT manager) and, secondly, the management of updated data which may be used at any time (this is the responsibility of the event manager)	Programmes detecting and blocking attempts to steal and delete data important for the company. Cyber attacks may be carried out by employees or by people from outside the company	Computer programmes making it possible to assign selected groups of words to employees' emotional states, intentions or attitudes	Active monitoring is a tool for the quick recording of information important for the company. If a document is marked as "important" and an employee for any reason deletes a fragment from such a document, the programme automatically records what has been deleted

Source: (Parloff 2016: 59)

punishment (they are described in the subchapter "Types of punishment"). However, the description presented here does not exhaust this interesting issue. There are obviously various types of punishment, maybe much more complicated and imposed in various configurations. The determination of the sources and manifestations of punishment in various circles and at various levels of power may be an interesting research topic. For example, there is no research on the use of informal punishment in management or supervisory boards.

Also, the knowledge of how subordinates punish their superiors is insufficient. This book provides only a few selected examples (e.g. such punishment may consist of establishing virtual alliances). The same should be said about the conditions in which punishment is imposed and related problems.

Further research may also comprise the complexity of tasks and structures, situational stressors and other contextual factors related to the application of punishment (Podsakoff 1982).

Research on punishment may be connected with analysis of organisational changeability and assumed risk. In management, it is assumed that risk should be minimised, but frequently, in order to achieve short-term objectives, companies agree to perform very risky actions (for example, if they are forced to do so). If risk management requires responsibility, adequate decision-making powers and, first of all, proper actions on the part of all employees, the question arises as to whether punishment is necessary in such comprehensive risk management processes and if so, what role punishment plays.

Also, little is known about the consequences of refraining from the use of punishment in the event of an evident violation of work discipline regulations. Sometimes very good effects may be achieved by refraining from the imposition of punishment. Such concessions motivate employees to work and, in particular conditions (e.g. conscious responsibility), increase their loyalty.

In the 1990s, in a certain factory, an employee of the mechanical department was celebrating his birthday. Despite the prohibition against the consumption of alcohol at work, he had drunk a few shots of vodka before the breakfast break. At 9 o'clock he decided to have breakfast in the company canteen. He had to leave his department building and go through the office building. There was a toilet on the third floor in the office building. When the employee was standing in front of a urinal, suddenly the company president came into the room. The drunk employee was so surprised by the sudden appearance of the president that he turned around and urinated on his trousers and shoes. In such circumstances, most managers would probably show no leniency. However, the president decided to exclude the employee from work because of his intoxication, but refrained from imposing any disciplinary punishment (the employee could have been dismissed on disciplinary grounds with immediate effect). For many years until his retirement, the employee performed his work the best he could and did not breach the work discipline regulations a single time. He was grateful to the president for his trust in him.
Source: the author's own work

An interesting research thread may be to establish how employees who face two mutually exclusive normative systems behave in particular organisations. If standards effective in the whole organisation are in conflict with norms followed in particular groups, a normative conflict occurs (employees do not know which rules they should follow and additionally are the subjects of pressure exerted by the informal leaders of various social groups, creating subcultures).

There is very little knowledge of the consequences of social control on the ethical sphere. For example, we do not know whether control exercised by voters is the reason for short-term actions performed for show or for the improper allocation of budgetary funds.

We know little about employees' controlling their own behaviour and about what happens among employees in an organisation. After all, people are capable of controlling their own behaviour. In organisations, people occupy various roles, take part in various relationships and build their own social networks. This process also influences how employees behave in various situations towards various people or groups. For researchers specialising in organisational behaviour, establishing the sources of control could be an interesting research subject. Such sources do not have to result from unfulfilled needs. So far the research practice has indicated that informal control is frequently caused by change processes.

The danger of transforming employee control into surveillance is another neglected research problem. This transformation is favoured by the development of such modern technologies as micro cameras, GPS location systems, listening devices to be installed in various equipment (Sewell 1998: 397–428). Further research should also comprise both negative and positive consequences of employee monitoring by means of modern technical tools. What requires special attention is the dilemma between ensuring a safe working environment and ensuring privacy for employees.

References

Allen, Mathew R., Gordon K. Adomdza, and Marc H. Meyer. 2015. Managing for Innovation: Managerial Control and Employee Level Outcomes. *Journal of Business Research* 68 (2): 371–379.

An Eye on Spyware. 2014. *Restaurant Business* 113 (2).

Arvey, Richard D., and Allen P. Jones. 1985. The Use of Discipline in Organizational Settings: A Framework for Future Research. *Research in Organizational Behavior* 7: 367–408.

Atuahene-Gima, Kwaku, and Haiyang Li. 2006. The Effects of Formal Controls on Supervisee Trust in the Manager in New Product Selling: Evidence from Young and Inexperienced Salespeople in China. *Journal of Product Innovation Management* 23 (4): 342–358.

Bacharach, Samuel B., Peter A. Bamberger, and William J. Sonnenstuhl. 2002. Driven to Drink: Managerial Control, Work-Related Risk Factors, and Employee Problem Drinking. *Academy of Management Journal* 45 (4): 637–658.

Ball, Kristine. 2010. Workplace Surveillance: An Overview. *Labor History* 51 (1): 87–106.

Baucus, Melissa S., and Caryn L. Beck-Dudley. 2005. Designing Ethical Organizations: Avoiding the Long-Term Negative Effects of Rewards and Punishments. *Journal of Business Ethics, Part 2* 56 (4): 355–370.

Bellizzi, Joseph A., and Ronald W. Hasty. 2000. The Effects of Hiring Decisions on the Level of Discipline Used in Response to Poor Performance. *Management Decision* 38 (3): 154–159.

Beyer, Janice M., and Harrison M. Trice. 1984. A Field Study of the Use and Perceived Effects of Discipline in Controlling Work Performance. *Academy of Management Journal* 27 (4): 743–764.

Bugdol, Marek. 2010. *Wymiary i problemy zarządzania organizacją opartą na zaufaniu.* Kraków: Wyd. UJ.

Cendrowski, Scott. 2015. ICBC Disciplined Staff for Taking Gifts From Lower-Level Employees. *Fortune*, December 8.

Chan, Andy W., and Zhanchao Tan. 2015. Employee Stock Options in China: Impacts on Employees' Psychological Ownership and Job Behaviours. *International Journal of Employment Studies* 23 (2): 38.

Chen, Clara Xiaoling, and Tatiana Sandino. 2012. Can Wages Buy Honesty? The Relationship Between Relative Wages and Employee Theft. *Journal of Accounting Research* 50 (4): 967–1000.

Chory, Rebecca M., Lori E. Vela, and Theodore A. Avtgis. 2016. Organizational Surveillance of Computer-Mediated Workplace Communication: Employee Privacy Concerns and Responses. *Employee Responsibilities & Rights Journal* 28 (1): 23–43.

Christ, Margaret H., Scott A. Emett, Scott L. Summers, and David A. Wood. 2012. The Effects of Preventive and Detective Controls on Employee Performance and Motivation. Les répercussions des nnova les de prévention et de détection sur le rendement et la motivation des employés. *Contemporary Accounting Research* 29 (2, Summer): 432–452.

Coletti, Angela L., Karen L. Sedatole, and Kristy L. Towry. 2005. The Effect of Control Systems on Trust and Cooperation in Collaborative Environments. *Accounting Review* 80 (2): 477–500.

Connellan, Thomas K. 1978. *How to Improve Human Performance: Behaviorism in Business and Industry*. New York: Harper & Row.

Cooper, Laura J. 2012. Discipline and Discharge of Public-Sector Employees: An Empirical Study of Arbitration Awards. *ABA Journal of Labor & Employment Law* 27 (2, Winter): 195–210.

Deci, Edward L., and Richard M. Ryan. 1980. The Empirical Exploration of Intrinsic Motivational Processes. In *Advances in Experimental Social Psychology*, ed. Leonard Berkowitz, vol. 13. New York: Academic Press.

Drummond, Helga. 1998. *W pogoni za jakością: Total Quality Management*. Warszawa: Dom Wydawniczy ABC.

Edwards, Richard. 1979. *Contested Terrain: The Transformation of the Workplace in the Twentieth Century*. London: Heinemann.

Fandt, Patricia M., Chalmer E. Labig Jr., and Andrew L. Urich. 1990. Evidence and the Liking Bias: Effects on Managers' Disciplinary Actions. *Employee Responsibilities & Rights Journal* 3 (4): 253–265.

Fox, Robert. 2000. The Boss Knows. *Communications of the ACM* 43 (2): 10.

Gallivan, Michael J., and Gordon Depledge. 2003. Trust, Control and the Role of Interorganizational Systems in Electronic Partnerships. *Information Systems Journal* 13 (2): 159–190.

Garson, Barbara. 1988. *The Electronic Sweatshop*. New York: Simon and Schuster.

Gonzalez, Gloria. 2015. Filming Comp Cheats Carries Privacy Risks. *Business Insurance*, 10/26/ 49 (22).

Góral, Zbigniew, ed. 2010. *Kontrola techniczna. Możliwości techniczne i dylematy prawne*. Warszawa: Wolter Kluver.

Hall, Laura, and Carol Atkinson. 2006. Improving Working Lives: Flexible Working and the Role of Employee Control. *Employee Relations* 28 (4): 374–386.

Herbert. 1997. *Organizacja i porządek pracy*. Bydgoszcz: TNOiK.

Inkpen, Andrew C., and Steven Currall. 2004. The Coevolution of Trust, Control, and Learning in Joint Ventures. *Organization Science* 15 (5): 586–599.

Jensen, Jaclyn M., and Jana L. Raver. 2012. When Self-Management and Surveillance Collide: Consequences for Employees' Organizational Citizenship and Counterproductive Work Behaviors. *Group & Organization Management* 37 (3): 308–346.

Kohn, Alfie. 1993. Why Incentive Plans Cannot Work. *Harvard Business Review,* September, October.

Kusari, Sanjukta, Daniel Cohen, Jagdip Singh, and Detelina Marinova. 2005. Trust and Control Mechanisms in Organizational Boundary Spanners' Cognitions and Behaviors. *Academy of Management Annual Meeting Proceedings* 2005 (1): D1, 6p–D6.

Leifer, Richard, and Peter K. Mills. 1996. An Information Processing Approach for Deciding Upon Control Strategies and Reducing Control Loss in Emerging Organizations. *Journal of Management* 22 (I): 113–137.

Miller, Seumas, and John Weckert. 2000. Privacy, the Workplace and the Internet. *Journal of Business Ethics, Part 1* 28 (3): 255–265.

Neves, Pedro, and António Caetano. 2006. Social Exchange Processes in Organizational Change: The Roles of Trust and Control. *Journal of Change Management* 6 (4): 351–364.

O'Reilly, Charles A., and Barton A. Weitz. 1980. Managing Marginal Employees: The Use of Warnings and Dismissals. *Administrative Science Quarterly* 25 (3): 467–484.

Parloff, Roger. 2016. Spy Tech That Reads You Mind. *Fortune,* lipiec.

Podsakoff, Philip M. 1982. Determinants of a Supervisor's Use of Rewards and Punishment: A Literature Review and Suggestions for Future Research. *Organizational Behavior and Human Performance* 29 (1): 58–83.

Podsakoff, Philip M., William H. Bommer, Nathan P. Podsakoff, and Scott B. Mackenzie. 2006. Relationships Between Leader Reward and Punishment Behavior and Subordinate Attitudes, Perceptions, and Behaviors: A Meta-Analytic Review of Existing and New Research. *Organizational Behavior & Human Decision Processes* 99 (2): 113–142.

Podsakoff, Nathan P., Philip M. Podsakoff, and Valentina V. Kuskova. 2010. Dispelling Misconceptions and Providing Guidelines for Leader Reward and Punishment Behavior. *Business Horizons* 53 (3): 291–303.

Podsakoff, Philip M., William D. Todor, and Richard Skov. 1981. Effects of Leader Reward and Punishment Behaviors on Subordinate Performance and Attitudes. *Academy of Management Proceedings* 1981 (1): 151–155. 4 Charts (00650668).

Ramaswami, Sridhar N. 1996. Marketing Controls and Dysfunctional Employee Behaviors: A Test of Traditional and Contingency Theory Postulates. *Journal of Marketing* 60 (2): 105–120.

Retailers Fight Theft at Every Turn. 2016. *Convenience Store Decisions* 27 (3).

Robbins, Stephen P., and David A. DeCenzo. 2002. *Podstawy zarządzania.* Warszawa: Polskie Wydawnictwo Ekonomiczne.

Rodrigues, Luiza Cristina Alencar, Filipe Coelho, and Carlos Sousa. 2015. Control Mechanisms and Goal Orientations: Evidence from Frontline Service Employees. *European Journal of Marketing* 49 (3/4): 350–371.

Rosner, Bob. 1999. How Do You Feel About Video Surveillance at Work? *Workforce* 78 (10): 26–27. (10928332).

Samani, Sanaz Ahmadpoor, Siti Zaleha Abdul Rasid, and Saudah bt Sofian. 2015. Perceived Level of Personal Control Over the Work Environment and Employee Satisfaction and Work Performance. *Performance Improvement* 54 (9): 28–35.

Sewell, Graham. 1998. The Discipline of Teams: The Control of Team-Based Industrial Work Through Electronic and Peer Surveillance. *Administrative Science Quarterly* 43 (2): 397–428.

Siang, Ch'ng Kean. 2012. Punishment as a Price to Pay. *Contemporary Economics* 6 (1): 86–97.

Smith, Russell L., Luigi F. Lucaccini, and Murray H. Epstein. 1967. Effects of Monetary Rewards and Punishment on Vigilance Performance. *Journal of Applied Psychology* 51 (5, Pt.1): 411–416.

Şngün, Ayşe Elif, and S. Nazli Wasti. 2007. Trust, Control, and Risk: A Test of Das and Teng's Conceptual Framework for Pharmaceutical Buyer-Supplier Relationships. *Group & Organization Management* 32 (4): 430–464.

Stępak-Miczek, Magdalena. 2015. *Kontrola pracownika przez pracodawcę.* Warszawa: Wyd. C.H. Beck.

Stoner, James A.F., R. Edward Freeman, Daniel R. Gilbert, and Jr. 2001. *Kierowanie.* Warszawa: PWE.

Strid, Steve, and Claes Andréasson. 2007. If You Want to Motivate, Forget Reward and Punishment. *Viking Manifesto,* 127–129.

Szczepankowski, Piotr. 2007. Kontrola i controlling. In *Zarządzanie. Teoria i praktyka,* ed. Andrzej K. Koźmiński and Włodzimierz Piotrowski. Warszawa: PWN.

The More the State Has to Say in Local Affairs. 2016. *The Worse,* 22 September, 8.

Tremblay, Michel, Christian Vandenberghe, and Olivier Doucet. 2013. Relationships Between Leader-Contingent and Non-contingent Reward and Punishment Behaviors and Subordinates' Perceptions of Justice and Satisfaction, and Evaluation of the Moderating Influence of Trust Propensity, Pay Level, and Role Ambiguity. *Journal of Business & Psychology* 28 (2): 233–249.

Vander Elst, Tinne, Anja Van den Broeck, Nele De Cuyper, and Hans De Witte. 2014. On the Reciprocal Relationship Between Job Insecurity and Employee Well-Being: Mediation by Perceived Control? *Journal of Occupational & Organizational Psychology* 87 (4): 671–693.

Woś, Rafał. 2016. A może żyjemy w XIX wieku. *Dziennik Gazeta Prawna*, nr 165 (4312) z 26 sierpnia.

Yang, Shu-Chen, and Cheng-Kiang Farn. 2009. Social Capital, Behavioral Control and Tacit Knowledge Sharing—Multi-Informant Design. *International Journal of Information Management* 29 (3): 210–218.

Zoghbi-Manrique-de-Lara, Pablo. 2011. Predicting Nonlinear Effects of Monitoring and Punishment on Employee Deviance: The Role of Procedural Justice. *European Management Journal* 29 (4): 272–282.

[www1]. http://www.zeit.de/politik/index. Accessed 4 Nov 2016.

[www2]. http://www.infor.pl/prawo/praca/rozwiazanie-umowy/702193,Zwolnienie-dyscyplinarne-czyli-rozwiazanie-umowy-o-prace-bez-wypowiedzenia.html. Accessed 8 Aug 2016.

4

Discipline and the Selected Manifestations of Employee Behaviour

4.1 Introduction

It needs to be clarified at the start that any classification of unethical behaviour constituting a direct cause of undertaking disciplinary actions, and also evidence that the work discipline system does not function properly, is ambiguous. For example, the word "fraud" as used in the literature on the subject refers to three related types of behaviour. Research into fraud comprises descriptions and analyses of the following:

- theft and improper use of an organisation's resources;
- corruption (corruption, exerting influence on an organisation's functioning and decision-making processes);
- falsifying financial reports (cf. e.g. Murphy and Free 2016: 41–56).

Theories of management describe the notion of counterproductive behaviour. There are many types of counterproductive behaviour; for example, annoying other employees (spreading gossip, being impolite and brusque—also to customers), lowering production output (e.g. by working deliberately slowly), damaging intermediate products, sabotage

© The Author(s) 2018
M. Bugdol, *A Different Approach to Work Discipline*,
https://doi.org/10.1007/978-3-319-74008-9_4

(e.g. leaving lights on after finishing work, damaging machines), theft, time fraud (coming to work late, leaving work early, faking an illness).

The direct manifestation of such behaviour is non-compliance with management procedures, personnel and systemic (quality, OHS, environmental, information security, etc.) policies. All these types of behaviour are also regarded as examples of a wider range of unethical behaviour (Cohen et al. 2013). Despite the lack of unambiguous classifications, a considerable part of research is conducted on the basis of the division of the types of unethical behaviour. Thus, sabotage, theft, financial fraud and corruption are described separately, although corruption is frequently connected with financial fraud, and theft can be an act of sabotage.

Selected examples of unethical and criminal behaviour are presented further in this chapter. This chapter is based on the conventional division into behaviour against property and behaviour against employees. But it has to be emphasised that what is harmful to property very often also constitutes a threat to employees. This division takes into consideration the directness of behaviour only (what is directly harmful to property or employees).

The beginning of this chapter is devoted to psycho-social and organisational causes of counterproductive behaviour (Cohen et al. 2013; Michel and Bowling 2013; Scott and Judge 2013; Wei and Si 2013; Kelloway et al. 2010; Jensen and Raver 2012; Priesemuth et al. 2013; Liu and Xu 2012; Bruursema et al. 2011; Shoss et al. 2016; Idiakheua and Idiakheua 2012; Flaherty and Moss 2007; Enns and Rotundo 2012; Klotz and Bolino 2013; Glińska-Neweś and Lis 2016).

The following sub-chapter describes the selected manifestations of unethical and criminal behaviour such as sabotage, theft and financial fraud. The presented description is not a detailed characterisation of unethical behaviour, but only an indication that the mentioned types of behaviour are strictly connected with work discipline. Therefore, if intending to explore the topic of unethical behaviour, the reader should refer to more thorough analyses. For example, sabotage is very well described in the works by Dubois (1979), Giacalone and Knouse (1990), Dibattista (1991, 1996), Ambrose et al. (2002), Sappington and Weisman (2004) and many other authors (Dibattista 1991: 347–353; Analoui 1995: 48–66; Dubois 1979; Dibattista 1996: 41–53; Giacalone and

Knouse 1990: 53–61; Sappington and Weisman 2004: 52–56; Ambrose et al. 2002: 947–968), theft in the works by Garbutt and Stalworth (1989), Bernardin and Cooke (1993), Gabor (1994), Tylczak and Sheets (1995), Kennedy (2016) and many other authors (Garbutt and Stalworth 1989: 21–31; Bernardin and Cooke 1993: 1097–1108; Gabor 1994; Tylczak and Sheets 1995; Gross-Schaefer et al. 2000: 89–100; Mahmutefendić 2014: 9–16; Kennedy 2016: 49–60).

Financial fraud (e.g. Chauhan and Kenkre 2011; Albrecht et al. 2012; Free and Murphy 2015; Han 2016; McNeal 2016; Beebe, 2016; Kutera 2016) and corruption (Andersen et al. 2011; Zadjali and Wright 2012; Pakdel et al. 2012; Roman 2012) have been the subject of numerous studies.

This part of the chapter focuses on the methods of reducing unethical behaviour.

The second part is devoted to selected types of behaviour harmful to employees. As already mentioned, such behaviour is negative for the whole organisation because it generates unnecessary economic and social costs. This chapter attempts to present the methods of identifying and reducing behaviour harmful to employees. For this purpose, the author has relied on the available literature concerning mobbing (e.g. Leymann 1990; Resch and Schubinski 1996; Zapf 1999; Vandekerckhove and Cmmers 2003; Ertureten et al. 2013; Eriksen et al. 2016); stalking (e.g. Rosenfeld and Lewis 2005; McEwan et al. 2009; Lewis 2014; Diette et al. 2014), harassment (Fitzgerald et al. 1988; Jiang et al. 2015; Steinberg 2016; Westcott 2016; Toker 2016; Wynen 2016; Good and Cooper 2016), and blackmail (Forward and Fraizer 1999; Block et al. 2000; Robinson et al. 2010).

4.2 Psycho-Social and Organisational Causes of Counterproductive Behaviour

Before a discussion of various manifestations of unethical or criminal behaviour, the main psycho-social and organisational reasons for counterproductive behaviour need to be identified (see the Table 4.1 below).

Table 4.1 Psycho-social and organisational causes of counterproductive behaviour

Causes	Research
Personality traits, e.g. a low level of guilt	Counterproductive behaviour depends on personality traits. For example, on a level of guilt manifested by employees. If it is low, there is a higher probability of the occurrence of such behaviour (Cohen et al. 2013)
Aggression, narcissistic attitudes	Counterproductive behaviour can be favoured by aggression and narcissistic attitudes (Michel and Bowling 2013)
Neuroticism, tendency to compromise, physical attractiveness	When the three related factors, i.e. employee personality (neuroticism, tendency to compromise), appearance (physical attractiveness) and negative emotions towards other employees, were examined, it turned out that the employees who were physically unattractive and unwilling to compromise more frequently experienced unpleasant behaviour than their attractive colleagues (Scott and Judge 2013)
Self-worth and managers' behaviour	Other factors influencing counterproductive behaviour include self-worth, managers' behaviour and locus of control. Affronting or humiliating supervision releases counterproductive behaviour, which manifests itself in acts of vandalism, sabotage and increased employee turnover (Wei and Si 2013)
Lack of satisfaction and injustice	It is believed that counterproductive behaviour is connected with employees' expressing their protest, is a manifestation of the lack of satisfaction and an attempt to cope in situations characterised by injustice (Kelloway et al. 2010). Employees who experience injustice are often emotionally exhausted. Research shows that people displaying counterproductive behaviour do this in order to deal effectively with emotional stress in the unjust work environment (Sidle 2010)
Contradictions between declared intentions and factual actions. The lack of preparation for changes	Counterproductive behaviour takes place when contradictions appear, especially between declared intentions and factual actions. It is enough to refer to the example of organisations that have tried to experiment with various forms of self-management. It turned out that when organisational forms of empowerment were being introduced and the managers, who had not got rid of the old habits, started to control the employees, the latter reacted to the new situation with counterproductive behaviour (Jensen and Raver 2012)

(continued)

Table 4.1 (continued)

Causes	Research
Functional dependence	It has been shown that the weaker the functional relationship in an employee group, the greater the probability of the occurrence of counterproductive attitudes and behaviour (Priesemuth et al. 2013)
Values and organisational adjustment	It is being increasingly accepted that counterproductive behaviour can result from the scope of the individual's adjustment to the organisation because behaviour is also determined by values (Liu and Xu 2012)
Boredom	Counterproductive behaviour can be also caused by boredom (Bruursema et al. 2011). Boredom in the workplace can result in offending and attacking employees, lowering production output, sabotage or theft
Stress, risks and social disorder	Employee behaviour and its riskiness are determined by the employee's opportunities, attitudes and needs. These three factors dominate in various situations. For example, in periods of economic crisis the importance of needs increases, which can trigger unethical behaviour. Under the influence of permanent stress, employees manifest unethical behaviour as an attempt to escape or defend themselves. In dishonest people, stress triggers the tendency to behave unethically and counterproductively. Unethical behaviour occurs where there is no social order (Idiakheua and Idiakheua 2012) Counterproductive behaviour constitutes employees' reaction to all events and situations which they perceive as bad. Its objective is to make employees feel better (Shoss et al. 2016)
Attempts to mark one's presence	Sociologists (Idiakheua and Idiakheua 2012) explain counterproductive behaviour as make-up behaviour. Make-up behaviour is displayed by employees who are poor, sometimes living in extreme poverty, and their conduct is to mark their presence. Despite being irrational, such behaviour is harmful to the whole organisation (Idiakheua and Idiakheua 2012)
Desire for revenge	A desire for revenge plays an important role in counterproductive behaviour (Jones 2004)

(continued)

Table 4.1 (continued)

Causes	Research
Intensity of competition and personality traits	Employee behaviour depends on the used methods of motivation, the level of identification with the group and the character of commitment. The extent of counterproductive employee behaviour can depend on many variables; for example, the level of competition among groups or employees' personality traits (Flaherty and Moss 2007; Enns and Rotundo 2012)
Citizenship behaviour	Counteproductive behaviour is juxtaposed with citizenship behaviour but, in practice, people exhibiting citizenship behaviour can also manifest counterproductive behaviour. Research shows that when employees display citizenship behaviour, they grant themselves the right to behave counterproductively. In the theory of management, such "grants" are called "moral licences" (Klotz and Bolino 2013). Counterproductive behaviour is explained by the theory of moral cleansing. Research into this theory shows that immoral behaviour stimulates people to pursue behaviour change that can symbolically cleanse them and help them to restore the sense of internal moral balance (Glińska-Neweś and Lis 2016)

Source: own work based on (Cohen et al. 2013: 45–53; Michel and Bowling 2013: 93–105; Idiakheua and Idiakheua 2012: 912–993; Jones 2004: A1–A6; Klotz and Bolino 2013: 292–306; Scott and Judge 2013: 93–113; Sidle 2010: 101–103; Wei and Si 2013: 281–296; Bruursema et al. 2011: 93–107; Jensen and Raver 2012: 308–346; Priesemuth et al. 2013: 230–257; Liu and Xu 2012: 133–139; Wu and Lebreton 2011: 593–626; Glińska-Neweś and Lis 2016: 265–274; Shoss et al. 2016: 571–587)

As it can be concluded from the table above, reasons for counterproductive behaviour comprise numerous situational, social, organisational or even economic factors. In practice, it is very difficult to conduct research into why employees breach work discipline. Researchers focus too much on the very manifestations of unethical or criminal behaviour and too little on their sources. Counterproductive behaviour is very difficult to assess. What depends on the possibility of identifying and subsequently assessing such behaviour is the effectiveness of undertaken preventive actions aimed at reducing the range of counterproductive behaviour. Some types of behaviour are noticeable immediately (e.g. the effects of destruction); others become evident only after some time (cf. Wu and Lebreton 2011).

It should be also remembered that the aforementioned factors are related to one another. For example, a sense of injustice causes strong stress which, in turn, is the reason for counterproductive behaviour (Saleem and Gopinath 2015: 683–699).

4.3   Behaviour Against Property

The following sub-chapter describes the selected manifestations of unethical and criminal behaviour such as sabotage, theft and financial fraud. They represent counterproductive behaviour referred to as behaviour against an organisation's property.

4.3.1   Sabotage

Sabotage has the following characteristic features:

- It is a deliberate, well thought out and planned action; sometimes it happens on an ad hoc basis.
- It usually causes losses/costs (not necessarily economic ones).
- It consists of reducing the value of an organisation's assets (its economic, human, technical and organisational resources).

It is also an action aimed at reducing the probability of acquiring expected benefits/profits.

Connections between sabotage and work discipline consist of the following:

- The objective of work discipline is to prevent all manifestations of sabotage.
- The unjust and biased treatment of employees can lead to acts of sabotage (performed also by specialists or managers).
- Proved sabotage is the cause of initiating disciplinary procedures (mainly disciplinary dismissals).

Sabotage appears in different forms. Traditionally, acts of sabotage include slowing down production processes, destroying property, creating chaos, causing destruction and a lack of honesty and loyalty.

Physical or simple sabotage consists of destroying property. Typical examples of simple sabotage comprise short-circuiting electrical devices, puncturing oil barrels, cutting tyres, stealing power cables, etc. In the office, on the other hand, decision-making processes are boycotted, formal organisational structures are destroyed and people pretend to work. In some cases, rather than stealing or destroying a company's property, employees take advantage of its resources; for example, if disgruntled employees plan to start their own business in competition with their employer.

In the past, sabotage was associated with destroying machines and technical equipment. Nowadays more and more attention is paid to Internet sabotage; it is stressed that actions aimed at destroying knowledge are undertaken by specially trained employees who are frequently employed by competitive companies.

It is believed that acts of sabotage take place for particular reasons, e.g. strong social pressure, inappropriate behaviour of supervisors or even customers. Sabotage happens when employees are very dissatisfied with the organisational climate, existing procedures or unjust treatment. Unfortunately, it is very often believed that so-called external customers are regarded as more important than internal ones, i.e. employees. People resort to sabotage when inappropriate dismissal methods are followed (see the example below). Under the influence of strong emotions and perceived injustice, employees tend to destroy property or knowledge.

In 1996 an employee of Omega Engineering Corporation, Tim Lloyd, destroyed the whole corporate computer system. The direct cause of such behaviour was the employee's dismissal. He decided that his employer had to be punished. His "computer bomb" cost the company 10 million US dollars. It had to spend an additional 2 million dollars on necessary repairs. The side-effect of this act of sabotage was the dismissal of eighty employees. The employee's actions resulted in the company's losing many customers and consequently lower sales. Lloyd had worked for Omega for eleven years. The court sentenced him to forty-one months' imprisonment. He was the only employee possessing detailed knowledge of the functioning of the company's operating system; it turned out that he had consistently refused to train other employees. But the tragedy would not have happened if the company had followed the appropriate dismissal procedure. He had not been deprived of access to the system at the proper time.

Source: (www1)

This example effectively illustrates that the lack of reaction to behaviour harmful to the interests of an organisation can lead to the loss of precious capital (in this case, customers and employees).

Acts of sabotage also occur during the process of introducing organisational changes. This is usually due to a lack of information about their purpose, the unclear rules concerning the division of resources, the lack of appropriate communication or anticipatory actions taken by managers.

Anticipatory actions are ones that cause particular changes in the functioning of an organisation without any previous improvement in the awareness of employees and justification for the appropriateness of such changes.

For example, during a reengineering implementation process, it is possible to observe the following sabotage tactics: undertaking actions aimed at wasting the positive energy of changes, boycotting and questioning established objectives and dispersing resources (Taher and Krotov 2016: 145–163).

Behaviour referred to as sabotage is characteristic of any particular occupational or hierarchical group. Sabotage is used by both manual workers and managers. Saboteurs are not only people who undertake deliberate actions against their organisations (e.g. in consequence of an unjust dismissal) but also all types of jokers. There is research indicating that employees with high competences are more likely to use sabotage (e.g. cf. Johnson and Salmon 2016: 673–696). However, it can be assumed that the larger the scope of possessed knowledge, the greater the possibilities of harming an organisation.

The paradox is that people possessing such knowledge are often regarded as trustworthy and treated preferentially. This is probably why, in large state-owned companies, sabotage prevention is the responsibility of external organisations (which monitor employees' emails, telephone conversations and contacts, examine documentation, etc.).

Work discipline is one element in the system securing an organisation against sabotage. The other elements include extended recruitment and selection processes, technical means of securing valuable assets, information security systems and knowledge management, including encouraging employees to share and protect knowledge properly.

Most management practitioners agree that preventing acts of sabotage requires that managers be trained to quickly recognise the manifestations of employee dissatisfaction. In preventing sabotage, it is very important to draw valid conclusions from individual episodes of employee behaviour. In the case of electronic sabotage, prevention usually consists of blocking access to the Internet (before a troublesome employee is dismissed), conducting talks about a dismissal on neutral ground, preventing employees who are to be dismissed from removing any equipment from company premises.

Fighting or preventing sabotage can also have many adverse consequences. For example, restricting access to databases does not foster the development of either knowledge or trust.

4.3.2   Theft

Theft, especially of databases or intellectual property, takes place when employees are to be dismissed or when dismissals are planned and announced to employees (Survey Highlights Dangers 2011: 6–6).

In the case of factual and planned dismissals, theft results from an employee's conviction that stolen data can help them in their new jobs. In this case, theft is an act of revenge, results from the employee's wish to hurt the employer, and is determined by a strong sense of injustice.

Not all thefts are discovered and reported to the law enforcement authorities. An undisclosed theft is classified as "hidden costs". Quality management specialists use the phrase "the second factory of costs". Some companies assume in advance the existence of pathological phenomena and increase the prices of their products by 2–3 per cent (Bugdol 2007).

It is not only money, tools or materials that can get stolen. Theft also takes place when employees extend work breaks or come to work late (time theft). Knowledge, patents or copyrights are increasingly becoming the subject of theft. Receiving undue remuneration (e.g. a bonus depending exclusively on the effort and commitment of subordinates) can also be regarded as theft.

Theft also comprises deliberate actions undertaken by employees-shareholders with a view to increase the prices of company shares (e.g. by providing untrue information influencing share price quotations on stock exchanges).

Theft is more often only an introduction to further criminal activities. A case in point is a theft of confidential (commercial, personal, health, etc.) information.

It is claimed that theft is a crime that not only affects large corporations; theft is particularly harmful to small businesses (Kennedy 2016: 49–60). For example, a theft of a database can prevent a business from conducting any activities. An additional barrier is the fact that small businesses cannot afford expensive and complex tools providing security against theft.

Research into the problem of theft leads to the following conclusions:

- There are people more likely to steal (they think about opportunities for theft more often than others).
- Managers are more tolerant and less repressive towards those who steal from other people.
- Managers believe that most people steal regularly and that employees are not loyal.
- The inclination towards theft results from low wages (rationalisation of theft) (Bernardin and Cooke 1993: 1097–1108).

In practice, the behaviour of superiors can often affect the risk of theft. It happens when management tolerates petty theft (see the example below).

> I run a small transport firm. I used to work as a driver myself. Sometimes I stole petrol from the car I drove. I would siphon off two to three litres of fuel and nobody said a word. Now I know that my drivers do the same. When they pilfer a few litres, I don't intervene, but I worry that the volume of stolen petrol may increase. Some people know no moderation.
> (the owner of a transport firm employing eight people)

Economists (e.g. Mahmutefendić 2014: 9–16) and management specialists believe that sometimes theft is justified (e.g. "I can steal the equivalent of what I haven't been paid", "I steal because I don't earn enough"). However, the law and existing work discipline systems do not provide any justification for theft. For this reason, research is conducted into the level of people's acceptance of theft. (You take two paper clips from the office. Is it already a theft?)

Organisations use various methods to prevent and detect theft. They not only use permanent monitoring systems but also honesty tests. In some professions, the consequences of dishonest behaviour are closely related to employees' proneness to theft. Some research has shown that, in the case of shop assistants, there is a strong correlation between diagnosed honestly and theft; as far as proneness to theft is concerned, there are no significant differences with respect to such categories as gender, age or ethnic origin (cf. Bernardin and Cooke 1993: 1097–1108).

It is believed that one of the methods of preventing, or rather reducing, theft is to increase employees' responsibility. For example, appointing the owners of processes or process stages can cause employees to feel responsible for resources entrusted to them. But the absolute condition is a full sense of ownership; process owners have to have real influence on decision-making processes. They have to be guaranteed autonomy concerning process improvement methods; in other words, they have to be empowered.

Another way to reduce theft is to introduce full transparency wherever possible. The chapter devoted to control highlights the advantages of social control. In fact, many businesses have been successful in reducing not only theft but also other manifestations of inappropriate behaviour by ensuring transparency with respect to all decisions, including financial ones.

Some companies have introduced systems that provide rewards for employees who detect and report acts of theft. Such systems are based on the assumptions that:

• employees are able to detect theft more quickly than controllers,
• social and group standards are more effective in theft reduction than formal legal regulations, especially intra-organizational ones.

4.3.2.1 Work Time Theft

An inspection carried out by tax officials in a certain office in Italy revealed that after clocking in, one employee went to a bar, another to the beach, and yet another to a massage parlour (for five hours).
Source: Fakty, 06.2016, 7.00 pm

Italian economists estimate that every day, one in five public administration employees does not come to work (Worker Absenteeism on Rome's ... 2016: 11–11). In discussing absence from work, we should distinguish clearly between justified absence caused, for example, by illness from unjustified absence resulting from employees' deliberate actions (e.g. acquiring medical certificates illegally). Absenteeism can be caused by many external and environmental factors. The most frequent external reasons for absenteeism include family duties and tragic economic events (e.g. Black Friday). Some research (e.g. research conducted in small- and medium-sized hotels) indicates that there is a link between absenteeism and the age of the employee. Managers perceive older people as more disciplined and less prone to absenteeism (Magd 2003: 393–401).

Therefore, on the one hand, work discipline systems should provide for punishments, e.g. for unjustified absence from work, and, on the other hand, they have to provide preventive measures (training, assignment of new tasks, empowerment, appreciation of commitment, flexible work time).

An important role is played by employee assistance programmes and health programmes. There is evidence that an appropriate health programme is able to reduce absenteeism. For example, surveys conducted

among BMW auto-dealers clearly indicate that corporate fitness programmes limit the number of absences (LaReau 2012: S026).

Absenteeism not only generates economic costs but also disorganises
work, especially if work organisation is based on employee teams. The
majority of well-managed organisations have special replacement plans in
place, but even the best replacement plan cannot guarantee that substitute employees will have the same skills and will be adjusted the same to
the requirements applicable to teamwork.

Advice given to managers can be summarised as follows:

- Identify the true reasons for absences.
- Inform employees clearly about the consequences of unjustified and
  unauthorixed absences.
- Do not tolerate absenteeism.

Another important thing is to review management styles and, if possible, to introduce a flexible work-time system.

If all these measures do not bring the expected results, an employee
prone to absenteeism can be suspended from duty or dismissed
disciplinarily.

Good results can be achieved by following various activation methods.
For example, introducing new management methods favouring employee
commitment can reduce their proneness to absenteeism. Considerable
research indicates that increased employee motivation (achieved by
assigning new interesting tasks to employees) contributes to improvement in productivity. However, such factors as pressure from customers,
boredom or monotonous work can be the direct cause of increased absenteeism (e.g. Ahamed and Sunderasan 2016: 37–43).

4.3.3   Financial Fraud

There are various manifestations of financial fraud. The most common
ones include falsifying financial statements, developing unrealistic budgets and financial plans, creating mechanisms aimed at obtaining undue
value added tax, and establishing offshore entities in order to avoid paying taxes.

The mechanism of financial frauds is explained by the fraud triangle theory proposed by D.R. Cressey. According to him, people are ready to commit fraud when opportunity, rationalisation and pressure come together.

Many real cases show that fraud is committed when an opportunity appears (Sometimes fraud is committed by trusted people or people in positions of power). After some time fraudsters start to rationalise and justify their criminal behaviour ("I earn too little"). However, in recent years Cressey's theory has come under strong criticism, mainly because it lacks comprehensiveness (Free and Murphy 2015: 18–54). It disregards many other factors that could influence fraudulent behaviour (e.g. greed). Research results indicate that there are connections between environmental or generational conditions and the manifestations of unethical behaviour. For example, research conducted in the US shows that materialism and love of money negatively influence young people's ethical judgement and that a considerable risk of unethical behaviour is connected to family, in particular the style of parenthood and parents' religiousness (Flurry and Swimberghe 2016: 91–108). The triangle theory does not take into consideration the so-called instrumental climate. It means that it does not examine unethical behaviour with respect to employees' personality traits, situational factors or standards in place in an organisation (Murphy and Free 2016: 41–56).

Sometimes fraud is committed by the most trusted employees (because they have access to resources) (Ombler 2016: M6–M8).

Research conducted so far indicates the following:

- Employees' collusion is of considerable importance for the existence of financial fraud.
- In almost half of the detected cases of fraud, employees colluded with one another (the mechanisms of fraud were established, controlled and secured).
- The larger the number of people participating in collusion, the larger the scope of fraud (Lim 2016).
- There is a correlation between the time of detecting a fraud and its scale, as well as a fraudster's position of authority (the greater the scope of authority, the greater the opportunities for fraud and the longer it takes to detect it) (Deluna 2016: 17–17).

- Particular types of work can aid financial fraud (e.g. people responsible for investment activities have opportunities for committing fraud by colluding with investment consultants (e.g. Beebe 2016: 36–41).
- Financial fraud has different manifestations and scopes (sometimes it starts with an "innocent" company credit card misuse).
- The longer the period of impunity, the greater the probability of other more risky and costly frauds (Beebe 2016).
- The most frequent motives for financial fraud include problems in personal life, poor business results, bad relations with superiors, living beyond one's means (www2).

Financial frauds are difficult to discover because their structures are often very complex. It is rare for a fraudster to simply withdraw money from a company account or steal financial resources at hand. Fraudsters take advantage of their own professional positions and create complex embezzlement schemes (see the example below).

> Alexander was a purchasing department manager in a large company listed on the stock exchange. He decided who would supply the company with raw materials, tools, office equipment, etc. Taking advantage of his position, he agreed with one wholesale business that it would be the company's sole certified supplier of selected equipment. The prices offered to the company could be high but, in return, Alexander expected deliveries of the same equipment at much lower prices to a small business established in the name of his brother-in-law. This allowed Alexander to buy and sell the equipment at competitive prices. The practice continued for many years until a detailed inspection of prices offered by the company's suppliers revealed all irregularities.
> Source: the authors' own work

The above example shows that despite many advantages of quality management systems and their role in limiting the scope of financial frauds, what really matters is employees' ethics and to what extent they are prone to take advantage of opportunities for fraud. In many cases, people are driven by sheer greed.

It is generally believed that limiting the risk of financial fraud involves the necessity of establishing, maintaining and improving numerous procedures constituting parts of an organisation's comprehensive normative system. Such procedures determine employee conduct in particular emergency situations (e.g. the appearance of suspicion of financial fraud). For example, A. McNeal (2016) recommends establishing detailed fraud prevention programmes. Such programmes should be based on training courses, organisational missions, reporting mechanisms and scopes of responsibility (McNeal 2016: 38–43). Naturally, it is necessary to take into consideration the limitations of such programmes, mainly their effectiveness and true impact on employee behaviour. It is common knowledge that even the best training programme is not able to prevent financial fraud and the fact that a company has a mission does not entail its general acceptance. Even the best formulation of a company mission is practically insignificant for changing employee behaviour, unless a mission is closely connected with a strong and well-established organisational culture.

Some management manuals indicate that the crucial moment in which it is possible to detect financial fraud is the time of approving financial documentation (e.g. Han 2016: 35–37). It is true that people who approve, for example, invoices for payment, check whether they are consistent with placed orders, executed agreements, applicable budgets, etc. However, restricting control activities to just one stage is hardly effective. Therefore, the public sector introduces the principles of managerial control. The problem is that people using such control systems are not fully aware of the significance of the so-called process control (the subject of control activities is not a single stage, but the whole financial management process).[1]

An effectively functioning quality management system can be an important factor in preventing financial fraud. Such a system introduces strict regulations concerning the monitoring of complete processes, e.g. the process of providing services (see the example below).

---

[1] During quality audits conducted in the years 2009–2013, the author used to check the status of the process approach in the Polish local government administration. Among 20 audited offices, only one had integrated the processes functioning within the scope of managerial control with the processes of the quality management system.

In one restaurant, the kitchen staff decided to supplement their meagre wages. The restaurant would buy a lot of butter and oil for frying purposes. But in fact, food was fried in old and used oil. Saved products were sold on the local market by the cooks' friends. However, when the owner introduced an HACCP (Hazard Analysis Critical Control Point) system in the restaurant, it became necessary to develop methods of controlling so-called critical points and conducting periodic audits. During one of the inspections conducted by the owner herself, it turned out that the control card included an entry about a change of oil. The entry was false. The implementation of permanent monitoring revealed that the employees made fictitious entries in the documentation and selected purchased products were stolen and removed from the restaurant.

Source: the authors' own work

It is believed that the most successful methods of preventing financial fraud include conducting regular audits and implementing management systems (comprehensive solutions comprising monitoring, product identification and data analysis), but the most important role is played by an appropriate organisational culture and an ethical system, which, firstly, depend on many factors and HR processes, and secondly, are difficult to shape. Despite numerous preventive solutions, financial frauds are rarely discovered, sometimes by accident (Ombler 2016: M6–M8).

Organisations in which managers manifest and promote ethical behaviour are less exposed to various types of fraud (Albrecht et al. 2012).

The following factors can fulfil an important role in combating financial fraud:

- a zero-tolerance policy (there is no tolerance for even the slightest fraud; guilty employees are punished accordingly);
- a very strict control of employees (their previous behaviour, the reliability of provided data);
- a whistleblowing policy;
- procedures limiting the risk of fraud;
- a control of the reliability of conducted audits (complete audit processes and auditors' competences) (Chauhan and Kenkre 2011: 8–17).

Actions oriented towards employee disciplining depend on, among others, the following factors:

- whether fraud is undertaken by individuals or groups of employees (to what extent such behaviour is isolated or approved by others);
- whether an organisation as a whole has an economic interest in the public exposure of financial fraud (e.g. the case of companies listed on stock exchanges, information on fraud can influence share prices or destroy reputation);
- corporate governance mechanisms (only the adoption of voluntary regulations influences employee behaviour; the impact of legal regulations is seriously limited);[2]
- the scope of authority possessed by people committing financial fraud (see the example below);[3]
- an organisation's overall tax policy and legal regulations;[4]
- the range of horizontal integration (complex supply and distribution chains favour financial fraud, make it possible to manipulate with prices or payments as well as to change suppliers or materials).

> Dr. Ogru was a director in an Australian biotechnological company. Between 2004 and 2013, together with two other employees, he swindled his employer out of 6.1 million Australian dollars. The mechanism of the fraud was based on issuing and approving false invoices. The criminal practice lasted for such a long time because it was the director who approved false invoices for payment. It took the company's controlling commission a few years to prove that many invoices approved by him were false.
> Source: (Lim 2016)

---

[2] For example, after the fall of Enron more attention was paid to corporate governance, which cannot be based on formal and normative solutions only as it depends on the adoption of voluntary standards.

[3] Some research proves that positions held by employees within a power structure influence their behaviour (e.g. Deluna 2016: 17–17).

[4] Almost 30% of the 700 largest British companies did not pay taxes in the years 2006–2007.

In 2012 it turned out that Starbucks had not paid taxes in the United Kingdom for three years. Tesco, an icon of British commerce, developed a special offshore structure of tax havens in order to avoid paying taxes.

4.3.4   Corruption

Similarly to all other notions used in everyday life and constituting the subject of scientific research, corruption has many definitions. According to one of them, corruption is "a practice consisting of acquiring wealth and power by means of illegal methods. Such practice is aimed at acquiring private gain and constitutes a public cost. A manifestation of corruption is the abuse of public power in order to achieve private gain". (based on: Pakdel et al. 2012: 194–204). Some researchers regard corruption as financial fraud (Murphy and Free 2016: 41–56). Corruption is studied from the perspective of relations occurring between the possession of broadly understood power (e.g. power resulting from a higher position in the hierarchy of authority) and the inclination to abuse such power to achieve private gain. Such behaviour constitutes a clear conflict of interests (an organisation's objectives do not coincide with an individual's objectives). Such relations are usually difficult to perceive because the consequences of corruption become noticeable, if at all, after a longer period of time.

In view of the difficulties of defining corruption, it is frequently its attributes that become the subject of research (cf. Zadjali and Wright 2012: 34–51). For example:

- deliberate actions (e.g. delaying or accelerating various decisions or actions in return for private or group gain);
- the possibility of exercising power in the manner facilitating an employee's involvement in corrupt practices;
- the inclination to conceal corruption motives and actions;
- acquiring money or other benefits to which a given person is not entitled;
- abusing the previously developed trust (e.g. in order to achieve private gain).

Corruption manifests itself in various types of behaviour. It can consist of employing relatives and placing particularly beneficial orders with them, using confidential information to increase the value of held shares and thus achieving private gain. The most frequent types of corruption are bribery, nepotism and collusion.

In the public sector, corruption crimes include passive bribery (venality), active bribery (corruption), paid protection, active paid protection (trade in influence), and abuse of a public post.

There are a few types of corruption that can be helpful practically in developing anticorruption strategies and programmes (Langseth 1999):

- Petty corruption—it is practised by employees whose salaries are so low that they have to look for other sources of income. It comprises bribes of a low value; sometimes such bribes are accepted by officials who try to supplement their income in order to maintain their families.
- Grand corruption—it is practised by officials/employees holding higher managerial positions who are motivated by sheer greed. Resources acquired by dishonest employees usually remain at their disposal; however, sometimes such funds are forwarded to political parties.
- Episodic corruption—it is characteristic of organisations where the majority of employees are honest and corruption behaviour is not a standard (dishonest employees are disciplined).
- Systemic corruption—it is characteristic of organisations where unethical behaviour is deeply rooted in a pathological organisational culture; corruption behaviour is not countered, it constitutes a standard. Resources received from corruption return to the social system (without such resources the system is not able to exist).

The literature on the subject and normative acts refer also to political corruption. This term is used by the World Bank. The notion of political corruption comprises such manifestations as bribery, presents, donations, nepotism, favouritism, budget abuse, supporting political or election campaigns. Researchers increasingly refer to so-called managerial corruption (see the example below).

According to Article 296a §I of the penal code:
"Anyone who, while in a managerial position in an organisational unit performing business, or in an employment relationship, a service contract or a contract for a specific task, demands or accepts a financial or personal benefit or the promise thereof, in return for abusing the authority granted to him or her, or for failing an obligation, could inflict material damage on the unit, or constitute an act of unfair competition or an unacceptable act of preference for the buyer or recipient of goods, services or benefits, is liable to imprisonment for between three months and five years."
Source: The Penal Code Act of 6 June 1997 (Journal of Laws 1997)

On the basis of previous experiences, it should be stated that preventing corruption has a positive influence on investors' decisions (investors more willingly move their funds to places where they are positive that the market game is played honestly).

Much research indicates close relations between corruption and poverty, a low level of economic development, social stratifications and a low level of life satisfaction.

In business activities, corruption destroys trust, which is a valuable element of social capital determining an organisation's development, the costs of such development, market opportunities, operational effectiveness, etc. When the range of corruption behaviour increases, the "market value of acts of corruption decreases" (Zadjali and Wright 2012: 34–51). A wide range of observed corruption behaviour persuades players to adopt and intensify such behaviour, but at the same time they become less capable of estimating the occurring phenomena and achieved profits. As a consequence, nobody trusts anybody and corruption becomes the primary cause of eliminating economically positive behaviour. Networks of cooperation are exposed to the risk of destruction.

The adoption of any anti-corruption system can increase the value of listed shares. On the other hand, a company's failure to comply with anti-corruption law entails not only financial penalties but also loss of reputation, reliability and trust of business partners.

Actions connected with preventing corruption can be divided into two groups.

Firstly, many countries establish legal, normative and ethical regulations whose main objective is to increase anti-corruption awareness.

Sometimes such programmes constitute parts of wider motivational programmes. For example, the US government encourages the authorities of Afghanistan to measure their level of corruption. In cooperation with the World Bank, the government of Ghana has introduced a programme increasing the transparency of decision-making processes on the basis of the common high-speed Internet connectivity. Anti-corruption programmes have been developed and improved in Russia, as well as in various Asian and African countries. Obviously, there are different reasons and motives for fighting against corruption. Sometimes this fight is an element of political games. A considerable part of recommendations concerning the limitation of corruption apply to the cultural sphere; emphasis is put, for example, on improving morale, increasing social expectations and implementing the ethical principles of conduct. Although fully justified, such advice is difficult to put into practice.

The other group comprises actions undertaken by organisations themselves. Particular emphasis is put on the importance of large business entities and the whole financial sector in limiting corruption.

It is generally believed that an important role in reducing corruption is played by employee training, which helps people to avoid corruption situations by providing them with detailed descriptions of various types of unethical behaviour. Such training also makes it possible for employees to cope in difficult situations that may lead to corruption.

A controversial, but often effective, idea is to increase employees' salaries (cf. Sato 2011: 56–63). Cultural habits and psychological traits (e.g. greed) are difficult to change, but pay rises and penalties for corruption can be effective.

It is stressed that one of the methods of counteracting corruption is to ensure the transparency of conducted operations. However, this method has many technical, social and organisational limitations. One of the problems is to distinguish the resources of explicit knowledge from tacit knowledge. Undertaken actions are not always effective because corruption is a complex problem dependent on many mutually related factors. It is known, for example, that corruption is not only a problem in poor countries. It is also known that financial motives are not the only ones contributing to the occurrence of corruption (cf. Roman 2012: 237–254).

Transparency is assessed on a scale from 0 to 10 points. For example, according to the data published in 2012, Statoil scored 8.3 points. The company not only established its own anti-corruption programme but also published information on its taxes, received subsidies (e.g. export subsidies) and profits earned in every country where it conducts business activities. ExxonMobil and Walmart scored 6.4 points each, General Electric—6 points, Coca-Cola—5.3 points, Amgen—5 points, Merck & Co.—4.9 points. In 2012 Toyota scored less than three points, similar to Gazprom and Amazon. At present 105 companies are the subject of the survey.
Source: (Lloréns Vélez 2012: 22–22)

Transparency is measured for a very simple reason: it is very difficult to identify the extent of corruption. What is more, it is also difficult to assess some forms of legal corporate behaviour (such as paying for mineral mining licences). There is no certainty as to how such funds are used and how their amounts influence possible subsequent government contracts. Formal fees are perceived in the category of bribes and therefore, it is only large corporations that are awarded contracts, permits, licences, etc. It is increasingly claimed that extensive social networks make it difficult to identify corruption ties. This happens not only within supply chains but also during changes in forms of ownership, mergers, acquisitions, etc. Therefore, an important task is to develop principles of transparent cooperation with all third parties such as consultants, agents, auditors, etc.

Companies' readiness to increase transparency is influenced by two groups of factors. One group comprises the environment or cultural factors connected with the traditions of conducting business activities (e.g. American and European corporations receive better ratings than their competitors from Russia or China). The other group of factors comprises companies' objects (it turns out that companies from the mining sector are more transparent).

However, the innovation index needs to be taken into consideration in such comparisons.

Computer programmes that increase the range of data accessibility are helpful in fighting corruption (cf. e.g. Andersen et al. 2011: 387–417). Clients or citizens are usually allowed to monitor decision-making processes and it is access to knowledge that is protected. For example, in public administration offices, it is possible to track all applications going through the stages of relevant procedures. Hence the customer knows whether there are any delays, preferential treatment, etc. However, such programmes have to be followed by the publication of detailed procedures for handling particular products or services. The majority of experts specialising in this subject agree that technical infrastructure can fulfil only a supplementary or auxiliary function.

It is also believed that organisations should undertake voluntary actions aimed at limiting corruption. In practice, this means the necessity of the following:

- conducting social research into corruption behaviour and situations;
- carrying out management reviews oriented towards preventing corruption and solving problems occurring in consequences of acts of corruption;
- taking into consideration the idea of a supply chain in an anti-corruption system (identifying opportunities for and consequences of corruption along a whole supply chain).

A very important role in anti-corruption systems is played by the credibility of various reports, statements and information that are provided not only to key stakeholders but also to all potentially interested parties. Therefore, the necessity of authenticating all information is strongly emphasised. Organisations have many tools at their disposal. It is worth paying attention to the following:

- requesting independent external audits and expert opinions;
- establishing relations between published information and so-called primary information (e.g. information constituting a basis for a particular report).

Corruption develops in various organisations where privileged elites appear, there are no established decision-making procedures or inevitable punishments for breaking the law. This is why an important role in limiting corruption can be played by various intra-organisational entities (e.g. works councils, trade unions, supervisory boards).

Action to increase anti-corruption awareness consist not only of conducting training courses for employees but also in establishing a permanent position of an anti-corruption consultant, conducting audits, using check sheets, undertaking preventive actions (without punishments for employees).

At present there are two approaches towards implementing anti-corruption systems. In the first approach, a system based on ISO standards is integrated with the requirements of an anti-corruption policy. The other approach is to include an anti-corruption programme in general ethical principles.

The methods of limiting corruption are described separately for the public sector and the private sector. For example, the public sector emphasises the importance of the following:

- ensuring relevant training courses for employees (such courses fulfil the informative function; in poor countries, education increases customers'/citizens' knowledge of their rights and conducted processes);
- increasing the transparency of decision-making processes;
- maintaining contacts with customers and suppliers (in particular, direct meetings are an opportunity for sharing information and opinions);
- introducing e-services that facilitate the monitoring of processes and decreases subjectivity) (more: www3).

There is no doubt, however, that limiting corruption requires integrated actions.

Specially prepared programmes specify precisely what actions should be undertaken by the government, the media, the management, the customs service, etc. One such programme (Mauritius National Integrity Action Plan) advises public sector entities as follows:

- to increase the role which can be fulfilled by ethical codes;
- to increase transparency (also with respect to financing political parties);
- to introduce necessary declarations (similar to those used in quality policies);

- to introduce resources monitoring;
- to increase managers' responsibility for made decisions;
- to introduce the monitoring of financial (banking, insurance, etc.) processes.

Simultaneously it is emphasised that the state should control monopolistic and quasi-monopolistic practices, and public entities have to act in coordination, educate society, increase people's awareness with respect to desired behaviour and publish reports on corruption (Langseth 1999).

Fighting corruption is not an easy task and related recommendations are characterised by a high degree of imperfection. For example, 'An Anti-corruption Manual for Public Officers' recommends as follows (An Anti-corruption Manual for Public Officers 2011):

- to introduce a reporting system (superiors are to be informed of their subordinates' actions; reporting is to be a disciplinary tool);
- to develop mechanisms of reporting all irregularities and even suspicions of irregularities;
- to limit latitude in decision-making processes ("the scopes of employees' tasks and duties should be precisely defined");
- to introduce job rotation and changes in the composition of the personnel;
- to introduce the principle whereby important tasks have to be performed by at least two employees;
- to prepare a map of corruption risks;
- to develop and implement a document circulation system.

It should be stated unambiguously that every good organisation, every quality management system, is able to limit corruption. Such systems regulate internal and external communication activities, introduce the necessity of monitoring processes, supervising documentation, etc. In practice, it turns out that what is difficult is not so much developing an anti-corruption system but making employees aware that it should be maintained.

Anti-corruption systems can also be the subject of benchmarking research.

4.4   Abuse Against Others

Abuse against others is behaviour that is physically or psychologically (intimidation, harassment, ignoring) harmful to employees and consequently to the whole organisation. Such behaviour manifests itself in various ways, increasingly in combination with modern technologies.

4.4.1   Mobbing

There is probably no other activity that has been the subject of such a large number of publications in the past decade. The concept of mobbing is universally known about, but not always correctly understood (see the example below). It is often used interchangeably with the following terms:

- bullying (this term is often regarded as a synonym for mobbing, although it is accepted that bullying is a form of physical aggression expressed by a superior);
- emotional abuse (the term used, among others, by L. Keashly);
- frustrating;
- tormenting (the term used, among others, by B. I. Raknes);
- inappropriate treatment (the term used, among others, by L. P. Spratlan).

In a certain district the rubbish collection company noticed that the inhabitants were not segregating their rubbish. Therefore, it put an announcement on notice boards reminding the inhabitants about the obligatory segregation of rubbish. One inhabitant declared that such behaviour constituted a case of mobbing.
Source: the authors' own work

Mobbing has been defined as "hostile and unethical behaviour (communication) expressed systematically by one or more persons against usually one employee (as the target of such behaviour)" (Leymann 1990: 120). "Mobbing means actions or behaviour concerning an employee or directed against an employee consisting in persistent and long-lasting harassment or intimidation, leading, in such an employee, to a lowered assessment of occupational usefulness, causing or meant to cause the humiliation or ridicule of an employee, their isolation or elimination from a working team" (The Labour Law Act of 26 June 1974: §2).

The most frequent form of mobbing is referred to as "downward mobbing". Managers are mobbers and their subordinates are the victims of psychological and physical attacks (Vandekerckhove and Commers 2003: 41–50). The victims of mobbing are usually weaker people, not strong enough to defend themselves.

If particular negative behaviour (e.g. humiliating others) is to be regarded as mobbing, it has to be repeatable and last for a long time. The relations between mobbing and discipline are as follows: firstly, strong, pathological discipline frequently entails the use of mobbing. All acts of employee intimidation, frustration, harassment or humiliation are used where discipline is based on coercion, where, in the practice of management, everything is subordinate to unrealistic deadlines or financial objectives. Secondly, proper work discipline is a perfect means of preventing mobbing (in this context, a particular role is played by a control system, zero tolerance for pathological behaviour and superiors' direct interventions).

It is generally agreed that a mobber is a person who:

- overestimates their own competences;
- has an exaggerated sense of self-worth;
- accepts no criticism from others;
- does not trust anybody;
- is cowardly.

Mobbing:

- is the cause of many health problems (mental disorders, apathy, lack of concentration, social phobias, withdrawal, various psychosomatic symptoms, depression, anger, anxiety), and therefore, victims of mobbing are frequently on medical leave and sometimes eventually quit their jobs (e.g. Zapf 1999: 70–85; Eriksen et al. 2016: 129–150);

- destroys trust, creativity and motivation (e.g. Федорова 2015: 118–125);
- decreases job satisfaction and employee commitment (e.g. Ertureten et al. 2013: 205–216).

Consequently, mobbing generates both economic and social costs.

Some research indicates that women and men react a little differently to mobbing (e.g. women spend more time on medical leave and are also less appreciated at work) (e.g. Tomić 2012; Eriksen et al. 2016).

Researchers study various manifestations of mobbing. For example: disregard, inappropriate compensation, rejection, ignoring, isolation, humiliation, gossip, ridicule, unjustified criticism, bad work assessment, excessive control, excessive workload, assignment of worse tasks, rejection of requests for holidays, threats, unjustified accusations, sexual harassment (Tomić 2012: 243–25).

Research shows links between the probability of acts of mobbing and management styles. For example, transformational leadership decreases the probability of mobbing, while the autocratic style increases such probability. Paternalistic leadership also favours mobbing (Ertureten et al. 2013: 205–216).

In many countries, legislators have included recommendations concerning prevention of mobbing in labour codes (or other legal regulations). For example, the Polish labour code[5] (The Labour Code Act of 26 June 1974) states unambiguously that employers are obliged to prevent mobbing. According to the same labour code, an employee who proves that the conduct of other people has caused "their health disorder, may claim a relevant sum of money from the employer as compensation for suffered harm" (The Labour Code Act of 26 June 1974: §3). According to the labour law, "an employee who has terminated their employment contract in consequence of mobbing is entitled to claim compensation from the employer in the amount of not less than the minimum remuneration for labour established under separate regulations" (The Labour Code Act of 26 June 1974: §4).

---

[5] According to K. Durniat (2014), Poland is the fourth European country (after Sweden, France and Belgium) to implement legal regulations concerning the protection of employees against mobbing.

Prevention of mobbing was an item on the agenda of the European Parliament, which in 2001 adopted a resolution on harassment in the workplace (2001/2339).

Organisations implement anti-mobbing procedures, but their effectiveness varies. Their goal is to inform employees about the nature of mobbing, how to react in a mobbing situation, where complaints should be filed, etc. Sometimes, however, cases of mobbing are not reported. It happens when reported cases of mobbing are considered by commissions consisting of the employees of the same firm (see the example below).

> For two years our company has had an anti-mobbing procedure. During that period we didn't have a single report of even suspicions of mobbing. We have changed the procedure recently; the anti-mobbing commission consists not of people from the outside—a psychologist, a lawyer and a trade union representative—but from a different company, our subsidiary. And do you know what happened? Now we have a lot of cases on our hands. Employees themselves started to get in touch with the commission.
> (the HR department director in a company listed on the stock exchange and employing 3500 people)

Earlier publications have indicated that fighting mobbing is difficult, but not impossible (the solutions applied in Germany are a case in point). It has been concluded that limiting mobbing is connected with changes in managers' behaviour or even with appropriate adjustments to work organisation systems (Resch and Schubinski 1996: 295).

Research conducted in Poland has shown that, in practice, the following actions are required:

- training allowing employees to become aware of the problem of mobbing (such training should be targeted first of all at employees, and not only managers or HR specialists);
- shaping an anti-mobbing culture which includes the following important elements: principles specified in ethical codes, clear and transparent rules of communication, managers' vigilance and concern for integration between superiors and subordinates, a concern for the proper allocation of resources (including authority), an environment free from time pressure, ensuring that employees are not overburdened with work;

- communicating unambiguously the absence of acceptance for mobbing;
- ensuring managers' active participation in solving difficult situations;
- conducting social research (e.g. into employee satisfaction or pathological behaviour) and various controlling activities;
- developing procedures for reporting and dealing with cases of mobbing;
- appointing people responsible for solving mobbing problems (Durniat et al. 2016: 83–95; Durniat 2014: 105–114.)

The aforementioned recommendations are very much correct. In practice, however, superiors do not know how to cope with mobbing. What is more, it is superiors' behaviour that frequently causes conflicts and accusations of mobbing. Consequently, research shows clearly that many cases are covered up and anti-mobbing procedures are often of little effectiveness (e.g. Durniat 2014).

Researchers note that "even in those organizations which have established ethical standards and mobbing reporting procedures, such standards and procedures are often dead and ineffective, and reported cases are sometimes referred for solution to accidental people (Durniat et al. 2016: 89).

Any anti-mobbing policy should take into consideration the results of competence tests (conducted not only at the selection stage). Although there are doubts about the effectiveness of various psychological tests, their result can help in making decisions about promotions or the allocation of new tasks, especially ones connected with managing employee teams.

The organisational causes of mobbing constitute a serious and underestimated problem. Acts of mobbing take place when resources are allocated improperly, employees are overworked and an organisation has financial objectives only. The worst situation is when management's remuneration depends on the level of employees' achieving financial objectives. It results in employee harassment, coercion and stiff competition.

Therefore, a significant role in an organisation's overall anti-mobbing policy is played by a remuneration system (salaries have to depend on the degree of achieving both qualitative and financial objectives) and process audits (see the list of audit questions below).

A checklist of audit questions for service sector organisations:

- Please describe activities undertaken on the audit day divided into eight hours' work time.
- Please describe the course of the decision-making process (including necessary consultations, parts of the process performed by other organisational units or employees).
- Please describe the possibility of performing process input.
- Please specify your own and other employees' shares in process monitoring.
- Please specify internal consultations (on the audit day, with other employees for the purpose of carrying out processes).
- How much time does it take you to enter data in databases?
- How much time does it take you to analyse received data?
- Which forms of communication with customers does the employee prefer (e.g. in order to verify applications)?
- What scopes of decision-making authority does the audited person possess?
- Who approves draft decisions/information?
- Who approves decisions?
- Does the employee have all data (including access to databases) connected with performing the process?
- How much time does it take the employee to wait for decisions or arrangements made by other employees or institutions?
- What document circulation system does the organisational unit use?
- How much time does it take the employee to perform additional required actions?
- How much time does the employee spend on reporting activities? (How often are reports prepared and sent?)
- Who is responsible in the organisational unit for monitoring processes (in terms of completing particular stages)?
- Who is responsible for identifying legal requirements?
- What is the impact of legal regulations on the duration of performing services (with respect to a particular example)?
- Does the employee notice any sources of wastage? If so, what are they?
- Do any actions require the superior's acceptance (e.g. in the process of communicating with the customer)?
- In which teams or commissions is the employee a member?

Note: verification has to be connected with documentation (selected examples) review.

4.4.2 Stalking

Stalking consists the most frequently of deliberate, persistent and long-lasting actions aimed against a particular person, with a view to humiliating such a person or disorganising their life. In the case of stalking, the causative act consists of persistently harassing another person or people close to such a person. As a consequence, "the stalked person's privacy is seriously invaded and the person themselves feels justifiably threatened" (www4).

Stalking has three characteristic features. It is:

- deliberate (actions are usually planned in advance, but sometimes depend on a concrete situation);
- malicious (it results from the stalker's intention to torment somebody and make their normal functioning difficult);
- repeatable (one-off actions are not stalking; stalking lasts from a few weeks to a few years).

Stalking appears in various forms, which include uncalled-for and frequent telephone calls, persistent emails or letters, and loitering around the victim's home or place of work. Research shows unambiguously that the longer the duration of stalking, the greater the psychological, physical and social losses (McEwan et al. 2009: 149–158). There is usually some relationship between a stalker and their victim. A stalker undertakes various actions because they feel rejected or ignored (McEwan et al. 2009). Research conducted in the 1990s found that stalking perpetrators were usually middle-aged males (70–90 per cent) (Tjaden and Thoennes 1998: 1). They suffer from various mental and personality disorders (Rosenfeld and Lewis 2005: 343–357).

The opinion that stalking is limited to other people, mainly celebrities or political personas, had been generally accepted until the 1990s (Diette et al. 2014: 563–580). At present stalking is also regarded as a serious problem occurring in organisations.

The most frequent causes of stalking in the workplace include the following (Lewis 2014: 8–9):

- a desire for revenge (e.g. a dismissed employee harasses their former boss or co-workers);
- previous relations (rejecting or leaving a person; terminating a relationship can result in stalking, according to the principle that communication between former partners intensifies in the first phase after a split-up);
- infatuation (a stalker can be somebody who has fallen in love with a person) (see the example below);
- a desire to maintain a previous relationship (stalkers are sometimes people who have previously received help from their victims, with whom their victims have spent a lot of time).

I am the director of a private medical clinic. A few years ago one of the employees became infatuated with me. For a few months she would send me text messages and letters. When I rejected her proposition, my wife received an anonymous letter informing her that I had a lover in the workplace. I was furious. I wasn't able to reason with the employee. She was eventually fired and after some time things got back to normal.
(a director in a medical clinic employing 80 people)
I am a private detective. Once I received a strange commission. A company wanted me to keep their chief accountant under surveillance. As a matter of fact, the problem didn't concern her, but the person who had worked with her in the past. He had fallen in love with the accountant and when she rejected him, he started to stalk her. Consequently, the poor woman wasn't able to function properly. It turned out that the company's suspicions were fully justified. After a month of close surveillance we reported the case to the police.
Source: the authors' own work

Stalking causes people to lose their efficiency at work and even give up their jobs. Research conducted in the United Kingdom has shown that more than eighty per cent of organisations do not have relevant procedures or policies for coping with stalking (Lewis 2014: 8–9).

The identification of stalking is a very difficult task. For this purpose, special computer programmes are used more and more often; they analyse some key words and the frequency of their occurrence. However, there are no proven methods of preventing stalking because it is difficult to foresee employees' behaviour, whether somebody will feel offended, rejected, etc.

4.4.3   Sexual Harassment

Sexual harassment appears in two forms.

Firstly, in the work environment there are people who take advantage of their position (not necessarily a higher place in the organisational hierarchy) and demand sex in return for some favours (e.g. positive testimonials, promotion, a higher salary). This harassment is referred to as "quid pro quo" harassment. Secondly, harassment can consist of deliberately creating a hostile work environment. This form of harassment occurs between a harassed person and a harassing person, i.e. a colleague, a superior or another person directly or indirectly connected with the organisation.

It is possible to distinguish the following five groups of behaviour, referred to as sexual harassment:

a) sexual assaults and/or rapes;
b) coercion of sex by means of threats, punishments, etc;
c) sexual bribery consisting of acquiring sex in return for promises of rewards and other benefits;
d) "seductive behaviour", i.e. behaviour that is unwanted, unaccepted, inappropriate and offensive to a person's sense of dignity;
e) sexist behaviour that offends and humiliates the other sex (regarding the other sex as worse) (Fitzgerald et al. 1988: 32152–32175).

It is possible to distinguish three research approaches (Bugdol 2007). The first of them, the so-called gender approach, analyses interactions taking place between women and men in the workplace. For example, it tries to explain to what extent the number and quality of interactions influence sexual behaviour.

The second approach, the so-called role approach, studies the roles played by women and men. Finally, the power approach focuses on examining the influence of power and political domination on sexual behaviour. Among other things, researchers study to what extent roles played by people in various environments influence sexual harassment and whether what is expected from women and men is transferred to the workplace.

Some specialists regard sexual harassment as an element of mobbing, but the decisive majority focus on it as a separate problem.

Current experience indicates that sexual harassment is fostered by the unethical work environment, in particular the lack of reaction on the part of top management. Therefore, the notion of a "harassment culture" has been coined (e.g. Steinberg 2016: 68–69).

Harassment is favoured by a culture whose characteristic feature is that superiors hold considerable power over subordinates and such power tends to be abused. Sexual harassment often starts with intimidating potential victims and making them realise their superiors' enormous influence on their professional careers (see the example below).

> Clara, a student of photography, was an intern in the editorial office of a daily newspaper. Her supervisor asked her whether she had ever had sex, sent her vulgar text messages and made lewd propositions. After some time he went even further and asked Clara to come to his home. He wanted to know whether "she would be willing to do anything for him". Clara refused a few times, but eventually she gave up. She was afraid that a negative opinion about her internship would be detrimental to her future career. When she came to her supervisor's flat she asked if they could watch a film together. He answered that it probably wasn't what she had come for. She was forced to have oral sex with him.
> Source: (Westcott 2016: 18–21)

What happens frequently is that particular people receive favourable treatment and managers promote those employees with whom they have closer and sometimes intimate relations.

Various research conducted for the purpose of identifying factors favouring sexual harassment has shown that such factors include not only an organisational culture but also a national culture (cf. Toker 2016: 625–643), a stereotypical and unethical perception of the role of women and the fact of holding power. Research carried out in the public sector has shown that harassment is linked to age (e.g. Wynen 2016: 345–358), which does not mean that older people are not harassed at all.

Sexual harassment occurs in various environments: in production or service companies, and even in academic circles, which are dominated by the hierarchical culture and relations of dependence. Sexual harassment also concerns relations between employees and customers (Good and Cooper 2016: 447–469). This problem is so serious that some businesses, especially in the service sector, hierarchise their customers, referring to them as "our kings, bosses".

Preventing sexual harassment consists of performing social research oriented towards acquiring information on risk factors (a so-called risk-culture survey) (Steinberg 2016: 68–69).

Superiors have to remember that articulating malicious or sexist comments about somebody's clothes, behaviour or appearance may be regarded as a manifestation of harassment. Therefore, an important role in preventing sexual harassment is played by training courses providing relevant information and communication procedures (not only ones related directly to harassment). Many authors emphasise that undertaking disciplinary actions, for example, suspending an employee from duty, does not suffice (e.g. Death threat? Yeah, that's reason to quit 2016: 1–2). Employees need to know and become aware of what sexual harassment is and how they should behave towards their colleagues.

Settling disputes among employees and fighting with the manifestations of sexual harassment is very difficult, not only because not all types of inappropriate behaviour can be classified as harassment but also because the behaviour of dispute participants varies considerably. Not all harassed people react by escaping. Some employees counterattack, which in practice is equally unethical.

In one company, a trainee came to the conclusion that she was being harassed sexually. She declared that her boss came to her when he had an erection. At the same time, internal documentation showed that she had been disciplined on a number of occasions. She refused to follow instructions. After some time the troublesome trainee was dismissed. A subsequent analysis of monitoring records showed that she had often run after her superior, followed him into an elevator, and attacked him physically and verbally.
Source: (*Retaliation? Not If You Can Prove You Would Have Fired Anyone Who Broke the Same Rule* 2016: 2–2)

It happens sometimes that sexual harassment is returned—the harassed person retaliates with the same behaviour as the perpetrator. Lawyers emphasise that there is no justification for such behaviour. Breaching work discipline rules for whatever reason has to entail punishment. People discriminated or harassed react differently. In some cases, victims fight not against their harassers but the whole organisation.

Another problem is that sexual harassment tends to be combined with other manifestations of unethical behaviour; for example, with racial discrimination.

The attitude of top management, especially a zero-tolerance policy, is of enormous importance when fighting with sexual harassment as well as other criminal or unethical behaviour. Research shows that employee commitment to fighting against harassment can increase when all negative incidents have been identified and practical methods of coping with harassment have been developed and implemented. In this commitment, an important role is played by the sense of harm, injustice, sorrow or despair (Jiang et al. 2015: 1–21).

Preventing and fighting sexual harassment is very difficult because many people experiencing harassment ignore it (at least at the preliminary stage), and decide to spend some time on medical leave instead of coming to work. Victims of sexual harassment:

- are afraid of losing their jobs;
- are afraid of being perceived as difficult employees;
- do not believe in the effectiveness of procedures;
- are afraid of being accused of sexual provocations.

4.4.4 Blackmail

Blackmail is defined in many different ways, the most often on the basis of three theoretical approaches. One of them focuses on a simple relation: somebody starts to blackmail a victim by declaring the possession of some secrets and promising not to disclose them if the victim follows their instructions. Consequently, blackmail is often defined as "forcing somebody to perform a particular action; extorting something (e.g. money) from somebody by means of intimidation or threats to disclose compromising events or documents" (Skorupka et al. 1969: 795). Blackmail is a threat to reveal somebody's secrets (Block et al. 2000: 593–622). Blackmail is facilitated by access to information and therefore, in contemporary organisations, blackmailers are often hackers (but also IT specialists with access to email systems can become blackmailers).

In the second approach, blackmail is a threat of getting involved in unethical or criminal behaviour (Robinson et al. 2010: 291–352).

The third approach regards blackmail as a social process with its input (acquired secrets), inside (a series of interactions and communications) and output (disclosure of secrets, termination of blackmail). It is an interactive game played by a blackmailer and a victim (The Social Cost of Review of Law & Economics 2011: 337–351). Blackmail is almost always connected with fear. Fear, in turn, can lead to many other types of counterproductive behaviour, reduced commitment or actions inconsistent with applicable standards or customs.

In terms of morality or ethics, blackmail is something evil, but as far as the law is concerned, the manifestations of such behaviour as gossip or accusation need not constitute offences. Blackmailers usually demand money, but sometimes also sex, promotions or privileged positions in a group. Blackmail can also be oriented towards destroying an employee emotionally.

With respect to the direction of exerted pressure, we distinguish between internal and external blackmail. Inside organisations, blackmail can appear in financial, emotional, sexual and positional forms. Financial blackmail consists of the following:

- demanding money (indirectly or directly) in return for concessions, benefits, decisions, not revealing secrets, hiding the truth, etc.;
- making financial support dependent on complying with demands or making considerable concessions.

Blackmail is based on greed for money and power.

Emotional blackmail consists of using expressed emotions, social engineering techniques, organisational games or alleged weakness to acquire particular behaviour or benefits from a victim. "However, at the roots of every type of blackmail there is a threat which can be issued in many ways: if you do not behave the way I want you to, you will suffer" (Forward and Fraizer 1999: 12).

There are four types of emotional blackmailers:

a) the prosecutor, who threatens and accuses continually;
b) the flagellant, who hurts themselves (e.g. drinks alcohol, uses drugs), threatens to hurt themselves;
c) the tempter, who uses the carrot and stick method;
d) the martyr, who plays the "guess-what-you-have-done-to-me" game, expects the victim to give them everything they want, feels abandoned and humiliated and blames the victim for this (Sobolewska 2006).

Sexual blackmail consists of threatening a person who is known to manifest sexual behaviour that is not acceptable in a given culture. In the case of sexual blackmail, sex is either the means or the end of obtaining other benefits. Blackmail victims are often threatened with the disclosure of some compromising information of a sexual character (Bugdol 2007).

In 2013 the police arrested a man who had been blackmailing a woman: in return for not disclosing her compromising photographs, he demanded more photographs and recordings. The blackmailed woman was convinced that she was participating in a research project. The blackmailer had sent her an invitation to participate in a study called "Various types of breasts and their perception". For participation in the alleged research project, the woman had been promised a high remuneration.
Source: (Feeney 2014)

Positional blackmail appears in two variants:

• It is an attempt to acquire a higher or privileged position within an organisation.
• It is a situation in which a blackmailer strengthens their demands, taking advantage of their own privileged position.

An organisation can be a blackmail victim itself, especially if its business activities are globalised or fulfil an important role in a given society.

Thus it is possible to refer to external blackmail. It is political blackmail if, for example, a management board is coerced into making particular decisions in return for not informing competitors about the victims' special privileges.

Organisations can be the victims of social blackmail attempted by various social groups (e.g. hackers, third-sector organisations, other institutions). Such blackmail can effectively prevent organisations from developing new projects. In this case, blackmail does not have to entail revealing any secrets; it becomes a transaction ("we do not criticise you or destroy your image, but you give us something in return"). Such blackmail can change the marketing orientation of a particular company.

Organisations can blackmail each other; for example, when they pursue benefits such as new contracts, tax reliefs, subsidies or location decisions.

There is little knowledge about how blackmail can be prevented. This results from a simple fact: secrets of blackmail victims are not necessarily connected with their professional duties. Blackmailers take advantage of the fact that somebody has a different sexual orientation, has some family problems, has committed some crime, etc.

One of the methods of preventing blackmail is restricting access to specific information (e.g. information connected with conducted financial transactions).

4.5   Further Research

Further research should establish relations between manifestations of citizenship behaviour and counterproductive behaviour. As has already been mentioned, in practice people exhibiting citizenship behaviour can also manifest counterproductive behaviour. Research shows that when employees display citizenship behaviour, they grant themselves the right to behave counterproductively. Thus, the following questions arise: what are individual motives for citizenship behaviour? How is it possible to prevent the negative consequences of such behaviour?

Research conducted so far into the causes of counterproductive behaviour is by no means complete. There must exist many other factors favouring counterproductive behaviour. Such factors can include, for example, the lack of the awareness of quality (the consequences of non-compliance with established quality standards) and improperly established objectives (e.g. the lack of connections between quality objectives and strategic objectives, establishing objectives that are impossible to measure). In quality management systems, it is assumed that employees' awareness of the role of quality is of primary importance for their behaviour. On the other hand, information on the achievement of quality objectives is important for employees' motivation and inclination to maintain a high level of commitment. The lack of such information and, what is more, the lack of the awareness of quality or the non-acceptance of quality objectives can also result in counterproductive behaviour.

There is much research concerning sabotage, but there is not enough knowledge about the mechanisms of extensive sabotage, for example, network sabotage. Destruction of the organisation's capital can be a planned and purposeful process often carried out not by one perpetrator, but by various groups of employees who are driven by the desire for revenge. They use different tactics, for example, they intimidate employees.

Sabotage consists also of destroying an organisation's formal structures. In practice, such behaviour involves saboteurs' establishing their own connections, cliques or networks of interests. Determining the possibility of destroying particular types of such formal structures can be an interesting research problem.

If receiving benefits that do not result from ownership, competences or commitment is regarded as theft, then receiving undue remuneration (e.g. bonuses depending exclusively on the effort and commitment of employees) can be considered theft as well. In practice, such situations are fostered by the existing employee assessment systems and remuneration systems. Pursuing ever higher financial results and higher efficiency contributes to fierce competition and causes unethical behaviour. Thus, another question arises: to what extent is such theft the cause of other types of unethical behaviour such as financial fraud or forging financial documents or economic analysis?

Preventing the theft of ideas or plans is a very difficult task. Even the best regulations are not able to prevent theft completely. Prohibitions against competitive activities can be ignored easily by establishing businesses in the name of other people. Theft is always related to trust. The problem of stealing intellectual property can be studied with respect to the attractiveness of such property, the sense of injustice experienced by thieves, pressure from the outside, a desire for revenge, personality traits, etc.

Theft of knowledge perpetrated by hackers is another interesting research subject. The following questions arise: to what extent is theft connected with the actions of employees themselves? What is the scope of cooperation between thieves and employees? To what extent are hacking attacks carried out by employees themselves?

Establishing to what degree various forms of flexible employment facilitate the theft of work time would be another interesting research problem. Flexible work-time forms are increasingly being introduced; for example, employees can participate in job-sharing programmes, flexibly lengthen and shorten their work time in return for an extra day off.

Assessing the theft of work time is another interesting issue. Such assessments can depend on what employees do during their extra work breaks (which situation is worse: when they drink coffee or when they surf the Internet?).

Employee absenteeism, especially if it results from the complete lack of any motivation to work, is a serious problem. However, we know little about the opposite phenomenon, i.e. employees' coming to work even when they are gravely ill. According to preliminary research into the phenomenon of "presenteeism", almost twenty per cent of employees are convinced that working long hours will help them in their careers and that employers expect employees to stay at work after regular working hours (Woods 2008: 26–26). Such convictions are close to the idea of citizenship behaviour and can result in, mainly unconscious, counterproductive behaviour.

Financial fraud increasingly adopts the form of establishing companies whose sole objective is to achieve profit quickly by means of unethical business activities. Such unethical criminal activities consist of using false customer service procedures (misleading customers, swindling money from them), offering products that are worthless or harmful for customers (e.g. some dietary supplements). Thus, the question arises as to how participation in such an "enterprise" influences the competences of employees who, after the downfall of their fraudulent employer, have to function in the new work environment.

There is no research analysing the influence of vertical integration on limiting the number of financial frauds. Does the integration which introduces the same quality standards contribute to greater control and consequently limit the range of unethical behaviour?

It is not known to what extent criminal behaviour of top management influences disciplinary actions undertaken by them. There is a correlation between the time of detecting a crime and the scale of fraud as well as the position of power (Deluna 2016: 17–17). Another question arises as to whether people committing financial fraud decrease in any way the level of control over their subordinates.

Greed and related behaviour definitely deserve further research, although it is not a common study conducted by organisations (e.g. Bruhn and Lowrey 2012: 136–150). On the other hand, there are many source materials concerning the greed of financial institutions or bankers (e.g. Dhiman 2008).

Organisations which have implemented anti-mobbing procedures face the topical problem of their effectiveness. It turns out that fighting mobbing depends not only on the composition of a commission, the weight of collected evidence, the commission members' interviewing skills, but also on employees' honesty, the level of fear, etc. Hence it should be determined to what extent a certain type of organisational culture facilitates the identification and limitation of mobbing and other forms of pathological behaviour.

Specialists in human resource management can conduct further research into the sources and manifestations of stalking in the workplace or connected with the workplace. Stalking is a relatively new notion; in the past it was believed that it only concerned relations outside the workplace.

We do not know how and to what extent the media coverage of legal disputes between employers and their former employees encourages others to fight such phenomena as mobbing, stalking or sexual harassment. Some researchers presume that such news encourages undecided people to start fighting unethical behaviour.

The question also arises as to whether knowing that there are other victims of harassment encourages particular individuals to put up a legal fight with their oppressors. This is what happens in the case of sexual harassment where a legal action taken by one person (e.g. Gretchen Carlson, a former Fox News employee) encourages other victims to follow suit. Strategies followed by immigrant employees with high aspirations and higher education against people harassing them in the workplace would constitute an interesting research subject. The following questions arise: Does the necessity of keeping a job in combination with high aspirations modify employee behaviour? Do immigrant employees react differently to harassment or mobbing?

References

Act of 26 June 1974 r. The Labour Law, art. 94, Dz.U.2014.0.1502.
Act of 6 czerwca 1997 roku. Journal of Laws (Dz. U. z 1997 r. Nr 88 poz. 553, z późn. zm.).
Ahamed, Shaik Raffi, and V. Sunderasan. 2016. A Study on Employee Motivation and Its Influence on The Performance of The Organisation. *ITIHAS—The Journal of Indian Management* 6 (3): 381–393.
Albrecht, W. Steve, Chad O. Albrecht, Conan C. Albrecht, and Mark F. Zimbelman. 2012. *Fraud Examination*. 4th ed. Mason, OH: Southm.
Ambrose, Maureen L., Mark A. Seabright, and Marshall Schminke. 2002. Sabotage in the Workplace: The Role of Organizational Justice. *Organizational Behavior & Human Decision Process* 89 (1): 947–965.
An Anticorruption Manual for Public Officers. 2011. Wydawnictwo Centrum Szkolenia Policji w Legionowie, Warszawa, dokument dostępny na stronie. http://www.cba.gov.pl.
Analoui, Farhad. 1995. Workplace Sabotage: Its Styles, Motive and Management. *Journal of Management Development* 7 (14): 48–65.
Andersen, Thomas Barnebeck, Jeanet Bentzen, Carl-Johan Dalgaard, and Pablo Selaya. 2011. Does the Internet Reduce Corruption? Evidence from U.S. States and across Countries. *World Bank Economic Review* 25 (3): 387–417.
Beebe, Lawrence R. 2016. Where Is Fraud Likely in Your Employee Benefit Plan? *Benefits Magazine* 53 (6): 36–41.

Bernardin, H. John, and Donna K. Cooke. 1993. Validity of an Honesty Test in Predicting Theft Among Convenience Store Employees. *The Academy of Management Journal* 36 (5): 1097–1108.

Block, Walter, N. Stephan Kinsella, and Hans-Hermann Hoppe. 2000. The Second Paradox of Blackmail. *Business Ethics Quarterly* 10 (3): 593–622.

Bruhn, John G., and Josiah Lowrey. 2012. The Good and Bad About Greed: How the Manifestations of Greed Can Be Used to Improve Organizational and Individual Behavior and Performance. *Consulting Psychology Journal: Practice and Research* 64 (2): 136.

Bruursema, Kari, Stacey R. Kessler, and Paul E. Spector. 2011. Bored Employees Misbehaving: The Relationship Between Boredom and Counterproductive Work Behavior. *Work & Stress* 25 (2): 93–107.

Bugdol, Marek. 2007. *Gry i zachowania nieetyczne w organizacji*. Warszawa: Wyd. Difin.

Chauhan, Arun, and Mark Kenkre. 2011. Fraud Investigations—Employee Fraud. *Credit Control* 32: 8–3/4.

Cohen, Taya R., A.T. Panter, and Nazli Turan. 2013. Predicting Counterproductive Work Behavior from Guilt Proneness. *Journal of Business Ethics* 114 (1): 45–53.

Death Threat? Yeah, That's Reason to Quit. 2016. HR Specialist: California Employment Law. 10 (10).

Deluna, Joann. 2016. Senior-Level Employees are Most Frequent Expense Fraud Offenders. *Business Travel News*, 6/13/ 33 (9).

Dhiman, Satinder. 2008. Enhancing Business Education: Bringing Ethics and Excellence to Classroom. *Journal of Global Business Issues* 2 (Spring): 7–11. Conference Edition. 1 Diagram.

Dibattista, Ron A. 1991. Creating New Approaches to Resource and Deter Sabotage. *Public Personnel Management* 3 (20): 347–352.

———. 1996. Forecasting Sabotage Events in the Workplace. *Public Personnel Management* 1 (25): 41–52.

Diette, Timothy M., Arthur H. Goldsmith, Darrick Hamilton, William Darity, and Katherine McFarland. 2014. Stalking: Does it Leave a Psychological Footprint? *Social Science Quarterly (Wiley-Blackwell)* 95 (2): 563–580.

Dubois, Pierre. 1979. *Sabotage in Industry. Home Worth*. Pelikan Books (tłumaczenie z j. francuskiego R. Shead).

Durniat, Katarzyna. 2014. *The Education of Human Capital in the Field of Mobbing Protection*. Research Papers of the Wroclaw University of Economics (350).

Durniat, Katarzyna, Agnieszka Krupa, and Beata Działa. 2016. *Organizacyjne mechanizmy prewencji i radzenia sobie z mobbingiem z perspektwy specjalistów HR*. Research Papers of the Wrocław University of Economics (430).

Enns, Janelle R., and Maria Rotundo. 2012. When Competition Turns Ugly: Collective Injustice, Workgroup Identification, and Counterproductive Work Behavior. *Human Performance* 25 (1): 26–51.

Eriksen, Tine L. Mundberg, Annie Hogh, and Åse Marie Hansen. 2016. Long-Term Consequences of Workplace Bullying on Sickness Absence. *Labour Economics* 43: 129–150.

Eratureten, Aysegul, Zeynep Cemalcilar, and Zeynep Aycan. 2013. The Relationship of Downward Mobbing with Leadership Style and Organizational Attitudes. *Journal of Business Ethics* 116 (1): 205–216.

Feeney, Nolan. 2014. Google Employee Arrested for Alleged Nude Photo Blackmail. Time.com. 10/28/, pN. PAG. 1p.

Fitzgerald, Louise F., Sandra L. Shullman, Nancy Bailey, Margaret Richards, Janice Swecker, Yael Gold, Mimi Ormerod, and Lauren Weitzman. 1988. The Incidence and Dimensions of Sexual Harassment in Academia and the Workplace. *Journal of Vocational Behavior* 32 (2): 152–175.

Flaherty, Shane, and Simon A. Moss. 2007. The Impact of Personality and Team Context on the Relationship Between Workplace Injustice and Counterproductive Work Behavior. *Journal of Applied Social Psychology* 37 (11): 2549–2575.

Flurry, Laura A., and Krist Swimberghe. 2016. Consumer Ethics of Adolescents. *Journal of Marketing Theory & Practice* 24 (1, Winter): 91–108.

Forward, Susan, and Donna Fraizer. 1999. *Szantaż emocjonalny. Jak bronić się przed manipulacją i wykorzystaniem*. Gdańsk: GWP.

Free, Clinton, and Pamela R. Murphy. 2015. The Ties That Bind: The Decision to Co-Offend in Fraud. *Contemporary Accounting Research* 32 (1): 18–54.

Gabor, Thomas. 1994. *Everybody Does It! Crimes by the Public*. Toronto: University of Toronto Press.

Garbutt, Cynthia Horvath, and Lamont E. Stalworth. 1989. Theft in Workplace: An Arbiter's Perspective on Employee Discipline. *Arbitration Journal* 44 (3): 21–31.

Giacalone, Robert A., and Stephen B. Knouse. 1990. Justifying Wrongful Employee Behavior: The Role of Personality in Organizational Sabotage. *Journal of Business Ethnic* 9 (1): 55–61.

Glińska-Neweś, Aldona, and Andrzej Lis. 2016. *The Paradox of Co-Existence of Organisational Citizenship Behaviours and Counterproductive Work Behaviours*. Wrocław: Research Papers of the Wroclaw University of Economics (422).

Good, Laura, and Rae Cooper. 2016. 'But It's Your Job To Be Friendly': Employees Coping With and Contesting Sexual Harassment from Customers in the Service Sector. *Gender, Work & Organization* 23 (5): 447–469.

Gross-Schaefer, Arthur, Jeff Trigilo, Jamie Negus, and Ceng-Si Ro. 2000. Ethics Education in the Workplace: An Effective Tool to Combat Employee Theft. *Journal of Business Ethics* 26 (2): 89–100.

Han, John. 2016. The "Anti-Fraud Moment". *Internal Auditor* 73 (1): 35–37.

Idiakheua, E.O., and G.I. Idiakheua. 2012. Counterproductive Work Behaviour of Nigerians: An Insight Into Make-Up Theory. *Interdisciplinary Journal of Contemporary Research in Business* 4 (7): 10.

Jensen, Jaclyn M., and Jana L. Raver. 2012. When Self-Management and Surveillance Collide: Consequences for Employees' Organizational Citizenship and Counterproductive Work Behaviors. *Group & Organization Management* 37 (3): 308–346.

Jiang, Kaifeng, Ying Hong, Patrick F. McKay, Derek R. Avery, David C. Wilson, and Sabrina D. Volpone. 2015. Retaining Employees Through Anti-Sexual Harassment Practices: Exploring the Mediating Role of Psychological Distress and Employee Engagement. *Human Resource Management* 54 (1): 1–21.

Johnson, David, and Timothy C. Salmon. 2016. Sabotage versus Discouragement: Which Dominates Post Promotion Tournament Behavior? *Southern Economic Journal* 82 (3): 673–696.

Jones, David. 2004. A Counterproductive Work Behavior Toward Supervisors & Organizations: Injustice, Revenge, & Context. *Academy of Management Proceedings*, A1–A6.

Journal of Laws. 1997. no. 88, item 553, as amended.

Kelloway, E. Kevin, Lori Francis, Matthew Prosser, and James E. Cameron. 2010. Counterproductive Work Behavior As Protest. *Human Resource Management Review* 20 (1): 18–25.

Kennedy, Jay P. 2016. Shedding Light on Employee Theft's Dark Figure: A Typology of Employee Theft Nonreporting Rationalizations. *Organization Management Journal (Routledge)* 13 (1): 49–60.

Klotz, Anthony C., and Mark C. Bolino. 2013. Citizenship and Counterproductive Work Behavior: A Moral Licensing View. *Academy of Management Review* 38 (2): 292–306.

Kutera, Małgorzata. 2016. *Nadużycia finansowe. Wykrywanie i zapobieganie.* Warszawa: Difin.

Langseth, Petter. 1999. (opracowanie), Prevention: An Effective Tool to Reduce Corruption. Centre for International Crime Prevention, Office of Drug

Control and Crime Prevention, United Nations Office at Vienna. Referat prezentowany podczas koferencji—The ISPAC conference on Responding to the Challenge of Corruption, 19 November 1999, Milan.

LaReau, Jamie. 2012. Store's Fitness Focus is a Win-Win for Losers. *Automotive News*, 2/10/NADA Show Daily Supplement.

Lewis, Grace. 2014. We Need to Talk About Stalking. *People Management*: 8–9.

Leymann, Heinz. 1990. Mobbing and Psychological Terror at Workplaces. *Violence and Victims* 5 (2): 119–126.

Lim, Matthew John. 2016. Combating Collusion. *Governance Directions* 68 (7): 418–420.

Liu, Zhen, and Meixin Xu. 2012. Preliminary Exploring the Influence of Person-Organization Fit on Counterproductive Work Behavior. *International Business & Management* 4 (2): 133–139.

Lloréns Vélez, Eva. 2012. Companies Still Must Do More to Be Transparent, Anticorruption Group Says. *Caribbean Business*, 7/26/ 40 (29): 22–22.

Magd, Hesham. 2003. Management Attitudes and Perceptions of Older Employees in Hospitality Management. *International Journal of Contemporary Hospitality Management* 15 (7): 393–401.

Mahmutefendić, Tahir. 2014. *Economics of Theft*. Zbornik Radova Ekonomskog Fakulteta u Istocnom Sarajevu (9).

McEwan, Troy E., Paul E. Mullen, and Rachel MacKenzie. 2009. A Study of the Predictors of Persistence in Stalking Situations. *Law & Human Behavior* 33 (2): 149.

McNeal, Andi. 2016. What's Your Fraud IQ? This Month: Employee Handbooks and Policies. *Journal of Accountancy* 222 (3): 38.

Michel, Jesse S., and Nathan A. Bowling. 2013. Does Dispositional Aggression Feed the Narcissistic Response? The Role of Narcissism and Aggression in the Prediction of Job Attitudes and Counterproductive Work Behaviors. *Journal of Business & Psychology* 28 (1): 93–105.

Murphy, Pamela R., and Clinton Free. 2016. Broadening the Fraud Triangle: Instrumental Climate and Fraud. *Behavioral Research in Accounting* 28 (1, Spring): 41–56.

Ombler, Kathy. 2016. Corporate Fraud: Who is Vulnerable and Why It Could Be Any Organization. *NZ Business + Management* 30 (4): 7–9.

Pakdel, Abdollah, Qader Vazifeh Damirchi, and Hafez Gholizadeh. 2012. Corruption and Anti-Corruption Policies in Developing Countries. *Interdisciplinary Journal of Contemporary Research in Business* 3 (9): 194–204.

Priesemuth, Manuela, Anke Arnaud, and Marshall Schminke. 2013. Bad Behavior in Groups: The Impact of Overall Justice Climate and Functional Dependence on Counterproductive Work Behavior in Work. *Units Group & Organization Management* 38 (2): 230–257.

Resch, Martin, and Marion Schubinski. 1996. Mobbing—Prevention and Management in Organizations. *European Journal of Work & Organizational Psychology* 5 (2): 295–307.

Retaliation? Not If You Can Prove You Would Have Fired Anyone Who Broke the Same Rule. 2016. HR Specialist: Minnesota Employment Law. 9 (10).

Robinson, Paul H., Michael T. Cahill, and Daniel M. Bartels. 2010. Competing Theories of Blackmail: An Empirical Research Critique of Criminal Law Theory. *Texas Law Review* 89 (2): 291.

Roman, Alexandru. 2012. The Myths Within Anticorruption Policies. *Administrative Theory & Praxis (M.E. Sharpe)* 34 (2): 237–254.

Rosenfeld, Barry, and Charles Lewis. 2005. Assessing Violent Risk in Stalking Cases: A Regression Tree Approach. *Law and Human Behavior* 29 (3): 343–357.

Saleem, Farida, and C. Gopinath. 2015. Injustice, Counterproductive Work Behavior and Mediating Role of Work Stress. *Pakistan Journal of Commerce & Social Sciences* 9 (3): 683–699.

Sappington, David E., and Dennis L. Weisman. 2004. Competition Policy, Parity Regulation and Self-Sabotage. *Info* 1 (6): 52–56.

Sato, Hideki. 2011. Raising Wages as a Strategy to Reduce Corruption. *Journal of Management & Strategy, Dec* 2 (4): –56.

Scott, Brent A., and Timothy A. Judge. 2013. Beauty, Personality, and Affect as Antecedents of Counterproductive Work Behavior Receipt. *Human Performance* 26 (2): 93–113.

Shoss, Mindy, D.K. Jundt, Allison Kobler, and Clair A. Reynolds. 2016. Doing Bad to Feel Better? An Investigation of Within- and Between-Person Perceptions of Counterproductive Work Behavior As a Coping Tactic. *Journal of Business Ethics* 137 (3): 571–587.

Sidle, Stuard D. 2010. Counterproductive Work Behavior: Can It Sometimes Be Good to Be. *Academy of Management Perspectives* 24 (3): 101–103.

Skorupka, Stanisław, Halina Auderska, and Zofia Łempicka. 1969. *Mały słownik języka polskiego*. Warszawa: PWN.

Sobolewska, M. Szantaż emocjonalny. http://www.biznestrendy.infor.pl/indexg.1 z dnia. Accessed 28 July 2006.

Steinberg, Richard M. 2016. A Culture of Sexual Harassment. *Compliance Week* 13 (153): 68–69.

Survey Highlights Dangers of Data Theft by Ex-Employees. 2011. *Manager: British Journal of Administrative Management* 74 (Spring).

Taher, Nader Asaad Bin, and Vlad Krotov. 2016. Business Process Reengineering: Addressing Sources of Resistance and Sabotage Tactics. *Journal of Competitiveness Studies* 24 (3): 145.

The Social Cost of Review of Law & Economics. 2011. 7 (1).

Tjaden, Patricia, and Nancy Thoennes. 1998. *Stalking in America: Findings from the National Violence Against Women Study.* Pp. 1–19 in Research Brief. National Institute of Justice.

Toker, Yonca. 2016. Perception Differences in Ambiguous Forms of Workplace Sexual Harassment: A Comparison between the United States and Turkey. *Journal of Psychology* 150 (5): 625–643.

Tomić, Mileta. 2012. Mobbing: The Incidence of Mobbing Activities and Differences Regarding Workplace and Gender. *Megatrend Review* 9 (1): 243–252.

Tylczak, Lynn, and Thomas E. Sheets. 1995. *Preventing Workplace Theft. They are Stealing from You.* Menlo Park, CA: Crisp Publications.

Vandekerckhove, Wim, and M.S. Ronald Commers. 2003. Downward Workplace Mobbing: A Sign of the Times? *Journal of Business Ethics* 45 (1–2): 41–50.

Wei, Feng, and Steven Si. 2013. Tit for Tat? Abusive Supervision and Counterproductive Work Behaviors: The Moderating Effects of Locus of Control and Perceived Mobility. *Asia Pacific Journal of Management* 30 (1): 281–296.

Westcott, Lucy. 2016. Stories No One Dares Tell. *Newsweek Global*, 9/16/, 167 (10).

Woods, David. 2008. Understanding Overwork. *Employee Benefits*, Special section.

Worker Absenteeism on Rome's New Mayor's "To Do" List. 2016. *Acuity* 3 (7).

Wu, Jane, and James M. Lebreton. 2011. Reconsidering the Dispositional Basis of Counterproductive Work Behavior: The Role of Aberrant Personality. *Personnel Psychology* 64 (3): 2011.

Wynen, Jan. 2016. Sexual Harassment: The Nexus Between Gender and Workplace Authority: Evidence from the Australian Public Service. *Australian Journal of Public Administration* 75 (3): 345–358.

Zadjali, Mahir Al, and Christopher S. Wright. 2012. A New Paradigm of Corruption to Aid in Its Control and Dispel Its Sweet-Spot Myth. *Journal of Leadership, Accountability & Ethics* 9 (1): 34.

Zapf, Dieter. 1999. Organizational, Work Group Related and Personal Causes of Mobbing/Bullying at Work. *International Journal of Manpower* 20 (1/2): 70–85.

Фёдорова, А. С. 2015. Efficient stuff cooperation as an essential component of formation of corporate culture of the enterprise[Эффективное взаимодействие в коллективе как важная составляющая формирования корпоративной культуры предприятия]. *Economy of AIC* (11).

[www1]. https://en.wikipedia.org/wiki/Omega_Engineering oraz https://www.entrepreneur.com/article/250920. Accessed 10 Oct 2016.

[www2]. https://mfiles.pl/pl/index.php/Oszustwo_finansowe. Accessed 22 Sep 2016.

[www3]. http: //www.youthkiawaaz.com/2010/08/5-ways-to-reduce-corruption. Accessed 27 Sep 2012.

[www4]. http://www.infor.pl/prawo/prawo-karne/pokrzywdzony/704421, Stalking-uporczywe-nekanie.html. Accessed 27 Sep 2016.

5

The Role and Tasks of Management

5.1 The Role of Management in Undertaking Disciplinary Actions

Most recommendations concerning the conduct of management come down to the following:

- continually strengthen and improve the rules in place in the organisation;
- ensure that employees know what they can do and what they must not do;
- adjust the severity of punishments to proven offences;
- undertake corrective actions (before imposing punishments);
- give employees credit of trust (create opportunities for improving behaviour).

Such advice is very much justified. It should be remembered, however, that its effectiveness can be influenced by a wide range of factors such as the level of trust in interpersonal relations, the method of establishing objectives, the development of employee assessment systems and remuneration systems, etc.

© The Author(s) 2018
M. Bugdol, *A Different Approach to Work Discipline*,
https://doi.org/10.1007/978-3-319-74008-9_5

Disciplining employees is one of the most challenging tasks to be fulfilled by superiors. Even conducting a disciplinary talk is extremely difficult. Employees react to disciplinary talks in various ways. Some of them are aggressive and do not accept even the most objective arguments; others openly express their dissatisfaction and start ignoring their bosses' opinions. Furthermore, an undisciplined employee proves that the team is badly supervised and/or organised and that its manager or foreman does not fulfil their duties properly.

This is why superiors avoid punishing their subordinates and turn a blind eye to manifestations of indiscipline. Disciplining employees can undermine morale and cause the social system to lose its integrity and the performance of any tasks to become very difficult.

However, it cannot be assumed that all employees are angels complying perfectly with work discipline rules. It is necessary to distinguish between small mistakes or negligence and serious ethical or even criminal abuses. Employees who cannot cope with work standards should be disciplined in a particular way. In such cases, the notion of discipline should be replaced with the notion of managerial support. On the other hand, employees who steal, spread false information, cheat, falsify data, etc. should be treated accordingly; in the case of unethical or criminal behaviour, the term "disciplining" (understood as punishing) is totally justified.

The tasks of management consist of the following: promoting ethical behaviour and pursuing the maintenance of moral order, treating discipline as one of the elements of the whole human resource management system, implementing, maintaining and improving the employee discipline system, providing managerial support, conducting—together with employees—improvement activities taking into consideration work organisation, establishing objective reasons for breaches of work discipline, and ensuring adequate organisational solutions.

These eight tasks should be in the category of general work discipline rules (at the operational level as opposed to the cultural level, where we deal with the shaping of value systems).

1. *Promoting ethical behaviour and pursuing the maintenance of moral order*

The promotion of ethical behaviour is referred to by a considerable number of management improvement models (e.g. the EFQM model).

Some organisations' motivational systems provide for rewards for following particular rules (e.g. for coming to work on time or taking care of one's health), but rewards of this type concern proper rather than ethical behaviour. The most important thing is to prevent the occurrence of an "ethical gap" between what superiors demand from their subordinates and their own true behaviour (see the examples below).

In 2015 one of the regional blood donation centres in the south of Poland was to be shut down. The previous director had had new headquarters built for the centre. The director had commissioned various construction works without having secured necessary funds in the budget. After a while it turned out that a few of the companies building the headquarters had not been paid. The arrears amounted to a few million zlotys. The director was dismissed and replaced by her deputy. Despite enormous debts and employee dismissals, the new director came to work by taxi every day, at the expense of her employer. Every week she would be absent for two or three days. Such behaviour caused employees' outrage.

In a factory specialising in the manufacture of cathode blocks, a new technical director was appointed. Instead of focusing on technological improvement and development, the new director started to implement strict control rules. He started to check employees' work time himself. Those who were a few minutes late were punished severely. The staff were all indignant at the director's behaviour, the more so that he himself did not comply with the work time rules.

Source: the authors' own work

Such "ethical gaps" cause employees to stop trusting their superiors (Employees know that management does not comply with the discipline requirements). The thesis that employees may also manifest more behaviour inconsistent with work discipline rules would require empirical evidence. "Ethical gaps" disturb moral order. Researchers have often paid attention to relations between discipline and morale. Haimann and Hilgert (1997) indicate that morale influences discipline. A high level of discipline (connected with punishments) is possible when morality is compromised. Such discipline, however, is based on fear and coerced obedience. And vice versa—positive discipline understood as the correction of behaviour based on training and support is possible only where morale is very high.

In practice, on the basis of punishments imposed in consequence of breaching OHS regulations, it can be observed that employees are punished severely (but not reprimanded or trained) in businesses whose owners take care of their own interests only (see the example below).

I worked in a firm dealing with the maintenance and repair of photocopying equipment. We had a lot of small accidents at work, usually minor cuts and wounds. We were always in a hurry, rushing from one customer to another. Our schedule was very tight and we were very few in number. I received the punishment of reprimand twice, despite the fact that I was not guilty. The equipment was very old, frequently unsafe to use. My boss never had enough money and the number of customers was growing all the time. But the number of employees was always the same. I couldn't stand it any more and resigned eventually.

(a student, an employee in a service company)

There is no doubt that organisational behaviour is influenced strongly by the morality of both owners and employees. When owners are focused on short-term profits, they create remuneration systems based on financial values only. Profit is pursued by all available means. Employees are subjected to socio-technical manipulation and their work is continuously competiting for bonuses awarded for achieved financial resources. Deming was one of the first researchers to observe that employee rankings caused intense rivalry. Employees are disciplined but they only pretend to fulfil their superiors' instructions. However, the shaping of positive discipline is not possible because employees take care of their own interests at the expense of the welfare of social groups.

2. *Treating discipline as one of the elements of the whole human resource management system*

The shaping of employee discipline starts at the selection and recruitment stage. During the process of selection, employee competences are examined (tests are conducted, documentation is examined, CV detectives are hired, community interviews are conducted, etc.). Each subsequent HR process has to favour the shaping of work discipline. The process of adaptation is of considerable educational importance. During the process employees become familiar with work standards, an organisation's functional principles, etc.

3. *Implementing, maintaining and improving the employee discipline system*

Organisations, especially large ones, should maintain and continually improve employee discipline systems. Every organisation has work rules; it is additionally assumed that employees are familiar with the labour code. (Some companies have their own work discipline procedures concerning such issues as theft, corruption, harassment, etc.). There is no comprehensive system comprising a work discipline policy, work discipline objectives, scopes of employee duties and responsibilities (including particular disciplinary actions, employees' participation in developing procedures and establishing objectives), methods of monitoring undertaken actions, work discipline reviews, examination of the effectiveness of HR processes aimed at shaping appropriate behaviour, supervision of external processes (discipline rules in the workplace for suppliers and customers), personnel audits, data analysis.

4. *Providing managerial support*

Employees who do not comply with work discipline rules do so for various reasons: they have such inclinations, they do not fit their teams, they try to take revenge on managers for their unjust treatment, etc. If there is a real chance to change the behaviour, a comprehensive managerial support system should be taken into consideration. Such support is included in the positive discipline model. What is of considerable importance in this system is superiors' conduct in the preliminary period of shaping work discipline. When errors, irregularities or deliberate breaches of work discipline occur, supervisors provide support to undisciplined employees. The support usually has the form of a disciplinary talk, but other measures such as toolbox talks, motivating talks, work monitoring and coaching are used as well.

The term "managerial support" indicates a degree to which employees have a general idea about how managers appreciate their work, take care of their well-being (the quality of life at a workplace) and provide them with necessary support (cf. Eisenberger et al. 2002). Such support is of enormous significance in work discipline systems because:

- it allows employees to trust superiors' good intentions;
- it makes it possible to develop jointly corrective programmes if an employee evidently fails to comply with work discipline rules).

Providing support, managers can increase employee satisfaction, lower their stress and sense of danger, and consequently reduce costs and improve productivity (Sawang 2010: 247–256). It is believed that the positive impact of managerial support is the reduction of stress and the creation of a sense of well-being (Jones et al. 2005: 1–22).

However, in practice, providing managerial support is something particularly difficult. Rather than a comprehensive approach, we observe individual approaches; few managers can appreciate their employees' contributions and care about the appropriate quality of interpersonal relations. Nevertheless, it is worth considering the introduction of various educational activities aimed at convincing managers that such support is very important and that a manager is not somebody who only demands the achievement of financial goals.

5. *Conducting joint improvement activities*

In this area, besides training, it is possible to also distinguish the following:

- manager and employee jointly analysing various cases of breaching work discipline (looking for causes, identifying remedial measures, thinking about sanctions and rewards);
- improving existing procedures (discussing proposed corrective or preventive actions);
- presenting overall costs incurred by an organisation as a result of non-compliance with work discipline;
- rewarding the best ideas put forward by employees for shaping work discipline.

Joint work on appropriate behaviour (in the case of positive discipline) can lead to employees' higher level of acceptance of disciplinary actions undertaken by managers. It is claimed that this type of acceptance is possible when (Schoen and Durand 1979):

- all disciplinary actions are undertaken immediately (based on the conviction that postponing a decision in the case of a breach of applicable standards is not good from an educational point of view);
- superiors inform employees in advance about the rules of cooperation and other standards in place in their organisation, the value systems they will have to deal with and possible punishments for a lack of discipline;
- superiors continually strengthen and refer to the applicable rules of discipline;
- people are convinced of the appropriateness of undertaken actions (what are the purpose and tasks of discipline?).

6. *Taking into consideration work organisation*

A work discipline system has to be based on the assumption that not only do individual differences among employees exist, but also differences among particular organisational units or conducted processes.

What counts in fast-food restaurants is the duration of serving a customer and consequently the time of work, accuracy of instructions and procedural discipline applicable to food preparation processes. Similarly in hospitals, discipline has a standardised character. Various accreditation procedures connected with numerous standardised quality management systems are oriented towards patient safety and require both procedural discipline and insuring discipline where direct supervision and the monitoring of undertaken activities play an important role.

Differences among particular organisational units result from the simple fact that in functional structures, work is divided among specialised divisions. In managerial practice, such a division constitutes a major problem in implementing uniform discipline standards. For example, a production division is obliged to comply with work-time discipline, while a commercial division does not necessarily have to because commercial divisions in many companies are guaranteed flexible work time (the same rule applies to consultants or employees working in research and development divisions). In such cases management is responsible for establishing precise, basic work discipline rules applicable to all employees and making them aware of the specific character of work in particular organisational units.

Problems with work discipline are to a considerable extent related to improper work organisation. Unfortunately, employees can be punished for the poor quality of products or services when an individual's work has no influence on quality and the low quality has been caused by bad work organisation. Therefore, the most important task for management is to manage processes properly, i.e. to identify processes, to look for relations among processes, to allocate resources fairly and to carry out regular process audits.

7. *Establishing objective reasons for breaches of work discipline*

Not every manifestation of non-compliance with work discipline requires that disciplinary actions be taken.

There are various reasons for employees' breaching applicable policies, standards or rules of cooperation. Such situations require that superiors assess objectively the circumstances in which work discipline rules have been breached. It is worth establishing the reasons for inappropriate behaviour. They are usually connected with the following:

- a lack of knowledge (e.g. employees do not know the quality objectives or have not participated in developing the quality policy, which has been imposed on them hastily);
- establishing excessive objectives (such situations can result from salary systems for managers who are rewarded for achieving results only);
- allocating resources improperly (e.g. deploying employees and their competences inappropriately; distributing material or technical resources inappropriately).

8. *Ensuring adequate organisational solutions*

Order in the workplace is both a manifestation and a source of good discipline. Recommendations concerning order in the workplace come down to ensuring appropriate organisational solutions. Employees are advised to focus on one activity, devote the first hours of a work day to solving the most pressing problems and turn off the media at particular times. Order in the workplace is connected with the notion of standardisation. It is *"an activity aimed, in particular circumstances, at acquiring a degree of order in a specified scope by establishing rules to be followed universally and repeatedly, and concerning problems which occur or can occur"* (The Standardization Act of 12 September 2002 in Poland). Standardisation is achieved frequently, thanks to detailed instructions for performing particular actions (the 5S method is a case in point). Standardisation favours work discipline and makes it possible to quickly correct even slight irregularities. It is also an important element of self-discipline. The risk connected with standardisation is of employees getting used to performing their work mechanically, without any reflection. Hence it is important to ensure continuous improvement of established standards.

Another factor playing an important role in maintaining discipline is systematics. It concerns not only work tools but also work documentation and records. Systematics is *"organizing and marking all elements of a workstation so that they are easy to use and put back in their place as well as easy to locate and identify by every employee"* (Lisiecka and Burka 2016: 89). Systematics, standardisation and self-discipline are important for maintaining discipline; however, what is much more important is the fact that they foster creativity. This is why lean management or kaizen philosophy specialists recommend maintaining strict organisational order in which order in the workplace is just one of many elements. The shaping of a lean culture starts exactly from tidying the workplace. This favours self-discipline. When an organisation starts to implement workplace order regulations, it usually specifies the methods of supervising documentation or materials and identifyies the course of production processes. Implementing such regulations without a previous thorough analysis of key processes is a frequent mistake. For example, document circulation rules cannot be established without considering the course of particular processes because a method of supervising documentation can either lengthen or shorten the duration of service provision processes. It is necessary to take into consideration which materials and documents are necessary at particular workstations, who supplies them and at what times.

A certain production company introduced strict work discipline rules. Turners were punished for exceeding the established work time limits. The workers felt it was very unjust for them because they had frequently notified the management that they were not able to control the duration of their operations. After a few years a new president decided to implement the concept of lean manufacturing in the company. Under the old work organisation system, every turner on the shop floor had had to collect materials and tools from a special distribution centre. The company measured the distances covered by all turners and realised that each of them had to walk about three kilometres every day between their workstation and the distribution centre. The management decided to divide work differently: in the morning before the start of a shift, foremen were responsible for delivering all necessary materials and tools to the lathes. The turners did not have to worry about it any more. In this way, the company eliminated losses resulting from wasted work time.

Source: the authors' own work

Unification is another factor playing an important role in maintaining order. *"Unification is the use of the same elements or assemblies in different parts of a machine, which decreases their diversity"* (www1).

5.1.1 Developing a Discipline Management System

Developing a discipline management system is one of the most important operational tasks within management's scope of responsibilities. A discipline management system should include, among others, the following activities:

1. Ensuring supervision over external processes.
2. Establishing normative requirements concerning discipline.
3. Establishing scopes of responsibility and decision-making authority.
4. Establishing objectives and plans related to work discipline.
5. Conducting periodic management reviews.
6. Diagnosing undesirable behaviour.
7. Undertaking preventive and corrective actions.

1. *Ensuring supervision over external processes*

Ensuring supervision over external processes is an important task for the following primary reasons:

Firstly, all manifestations of non-compliance with work discipline or, more broadly, cultural standards, exert a negative influence on a company's image (see the example below).

Unfortunately, despite precise supply chain management procedures, sometimes employees of suppliers or cooperators work in conditions that have nothing in common with occupational health and safety. The quality of life in the workplace is very low. Work discipline standards are breached. Employees work overtime, sometimes even seven days a week, and live in congested accommodation. Non-compliance with the basic OHS regulations causes employees to frequently fall ill. There are many documented cases of employing underage workers. It is suspected that work-time standards are violated and employment documentation is falsified. In 2010, in a certain factory located in the east of China, 137 employees were poisoned by a chemical used to clean iPhone screens. Two explosions in Chinese factories killed 4 and seriously wounded 77 workers. The representatives of the National Advisory Committee on Occupational Safety and Health claim that if Apple representatives had been notified about the appalling work conditions, they did not react adequately to the scale of the threat. In 2005 the Apple management developed a set of various rules applicable to cooperation with suppliers. During the past three years (2009–2012), 312 audits were conducted. Auditors identified a few score serious deviations from the established procedures. Simultaneously, employees received training aimed at providing them with information on their employee rights and safe work methods.

In 2011, a report on social responsibility in value chains was published. It showed that work conditions had improved. However, Apple is not the only big company having problems with ensuring appropriate quality in supply systems. Similar problems have been studied in such corporations as IBM, Nokia, Toshiba, Motorola, Lenovo and Hewlett–Packard.

Source: (—) Apple and the American economy, *The Economist* 23.01.2012

Secondly, at present we are witnessing the trend of returning to vertical integration. Consequently, a problem arises of ensuring the same discipline standards along the whole supply and distribution chains. *"Vertical integration is a term denoting the acquisition of a distribution or supply company, which contributes to the broadening of the scope of operations. Such integration is one of the stages in the development of an organization. By broadening the scope of its operations, it pursues higher profitability"* (Stoner et al. 2001: 285).

Thirdly, a division of employees into those who work for outsourcing companies and those employed by entities which outsource various services and operations is not good for work discipline. Employees of outsourcing companies are supervised both by their own bosses and by the managers of a subcontracting firm. Depending on their status, employees are treated differently (those employed on a full-time basis are treated better, while those on temporary contracts, worse).

Therefore, when developing a discipline management system, managers should remember the following:

- establish individual responsibility for supervising external processes (at present this requirement is too often ignored and responsibility is blurred);
- implement the same management standards along the whole quality chain;
- oblige cooperators to adopt uniform standards.

2. *Establishing normative requirements*

Establishing normative requirements concerning discipline appears to be a simple task. Some organisations follow the principles according to the requirements laid out in the labour code, but simultaneously silently assume that employees are familiar with internal and customer requirements.

In order to establish discipline requirements effectively, it is necessary to possess (and continually improve) knowledge of the following:

- customers' expectations (which types of behaviour are acceptable and which are not);
- suppliers' expectations;
- intra-organisational requirements (which types of behaviour improve the quality of interpersonal relations).

The problem is that discipline should not exclusively concern legal regulations, should not be limited to rules specified in ethical codes and work regulations, and should take into consideration the requirements of all stakeholders of an organisation (as long as they are not contradictory).

3. *Establishing scopes of responsibility and decision-making authority*

Establishing scopes of responsibility and decision-making authority is an important element of any discipline management system. And such responsibility and authority concern the use of disciplinary measures and actions rather than the performance of everyday work. An organisation has to unambiguously determine who conducts disciplinary talks, identifies sources of inappropriate behaviour, selects remedial measures, undertakes corrective actions, etc.

4. *Establishing objectives and plans related to work discipline*

Another element in a comprehensive discipline management system is establishing objectives and plans related to work discipline.

The general objective of discipline is not only to minimise the number of employees breaching discipline rules or the number of unethical behaviour manifestations, but first of all to improve the quality of life in the workplace and increase employee satisfaction.

It should be explained that both objective and subjective quality or satisfaction indexes can indicate that an organisation provides appropriate work conditions, the quality of interpersonal relations is satisfactory and HR processes are effective. Large organisations should conduct regular audits of the quality of life in the workplace as well as employee satisfaction. It should be remembered that job satisfaction does not have to correlate positively with compliance with work discipline. Nevertheless, it constitutes a certain foundation for ethical behaviour. This is because satisfied employees have fewer reasons to use sabotage or harm an organisation in which they feel comfortable.

Plans and objectives related to work discipline have a collective dimension (they concern a whole organisation) and an individual dimension. They can be established for employees who, for various reasons, have problems with work discipline. Similar solutions are used by the automotive sector with respect to its providers of goods and services. If standards are not followed, the supplier has to prepare a corrective plan which is subsequently supervised by the client (or usually by an appointed auditor).

5. *Conducting periodic management reviews*

Periodic management reviews are indispensable in places fraught with serious problems with work discipline. It is necessary to identify the true causes of non-compliance with discipline rules, whether they result from bad work organisation, a management system, a lack of competences or knowledge, bad habits or inclinations to manifest unethical behaviour). Input data for such reviews should include the following:

- the results of examining employee satisfaction and quality of life in the workplace;
- the identified manifestations of non-compliance with discipline rules;
- the identified causes of accidents in the workplace;
- complaints submitted by employees;
- complaints submitted by customers;
- the results of cultural, process-related and personnel audits;
- analyses concerning employees' resignations;
- competence and employee assessments,
- the status of corrective and preventive actions.

Input data also comprise decisions made by management together with employees and concerning improvements in the discipline management system. They can concern, for example, transferring employees to other positions, training employees, developing new procedures, changing the allocation of resources, improving human resource management processes, changing work requirements and standards.

6. *Diagnosing undesirable behaviour*

Interviews are a useful tool for diagnosing undesirable behaviour. They are conducted with employees who are observers of disciplinary events and/or have experienced various punishments. Interviews are used to get to know employees' opinions on the effectiveness of various forms of discipline, as well as differences between the opinions of subordinates and those of superiors (cf. e.g. King and Wilcox 2003: 197). As has been mentioned above, all types of audits, especially process and personnel ones, and in-depth analyses of employee behaviour can also be used as diagnostic tools.

7. Undertaking preventive and corrective actions

Work discipline should be the subject of continually undertaken preventive and corrective actions. Many organisations, particularly those which have introduced standardised management systems, use specially developed registers of corrective and preventive actions. Entries in such registers comprise areas of inappropriate behaviour (organisational units or processes), dates of identifying inconsistencies, types of inconsistencies (serious or slight inconsistencies), risk assessments, proposed corrective actions, resources necessary to resolve (financial, operational, etc.) inconsistencies, responsible employees, deadlines and reviews of the effectiveness of undertaken actions. All manifestations of non-compliances with work discipline can be entered in such registers and subsequently analysed and supervised by appointed employees.

5.1.2 Possibilities of Using the Existing Quality Management Systems

A work discipline system has to be connected with quality management systems.

Irrespective of what system is followed, the implementation, maintenance and improvement of any quality management system usually brings about organisational order. This is so because the implementation of a system itself regulates the methods of supervising records and documents and introduces uniform principles of supervising provided services and products, a strict supervision over customers' property, and monitoring of processes. In quality management systems, an important role is played by quality audits (whose character is not restrictive, but preventive) and management reviews. One of the main advantages of properly functioning systems is undertaking improvement actions on a continual basis (see the example below).

A certain hospital implemented accreditation standards. For many years it had maintained a quality management system based on the ISO 9001 standard. The hospital's quality management representative prepared a list of undesirable events. The list included, for example, needlestick injuries, patients' falls and nurses' mistakes. According to the principles in place in quality management, every employee could enter undesirable events on the list. For example, if somebody mixed up medicines, they entered such an event on the list and subsequently employees analysed why the mistake had happened and who was to blame. It was not always nurses who were responsible for such mistakes. Sometimes pharmaceutical companies ignore marking drugs correctly and put drugs from different groups in similar packages. Entering events on the list was aimed mainly at improving quality. An employee who admitted having made a mistake was not punished. During the whole period that the principles were in place, only one nurse failed to make a relevant entry. When it turned out that a patient had been given the wrong medicine, the nurse asked for sick leave. Because she had concealed her own mistake, she was punished with a caution.
Source: the authors' own work

The essence of the functioning of any system is relations between its particular parts. In practice, it means that neglecting just one criterion of a quality standard can bring about negative consequences (see the example below).

A certain district hospital had maintained a quality management based on the ISO 9001 standard for three years. According to paragraph 7.6 of the ISO 9001 standard, *"The organization shall determine the monitoring and measurement to be undertaken and the monitoring and measuring equipment needed to provide evidence of conformity of product to determined requirements. Where necessary to ensure valid results, measuring equipment shall: be calibrated or verified, or both, at specified intervals, or prior to use, against measurement standards traceable to international or national measurement standards; where no such standards exist, the basis used for calibration or verification shall be recorded, shall be adjusted or re-adjusted as necessary"* (clause 7.6, ISO 9001:2008). In the vast majority of cases, this criterion of the standard was supervised strictly (after all, a patient's life depends on the correct functioning of measuring equipment). Unfortunately, employees often decide that provision of quality standards is impractical or exaggerated. Visiting his mother in hospital, one man noticed that her face was red. When he touched her forehead, it was very hot. He asked a nurse whether his mother's temperature had been measured. The nurse answered that it had been measured a few times. Two days later the man brought his own thermometer to the hospital and measured his mother's temperature. It was 38 degrees. He asked the ward nurse about his mother's temperature again and the nurse said again that it had been measured and had been correct. But a few days later the woman died. Her son filed an official complaint against the medical personnel. The hospital director appointed a special committee to investigate the reasons for the woman's unexpected death (accredited hospitals are obliged to carry out such investigations). It turned out that a few thermometers had not been calibrated and consequently their readings were wrong. Nobody had taken the trouble to compare such readings with those of a calibrated or verified thermometer.

Source: the authors' own work

If a quality management system is to foster the maintenance of work discipline, the following conditions have to be met:

- Conducted quality audits cannot end with conclusions suggesting that employees be punished (such conclusions have to have a preventive character).
- The proper (i.e. performed in accordance with applicable criteria) identification of key and auxiliary processes is necessary (otherwise resources will be allocated improperly, employees will be overworked, which, in turn, will evoke a sense of injustice).
- Improvement activities should be conducted continually and on a bottom-up basis (and not in consequence of internal audits only).
- Employees have to be guaranteed possibilities of learning from their own mistakes.
- Control should be substituted by self-control.

5.1.3   The Shaping of Organisational Justice

In the 1990s, research confirmed that organisational justice was of considerable importance for effective work discipline (e.g. Ball et al. 1992:
307–333). A sense of injustice is the cause of counterproductive behaviour (e.g. Flaherty and Moss 2007; Yang and Diefendorff 2009; Sidle
2010; Kelloway et al. 2010; Liu and Xu 2012). The unjust treatment of
employees or customers releases negative emotions which subsequently
manifest themselves in counterproductive behaviour (Yang and
Diefendorff 2009). A sense of procedural injustice increases the possibility of the occurrence of behaviour aimed against a whole organisation,
while interactional injustice manifests itself in destructive behaviour
occurring in relations between superiors and subordinates (Flaherty and
Moss 2007). However, the problem does not consist in that types of punishments, disciplinary procedures or disciplining skills can exert a positive or negative influence on a sense of justice, but in that the process of
employee disciplining takes place in a particular environment characterised by various types and levels of justice.

Punishments that are too severe destroy a sense of justice and therefore, both labour codes and disciplinary procedures in place in various
organisations provide for a gradual increase in the severity of punishments. The exception is situations in which an offence or crime is evidently committed (e.g. a theft is revealed). In this context, the following
assumptions are made:

- Punishments have to be commensurate with offences (which is a very
  difficult task and results mainly from established procedures).
- Punishments have to have an educational effect (which is not always
  easy to achieve).
- Lesser offences committed repeatedly result in increasingly severe punishment (in progressive discipline models).

M. Armstrong (2011) introduced the principles of natural justice into
employee disciplinary procedures. According to these procedures:

- Employees should know work discipline rules and performance
  standards.

- An employee should be given a clear explanation as to the nature of their guilt.
- An employee has to be given a chance to explain their behaviour.
- Before the initiation of a disciplinary procedure, an employee has to be given a chance to improve their behaviour (this principle does not apply to the most serious offences).

Some of these recommendations refer directly to the notion of organisational justice. In order to ensure organisational justice, the following recommendations have to be kept in mind:

- All employees in an organisation have to follow the same rules of discipline, irrespective of their positions in the power structure, form of employment, social or ethnic origin, or education.
- Disciplining employees must by no means destroy a superior's authority (which can happen if a superior exceeds their rights).
- Decisions concerning work discipline have to be made on the basis of facts—discipline cannot be based on rumours or gossip.
- A discipline policy has to be clearly communicated and continually improved.
- Disciplinary actions have to be taken immediately after inappropriate conduct has been identified (delaying the administration of punishments is a bad practice).
- Superiors have to express trust in those employees who have had problems with work discipline (neither party can feel hurt after disciplinary tools have been applied).
- An optimum discipline level needs to be determined (neither severity nor leniency is recommended).
- It is necessary to focus on factual problems, situations and events, and not on employees who breach work discipline rules,
- It is necessary to maintain employee files, including information on work discipline (Guffey and Helms 2011: 111–118).

The research conducted so far indicates that the effectiveness of both punishments and rewards used in work discipline systems depends on the level of justice and on conditionality, which means that a punishment and a reward should result from something; they cannot be accidental or depend on short-lasting emotions or moods (Podsakoff et al. 2006: 113–142.).

The majority of research is based on the assumption that there are many types of justice which depend on one another. In the context of work discipline, we can distinguish the following types of justice: informative, distributive, retributive and procedural. There is also justice understood as impartiality. Developing work discipline rules, organisations need to keep in mind the aforementioned types of justice as they make it possible to precisely formulate recommendations concerning work discipline. There are strong connections between the distributive, procedural, informative and interactional types of justice and various methods of disciplining employees. Research results indicate that the type of offence and the severity of a punishment considerably influence the perception of these types of justice (Cole 2008: 107–120). In practice, it means that, in their disciplinary actions, superiors refer to existing procedures. If breaching work discipline rules, an employee has to be aware that their superiors' behaviour (reaction) depends on what procedures are in place in their organisation. And it is much easier to shape work discipline if employees are able to participate in the development of such procedures (such possibilities are provided, for example, by standardised quality management systems).

According to distributive justice, work discipline rules have to prevent favouring some employees at the cost of others. If justice manifests itself in a just distribution of goods and burdens, then both punishments and rewards have to depend on commitment, allocated tasks and the difficulty of achieving particular objectives. Superiors have to be able to assess their subordinates justly (with respect to what other employees do).

Superiors' skills fulfil an important role in the shaping of justice. There are many such skills, but two of them deserve special attention: conducting disciplinary talks and developing procedures (which are of key importance in the shaping of procedural justice).

Disciplinary talks are important for maintaining justice (Cole 2008: 107–120). They have various objectives. One of them is to show an employee how they could improve their work, but disciplinary talks can be also used to warn or even to intimidate employees (Graham and Bennett 1995). Talks concerning work improvement or preventive actions (especially ones proposed by an employee), as well as corrective actions, are not disciplinary in character. Furthermore, during a disciplinary talk its participant can acquire new information connected with new circumstances. For example, it can turn out that an employee is not guilty and their behaviour resulted from improperly organised work or unreasonable objectives. In such circumstances a disciplinary talk can turn into an advisory talk. The decisive majority of manuals on conducting disciplinary talks advise the reader to become thoroughly familiar with facts before undertaking any disciplinary actions. It means that a person conducting such talks has to be properly prepared. It is necessary to talk to the witnesses of events and to gather information on the cause of unacceptable behaviour. In practice, unfortunately, it turns out that the person conducting disciplinary talks does not know how the work is divided and how employees tend to behave. H.T. Graham and E. R. Bennett (1995) recommend informing employees about the sources of information. However, such recommendations are usually ignored. Superiors do not want to let their employees know how they have found out about breaches of work discipline because what they often have at their disposal is not objective facts (e.g. statistical data, monitoring records), but information coming from employees' managers, co-workers or even auditors (which constitutes a breach of auditing rules). A very important issue is who conducts disciplinary talks. It does not have to be a direct superior; sometimes it is a personnel department manager or another member of the management team. If this is the case, communicated information can be distorted even further. It is also important what factors determine social relations in an organisation (see the example below).

I used to work as a marketing department manager. My employee had an affair with the personnel department manager; he would disappear for long hours and neglect his duties totally. Every morning he took the keys, saying that he was going to the advertising materials warehouse. I had friendly relations with that employee. I couldn't talk to him about his behaviour, let alone undertake any disciplinary actions. I asked my direct superior for an intervention. He had a short conversation with my subordinate, but its consequences were pitiful. I had a row with the employee and his further conduct was even worse. I decided to do nothing. After some time the problem solved itself.
Source: the authors' own work

It is also recommended that employees have an opportunity to present their positions on allegations made against them. It is important to ensure that other people, for example, trade union representatives, can be invited to disciplinary talks if employees request this. It should be remembered that a method of conducting a talk and communicating information (face to face or in the presence of other people) influences a sense of justice. In the process of communication, an important role is played by the ability to articulate the following:

- reasons for using these and not other types of punishment;
- existing (mutual) expectations.

Some management manuals recommend that an employee be informed in advance about the time and place of a disciplinary talk. However, this should not be done when an employee is involved in work, especially that of a dangerous nature. The very fact of calling an employee on the carpet causes stress and, in extreme cases, allows them to exert influence on the conduct of other people (e.g. forcing witnesses to change their statements).

A disciplinary talk does not have to end with concrete conclusions. It may be necessary to further examine the circumstances of an event in order to establish new facts and interpret new findings.

Another important skill is developing disciplinary procedures. Such procedures have to be reviewed periodically and, if necessary, amended in order to guarantee their influence of ensuring procedural and corrective justice. The principles of developing disciplinary procedures are as follows:

- They have to be agreed upon with employees or their representatives.
- When formulating particular provisions, it is necessary to remember existing legal requirements (organisations can also take into consideration specific industry standards or customer requirements).
- Every employee should become acquainted with the procedures.
- It is necessary to establish both punishments for non-compliance with organisational requirements and rewards for proposed procedural improvements or long-lasting compliance with work discipline rules.
- The procedures have to take into consideration particular roles performed by employees (e.g. who conducts disciplinary talks, who is

authorised to impose punishments, who decides which events are classified as breaches of work discipline).

- The procedures should include the opportunity to appeal and rules of corrective justice (if somebody has suffered damage, how such damage will be repaired).
- The duration of particular punishments has to be clearly determined (e.g. when a punishment of caution will be deleted from an employee's personnel file).

5.2   Managing Difficult Employees

The notion of a difficult employee has not been defined unambiguously yet. It can be assumed that any classification of an employee as difficult is not an easy task, for various reasons. Thus, the question arises as to who or what (what personality traits or behaviour) determines whether a given person is regarded as a difficult employee. An employee can often be competent, loyal and well-motivated, but despite this, be considered as difficult, resulting from bad work organisation, improper allocation of an employee to a team, biases, stereotypes, misleading information and poor decisions. In fact, a difficult employee can be very creative. An employee can be regarded as difficult if they work better than others (they constitute a threat to status quo, a team's standards related to the quantity and quality of work).

There are two approaches in this respect. The first one consists of attaching the label of difficult employee to those who intentionally or unintentionally fail to comply with certain standards and disregard company rules. The other approach is regarding employees with health problems or mental disorders as troublesome. Some classifications take into consideration both these approaches and, consequently, difficult employees are those who have problems with alcohol or narcotics, do not follow social standards, behave unethically or commit offences (e.g. steal or intentionally destroy property), refuse to follow orders or do not want to share their knowledge with others (Gladis 2015: 78–81; McCafferty 2014a). Employees who complain continually are also classified as difficult (The Breakroom 2016: 4–4). The majority of publications on the subject of difficult employees suggest that such employees harass (both passively and actively) others, use mobbing, lying, etc. There is no doubt that the category of difficult employees includes those who intentionally use various games or behave unethically (e.g. spread gossip).

Troublesome employees are even those who ostentatiously exercise their rights and take advantage of unclear legal regulations. For example, some states in the US have allowed the use of marijuana for therapeutic purposes. But does this mean that such use is allowed in the workplace? Instead of smoking traditional cigarettes, some employees use e-cigarettes. The issue arises as to whether e-cigarettes can be used in the workplace. HR specialists increasingly have to deal with such questions (e.g. cf. Yarbrough 2015: 22–25). Difficult employees are those who try to offload emerging problems onto their bosses (Liff 2007: 69–92). They include also those who are late for meetings, neglect their duties or cause chaos at work, for example, by spreading gossip, complaining about everybody and everything, holding unrealistic expectations and articulating them stubbornly, despite explanations from management. Difficult employees even include those who fulfil their duties well but, in various situations, behave unprofessionally and contrary to their superiors' expectations (Difficult Employee? Time for "The Chat" 2014: 1–1). People who, for various reasons, fail to perform tasks entrusted to them are also regarded as difficult. This is most often as a result of unrealistic objectives, a lack of common interests, adequate training or work performance standards (Zabriskie 2016: 8–8).

The second approach regards dysfunctional people as difficult employees (Miller 2009: 186–189). In discussing difficult employees, we should remember that people differ from one another. L. Miller suggests the following personality types: avoiding, dependent, emotional, narcissistic, antisocial, obsessive compulsive, paranoid, schizoid, passive-aggressive. People with different personality styles think and behave differently. For example, an employee with a paranoiac personality tells themselves, "Be careful, be one step ahead of your enemy, do this to them before they do this to you, people can't be trusted, business is war". People with obsessive-compulsive disorder think to themselves, "I must be 100% perfect, God is in the detail, look before you leap, if you want something to be done well, do it yourself, keep an eye on everything the whole time" (Miller 2008). Difficult employees manifest various disorders, for example, mental, dissociative or simulated disorders (Miller 2008). In the literature on the subject, some researchers use an alternative notion of a toxic employee (e.g. McCafferty 2014a).

Writing about the dangers of dividing employees into difficult and non-difficult or "healthy", we should remember that the category of employees who do not cause serious problems and contribute to the achievement of organisational objectives includes those who:

- do not worsen the quality of interpersonal relations by their behaviour or attitudes;
- are fully adjusted to the existing organisational culture;
- pursue established objectives without much disruption;
- constitute a model of a good worker for others;
- care about their own health and the health of their colleagues;
- work in accordance with management standards and rules;
- undertake and develop various quality-oriented initiatives.

Similarly, to all types of employee rankings, existing classifications are dangerous not only for ethical reasons but also because of the undeniable fact of the existence of various expectations. The character of a particular classification can be determined by what superiors expect from their employees. Paradoxically, employees manifesting citizenship behaviour can be classified as difficult (cf. research of Klotz and Bolino 2013). Such employees undertake tasks that go beyond their duty, but the problem is that they are not always driven by ethical motives.

Summing up, a difficult employee is a person who, despite correctly conducted human resource management processes, manifests attitudes and behaviour inconsistent with an organisational culture (values, convictions, standards).

5.2.1 The Types of Difficult Employees and Dealing with Them

It is believed that in order to prevent consequences of unethical behaviour, difficult employees should be dealt with in various ways. Dealing with difficult employees improperly results in stress, managers' losing their credibility, and decreased productivity and creativity (Kaushik 2014: 53–55).

Management manuals are full of advice such as "act immediately when something bad happens, explain to the employee what cooperation is all about, make sure that the employee knows your expectations" (5 Tips for Dealing with an Uncooperative Employee 2016: 4–4).

For example, McCafferty (2014b: 1–1) has formulated a list of recommendations for people who have to deal with toxic employees. He advises as follows:

- Do not imitate the behaviour of toxic employees (full professionalism has to be maintained).
- Place difficult employees in the same groups so that they are busy with one another.
- Allow difficult employees to express their opinions openly (but in a manner which does not harm other people).
- Do not show fear in front of difficult employees (unethical and criminal behaviour feeds on the fear of other people; therefore it is important to keep calm).
- Keep records of conducted observations.
- Assign difficult employees tasks that are as time-consuming as possible (McCafferty 2014b: 1–1).

Strategies of coping with difficult employees individually consist of the following:

- avoid contact;
- using the same types of behaviour towards difficult employees;
- pretending.

Some HR specialists recommend the method of a special talk with difficult employees based on the DIS (D-Direct, I-Immediate, S-Specific) model. According to the model, a talk with a difficult employee has to be conducted directly (in a blunt manner). The employee has to be informed about the superior's expectations and why, in the superior's opinion, their behaviour is inappropriate. Information on inappropriate behaviour has to be conveyed immediately (at the time when the superior witnesses it). This rule is based on the assumption that punishments administered immediately are more effective than ones imposed after some time. During the talk it is necessary to discuss concrete examples of inappropriate behaviour. The form of the presented comments is important (they cannot be offensive). After the talk the employee should know and understand how inappropriate behaviour influences productivity and morale (Difficult Employee? Time for 'The Chat' 2014: 1–1). In order to deal with difficult employees effectively, the traditional methods of reducing the number of such employees (e.g. by means of tests used in recruitment processes) may not suffice. The more important task is to improve the awareness of all employees with respect to unethical or criminal behaviour. For example, employees should know what mobbing is and how it manifests itself. The starting point is the assumption that changes in behaviour require effective feedback. Employees have to know when their behaviour is acceptable and when it is not. Therefore, documenting inappropriate forms of behaviour is very important (Think You Need to Fire a Difficult Employee? 2014: 4–4). Difficult employees are the targets of individual training programmes based on the most realistic scenarios (Kurtz and Kucsan 2009: 28–30).

In order to deal with difficult employees effectively, it is necessary to take into consideration their individual types. The table below presents a simple classification of difficult employees (Table 5.1).

The true practical value of the methods of dealing with difficult employees presented in the table above is that before we start resolving any problem, we have to know what types of people are involved and what particular corrective measures have to be employed in their case. In practice, however, very few superiors have the adequate competences to identify difficult employees, express opinions, or conduct corrective or recovery talks. In order to manage difficult employees effectively, it is necessary to be aware of an employee group's pursued objectives, its composition, interpersonal relations and reasons for playing personal games; it is also advisable to adopt assertive attitudes. In other words, superiors are expected to possess the skills of qualified and experienced labour psychologists and to act as true coaches. Such expectations are very optimistic and, unfortunately, unrealistic in the majority of cases.

Table 5.1 The types of difficult employees and the methods of dealing with them

Type	Description	Methods
Attacking	People hostile towards others, loudly expressing their opinions	It is necessary to distinguish between useful "aggression" (which does not result from any ill will and which can be utilised) and spiteful attacks Express your position and opinions assertively. Try to keep calm
Victim	People who are victims avoid contact with co-workers, adopt hostile and defensive attitudes Some employees express regression, compensate	It is important to establish reasons for somebody's being a victim. Maybe such a person is attacked intentionally by other people? (This happens, for example, when a group attacks one of its members in order to harass or get rid of such a person) It is advisable: • to listen to the employee carefully • to establish reasons for incidents • to attempt to define problems and related tasks • to identify problems on a regular basis and to assign responsibility for resolving them
Pessimist	A pessimist expresses negative opinions, consistently negates the sense of undertaken activities, is pessimistic about tasks and goals assigned to them	It is advisable: • to focus on small achieved objectives • to try to establish objectives so that the pessimist is focused on performing tasks and pursuing objectives • if possible, to combine the pessimist's work with the primary goals pursued by the employee group • to draw the pessimist's attention to their small successes • to highlight achieved progress
Rescuer	Such a person helps others willingly, but unfortunately often at the cost of their own work	It is advisable: • to precisely specify priorities related to assigned tasks • to emphasise individual responsibility of such people • to encourage such people to improve their time management skills

(continued)

Table 5.1 (continued)

Type	Description	Methods
Quiet	No reactions; attempts to avoid getting involved in anything	It is advisable: • if possible, to express trust (in other people, superiors) in every situation on an ongoing basis • to ask open questions during a talk, to avoid interruptions and moments of silence during a talk • to establish true reasons for the lack of commitment
Complaining	Such a person does not get involved in tasks assigned to them, complains about everybody and everything, always negates the sense of what is being done, blames others	It is advisable: • to let such a person know that such attitudes and behaviour are unacceptable • during a talk, to insist on such a person's identifying the manner of the discussion and its results • during a talk, to try to explain who was responsible for what in the performance of particular tasks and what the complaining employee's share was

Source: the author's own work based on (Kaushik 2014: 53–55)

In practice, the following questions should be asked:

1. What caused the situation in which we have to deal with a difficult employee?
2. Is an employee who is regarded as difficult in fact difficult?
3. Is it worth taking any action?

1. If we already have to deal with an employee who is regarded as difficult or toxic, we have to identify reasons for this.

There may be many different reasons. The least probable cause is a sudden appearance of new personality traits or changes in an employee's personality. The most frequent causes are related to improperly conducted human resource management processes. For example, during the recruitment process the candidate was not checked, their competences were assessed incorrectly; the employee was not trained and did not participate in any adaptation programme adjusted to the employer's organisational requirements. A frequent mistake is making decisions to employ candidates on the basis of conversations (and not special interviews) held by people from outside an employee team. In this respect, there are a few solutions that can help to avoid making bad employment decisions. It is possible:

- to carry out comprehensive and complex assessments of competences;
- to involve potential future co-workers in selection processes;
- to create opportunities for future employees to become familiar with the character of work and more broadly with the organisational culture before any final employment decisions are made.

It can turn out that somebody has become a difficult employee as the result of an unjust employee assessment system or conflicts.

There are considerable risks connected with outsourcing the recruitment process to external companies that may not be familiar with the specific character of an organisation for which they provide services.

2. Let us assume that the processes of recruitment, training, competence improvement and adaptation have been conducted properly (although we still have doubts as to the reliability of the applied assessment tools). A detailed personnel audit has been carried out and no unjust distribution of resources has been identified. Then doubts appear as to whether an employee regarded as difficult really is difficult. In order to establish objective reasons for negative behaviour, it is necessary:

- to conduct an analysis of employee satisfaction surveys;
- to conduct an analysis of reasons for employee resignations (based on interviews with resigning employees);
- to conduct a survey of the quality of interpersonal relations within an employee team;
- to examine the efficiency of a team based on a comparative scale.

It can turn out that an employee is regarded as difficult because of one negative quality (e.g. an employee does not to share their knowledge with others, see the example below). It is necessary to establish whether such a quality is connected with the employee's character or work organisation (maybe the employee does not know that knowledge should be shared or feels that their position is threatened according to the principle that knowledge is power). It can turn out that an employee is considered difficult because they work harder or longer than other members of their team and is a victim of personal attacks.

A certain company manufacturing cathode blocks employed a very good specialist—one of the best in the world. He dealt with calculating the durability of used raw materials and developing new improved technological recipes. Unfortunately, few other employees wanted to work with him. He reacted very badly to all requests for information and wanted to keep his professional knowledge to himself. The effect was that he did not have any followers or a team of co-workers who could learn from him or share their own experiences with him. The head of the personnel department tried to talk to the specialist about the problem many times, but he would not change his ways. Attempts were made to introduce new employees into the assembly teams (the specialist supervised their operations performed on customers' premises). But nothing worked. Threats also proved ineffective. The problem was solved by accident. The company was acquired by a large international concern and the specialist was appointed the manager of the research team. In this position, he had no option but to share his precious knowledge with other members of his team.
Source: the authors' own work

3. Even if we conclude that we are dealing with a difficult employee, another question arises: is it worth taking any action? In order to answer this question, we have to address the following detailed questions:

- What are the economic and social costs of corrective actions?
- Do such actions guarantee the improvement of the organisational climate?
- Which employee causes the most problems in the team?
- What is their value?
- Does the knowledge held by the difficult employee threaten the existence of our organisation?
- Is it possible to utilise some unique competences possessed by the difficult employee?
- Can the difficult employee be helped effectively?

In many cases, despite actions taken, the dismissal of a difficult employee may be inevitable.

5.3   Procedures Limiting Unethical Behaviour

It is accepted that, to a certain extent, it is possible to prevent breaches of work discipline by means of various management procedures. This is so, among other things, because their existence reduces the scope of informal practices (cf. e.g. Crafting Performance Measurement Systems ... 2007: 23–33). It should be remembered that procedures constitute only one element of a comprehensive work discipline management system.

When developing procedures aimed at limiting unethical behaviour, we should take into consideration the following principles:

- Identify areas/processes in which unethical behaviour can occur (taking into consideration various manifestations of such behaviour and its scale of risks).
- Ensure employees' participation when developing the procedures.
- Verify the usefulness of the procedures in accordance with the PDCA cycle.
- Remember to assess periodically the usefulness of particular provisions as well as complete procedures.
- Ensure training for employees in both the methodology of developing procedures and unethical behaviour (especially with respect to its identification and prevention).
- Connect the existing procedures with the work discipline policy and personnel audits.
- Ensure that the existing procedures are consistent with legal requirements.

A very important task is to ensure that procedures take into account specific features of particular manifestations of unethical behaviour. Consequently, developing anti-corruption procedures, we should:

- indicate unambiguously what types of behaviour constitute corruption and what types should be regarded as appropriate (consistent with the social standards in place in the organisation);

- disregard cultural values (corruption behaviour is assessed differently in different cultures, e.g. accepting an expensive gift can be acceptable in one country, but unacceptable in another; such differences make it difficult to introduce anti-corruption procedures in organisations conducting business activities in many various countries);
- take into consideration the relations occurring between behaviour, results and consequences;
- concentrate more on manifestations of corruption and less on motives for corruption behaviour (motives are difficult to identify or examine);
- take into consideration, as far as possible, the measurability of caused damage;
- take into consideration so-called redistributive justice (Zadjali and Wright 2012: 34–51).

There are many different ways to develop procedures. Their number, degree of formalisation and detail, as well as scope, have to be determined by organisations themselves. The table below presents a few examples of such procedures based on the analysis of selected case studies.

5.3.1   A Corruption Risk Assessment Procedure

A well-established anti-corruption system takes into consideration legal risk, financial risk, and non-compliance risk (Sherman and Cook 2011: 11–15). Legal risk frequently occurs in merger or acquisition processes. In such circumstances, one organisation's earlier obligations may be transferred to the other. In order to reduce legal risk, in-depth analyses of the legal situation are required. Non-compliance risk concerns the future, while financial risk is a derivative of non-compliance risk and legal risk.

Various auxiliary questions are usually formulated. For example:

- Where do organisations conduct their business activities? In connection with their business activities, do they take into consideration the existing risk level or opinions of independent institutions (e.g. the Transparency International Corruption Perceptions Index)?
- Has the risk connected with relations between the private sector and the public sector (e.g. the history of such relations, opinions of other organisations) been assessed?

- Is the risk of losing credibility and reputation assessed before establishing new relations?
- Has the organisation developed and implemented general rules for maintaining business relations with public administration representatives?

5.3.2 Anti-corruption Procedures

There are very many procedures aimed at limiting corruption; for example, procedures regulating cooperation with citizens/customers, the acceptance and giving of gifts, the hosting of delegations or guests (see the Table 5.2 below).

5.3.3 Procedures Regulating External Relations

There are many procedures regulating internal relations. The aforementioned business guest-hosting procedure is one of them. Other procedures in this area concern, for example, unethical behaviour in franchising, export transactions or appropriate relations in quality chains.

5.3.4 A Procedure Aimed at Limiting Unethical Behaviour in Franchising

In many companies, caring about ethical behaviour also manifests itself in particular structures of franchising packages. Such packages usually contain recommendations concerning the obligation to acquire goods from a particular supplier, employee training, mutual benefits, protection rights, control, advertising campaigns, etc.

5.3.5 A Procedure Concerning Export Transactions

Companies which sell their products or services abroad follow additional procedures applicable to export transactions. Such procedures usually regulate the activities of export agents (transparency of conduct

Table 5.2 Examples of anti-corruption procedures

Procedure	Description	Notes
Cooperation with citizens/customers	The procedure should be based on the assumption that a citizen/customer: • is guaranteed the right to file complaints about the negligence or inappropriate performance of tasks by particular entities or their employees • can take advantage of legal advice provided by various associations and foundations • has the right to have the existing legal regulations enforced • can ask assistance from specialist law enforcement authorities (e.g. the police or the Internal Security Agency) • has the right to notify competent law enforcement authorities of committed offences or crimes	Such procedures are extremely valuable in limiting unethical or criminal behaviour in the public administration
Accepting and giving gifts	It is emphasised that any anti-corruption system should include a procedure (a set of rules) applicable to accepting and giving gifts. The most frequently used solution is determining acceptable values of gifts (which are often elements of promotional or sales campaigns)	Organisations can establish registers of gifts (e.g. in public administration offices—such registers are obligatory)
Hosting delegations or guests	Anti-corruption procedures also contain specific recommendations concerning the hosting of business delegations. With respect to hosting business guests, some companies avoid making reservations in the best hotels, costs of entertainment[a], costs related to the presence of the family members of official business guests, etc	Similar rules are developed by companies receiving business guests from abroad

Source: (Jaeger 2011: 20–21; Kolasiński ed. 2005)
[a]Trips with a delegation, taking clients to the theater, operas, and so on, are few examples of costs of entertainment

and representation), the performance of financial operations and the conduct of audits. It is important that:

- export agents not take advantage of asymmetry of information (after some time their position becomes very strong and the knowledge of the market is larger than that of the employing organisation);

- export agents do not work on the basis of a competitive commission system (which can be a source of corruption behaviour).

5.3.6 A Procedure Ensuring Appropriate Relations in a Quality Chain

There is a high risk of unethical or criminal behaviour along the whole length of quality chains. Examples of such behaviour include corruption, financial fraud, mobbing and lowering quality deliberately. A procedure ensuring appropriate relations in a quality chain has to take into consideration the following:

- the transparency of decision-making processes;
- audits of suppliers and distribution chains;
- periodic inspections of financial reporting;
- document circulation systems;
- surveys of interpersonal relations (e.g. based on interviews conducted by specially trained people).

Separate procedures are developed for dealing with whistleblowers.

5.3.7 A Procedure for Dealing with Whistleblowers

When revealing criminal acts, whistleblowers become particularly exposed to various forms of personal attack. The most common problems related to dealing with whistleblowers occur when whole organisations manifest unethical behaviour. Even if there are relevant management procedures, they do not protect whistleblowers against dismissal, slander, accusations or lawsuits. However, procedures for dealing with whistleblowers can prove extremely effective in network or multi-divisional organisations and where unethical behaviour occurs in one particular group of employees. The primary objective of such procedures is to ensure safety for people disclosing manifestations of various types of unethical or criminal behaviour. Some procedures, as well as some legal regulations, provide special financial incentives for people who report criminal acts. For example, the US has a special motivational system (consistent with the Dodd-Frank Act) rewarding those who report breaches of the regulations included in the Foreign Corrupt Practices Act. A person who reports a breach of the anti-corruption regulations and contributes to the culprit's paying a fine receives ten to thirty per cent of the fine (cf. Morley et al. 2011: 32–33). Similar regulations can be introduced in business organisations. However, what has to be kept in mind are the dangers of using a financial system (cf. Aguilar 2011: 11–12). Financial incentives can be a source of other unethical behaviour. There are also doubts as to whether rewarding whistleblowers is ethical (Seitz et al. 2015: 68–90).

5.3.8   An Anti-Mobbing Procedure

An anti-mobbing procedure should specify basic definitions (what is mobbing?), preventive actions, emergency measures, methods of providing help to people experiencing mobbing, data access rules, employee rights and obligations, a detailed description of actions taken if a case of mobbing is reported, and methods of conducting social analyses connected with mobbing.

Furthermore, an anti-mobbing procedure should take into consideration the following three types of prevention (based on: Basińska 2015): primary, secondary and tertiary. Primary prevention comprises mainly training in issues related to mobbing (its sources, manifestations, consequences, methods of dealing with mobbing, management's tasks). Secondary prevention is connected with determining employee competences. *"Such prevention comprises also developing a procedure for monitoring and documenting behaviour bearing the hallmarks of mobbing (this is to protect the victim against any such further behaviour) as well as procedures for filing and considering complaints related to mobbing"* (Basińska 2015). Tertiary prevention includes activities aimed at providing legal, psychological and other assistance to victims of mobbing.

5.3.9   A Harassment Prevention Procedure

Such a procedure can constitute a part of an overall procedure aimed at preventing mobbing or discrimination. The structure of a harassment prevention procedure includes its objective and subject matter, the scope of application, particular stages (from receiving a report from a victim about an alleged or factual case of mobbing, through the scope of provided assistance to a detailed description of action taken and duties of particular employees), required documents, methods of communication and methods of modifying and controlling the procedure.

Furthermore, it should also specify which types of behaviour are undesirable and describe in detail how the privacy of victims of harassment is to be protected. Specialists dealing with the problem of harassment emphasise the necessity of checking the reliability of testimonies, ensuring confidentiality and limiting opportunities for any retaliatory actions, which is of enormous importance (e.g. Wagner 1991).

Obviously there are many possibilities of developing procedures aimed at limiting the occurrence of unethical behaviour and presenting practical advice on how to cope with difficult behaviour and situations. However, such procedures have to constitute parts of broader programmes of shaping organisational cultures. They regulate only the normative sphere of such cultures and fulfil the educational function. Their effectiveness depends not only on the aforementioned principles of development but also on the experiences of victims of harassment and their conviction that they are effective.

5.4 Behaviour Modelling Training

Behaviour modelling training (BMT):

- provides employees with information on desirable models of behaviour;
- teaches employees practically how to behave appropriately;
- emphasises the importance of applying acquired knowledge in everyday practice (Bugdol 2007).

There are both supporters and opponents of organising special training aimed at modelling employee behaviour. Opponents question the effectiveness of the methods checking the impact of training on employee behaviour. They claim that there is no convincing evidence that such training is more effective than other types of training (Mayer and Russell

1987: 21–41). On the other hand, if training in the area of ethics is taken into consideration, the conducted meta-analysis indicates the effectiveness of such training (Steele et al. 2016: 319–350). Research carried out in the banking sector has shown that training in ethical behaviour brings about positive results. Employees' ability to identify unethical behaviour and tendency to manifest them has increased (Warren et al. 2014: 85–117). If such training is organised, employees receive a clear message: the management care about us and are interested in ethical issues; consequently, the level of employee satisfaction can rise (Valentine 2009: 227–242). In practice, BMT training turns out to be effective in shaping the awareness of safe behaviour, in particular if such training is combined with awareness-raising talks and if a considerable amount of time is spent on practical training (Burke et al. 2006: 315–324).

Behaviour modelling training can be regarded as effective for increasing mediators' skills in peer groups, improving interpersonal and communication skills, decreasing anxiety, and increasing assertiveness and empathy. At the same time, however, badly conducted training (e.g. where unambiguous definitions of breaching work discipline rules are ignored) can cause employees to start filing unjustified complaints against their co-workers. What previously has been treated as a friendly gesture can be interpreted as a manifestation of non-compliance with work discipline or unethical behaviour.

The reason why training concerning ethical behaviour tends to be effective is simple. If such training is conducted well, it improves employees' knowledge of what is good and what is bad. It increases their awareness of possible consequences of unethical behaviour. Therefore, it is very important to provide training participants with knowledge concerning the economic and social consequences of unethical behaviour and non-compliance with work discipline rules.

BMT training can be effective if the following conditions are fulfilled (Taylor et al. 2005: 692–709; Laff 2006: 12–13):

- training cannot be too long;
- training has to have clearly defined objectives;
- training content has to contain both positive and negative examples of employee behaviour;

- the possibility of doing practical exercises has to be ensured;
- people supervising training processes have to be properly trained,
- a training system has to include both rewards and sanctions.

Organisations spend billions of dollars on training courses whose objective is to change employee behaviour. However, knowledge acquired during training is frequently not transferred to practice. An additional problem is that the effectiveness of training is difficult to measure (unless we reduce such effectiveness to cognitive, as opposed to application objectives). Besides, the effectiveness of such training is influenced by many other factors. For example:

- factors related to trainees' personality traits (cognitive abilities, a sense of one's own effectiveness, motivation, perceived usefulness of training);
- factors connected with the course or process of training (behavioural modelling, mistakes management, training environment realism degree);
- factors related to the work environment (climate, support, opportunities for performing tasks and observations) (Grossman and Salas 2011: 103–120).

In BMT training, behavioural modelling consists, among other things, of ensuring that participants are convinced of possessing their own effectiveness and ability to change things (e.g. to improve relations with other people).

5.5   Further Research

Haimann and Hilgert (1997) indicated that morale influenced work discipline. This particular assumption deserves further research. The ethical and moral behaviour of leaders shapes the organisational climate and constitutes an important element of the organisational culture. In this context, the following question arises: Don't manifestations of ethical behaviour cause employees to lose their focus, or create situations in which employees no longer appreciate such behaviour?

Research has shown that by providing support, managers can increase employee satisfaction, lower their stress and sense of danger, and consequently reduce costs and improve productivity (Sawang 2010). Thus subsequent questions appear. To what extent do superiors in various organisations possess the abilities and opportunities to provide managerial support? Is it possible to achieve higher productivity not only in the service sector but also in organisations where productivity depends strongly on a social and technical system (where work results depend on the correct functioning of technical equipment)?

Further research should also comprise relations among systematics, standardisation and self-discipline. In practice, the problem is that standardization and systematics favour "dead self-discipline" or self-discipline that is not active or quality-oriented. Standardised methods of conduct are very much needed, but they can be a reason for the lack of quality-oriented commitment in employees. There appears a problem with motivating employees effectively and encouraging them to look for various quality-oriented solutions on a continual basis.

As has already been mentioned, the research conducted so far indicates that a sense of procedural injustice increases the possibility of the occurrence of behaviour aimed against a whole organisation, while interactional injustice manifests itself in destructive behaviour between superiors and subordinates (Flaherty and Moss 2007). This relationship has been proved empirically. In further research, however, another question should be posed: To what extent is interactional injustice a source of procedural injustice (the lack of a proper quality of interpersonal relations makes it impossible to develop either documented procedures or procedures constituting standardized methods of conduct)?

Superiors who cope well with difficult employees and provide them with proper support are exposed to the risk of being assessed negatively and becoming difficult employees themselves (after all, they do it at their own cost). An interesting research thread could be to establish to what extent such superiors' behaviour is accepted by top managers (their opinions on dealing with difficult employees can be radically different).

Manuals on dealing with difficult employees are full of advice and recommendations that are usually too general and fail to answer the question: How? There is a lack of research suggesting how to determine whether superiors possess competences necessary for managing difficult employees, how such competences can be developed and by means of what methods.

Superiors use various disciplinary tactics (see the Table 5.3 below). But we know little about the true consequences of particular tactics.

Table 5.3 Examples of disciplinary tactics

Tactic	Description	Notes
Intimidation	Intimidation can have a direct character (e.g. a manager threatens an employee with dismissal) or an indirect character (this function is more and more often fulfilled by intranet messenger programmes or other employees being in cahoots with a manager)	Intimidation can be an effective tactic only in the case of people who neglect their duties In most cases, intimidation causes a decrease in motivation and damages management's image
Advance information	Advance information indicates a proper hierarchy of decisions (what is more important: occupational duties or personal matters?) It has a character of threat (if you do not do something, you will lose your job, bonus, etc.)	Advance information is not always effective. It proves the weakness of communication processes. However, in some cases, it is a necessary tactic (e.g. when despite ordinary requests, an employee does not change their behaviour)
Delaying actions	For various (often personal) reasons, managers impose punishments on employees for actions committed in the past This results from the conviction that, for example, a disciplinary talk requires appropriate conditions (e.g. it takes place after management's recommendations have contributed to some success or an employee's behaviour has led to some failure)	Such a tactic is not consistent with the principles of punishment (punishment should be administered as soon as possible so that it is associated with a forbidden action)
Omission	Omission of actions results from the lack of a possibility to replace an employee	Omission can strengthen negative and inappropriate behaviour

(continued)

Table 5.3 (continued)

Tactic	Description	Notes
Employee transfer	When management have many talented employees at their disposal, they can decide to transfer an undisciplined employee to another, less demanding position	Although necessary in many situations, employee transfer does not take into consideration how a transferred employee will function in a new position and how the transfer will influence other employees
Passing over	Undisciplined employees are often passed over (e.g. they are not invited to important events or appointed as members of important teams)	Passing an employee over is a severe punishment. However, a punished employee is not always aware of the true reasons for their being passed over
Broken communication	Managers decide to break all communication with undisciplined employees	Broken communication can be an effective tactic only if relations between the superior and the subordinate were good and the employee is able to analyse reasons for changes in another person's behaviour
Exclusion	An undisciplined employee is excluded from the "game" (e.g. they are deprived of the function of a member of a project team)	Exclusion is a failure. It means that the discipline system does not function well (some mistakes have been made)
Assignment of additional tasks	Undisciplined employees are given additional tasks to perform	Assigning additional tasks is a doubtful tactic; work cannot be punishment
Transfer to another organisation	Undisciplined employees can be transferred to other organisations (e.g. to local branches or suppliers)	Similarly to transferring an employee to another position within the same organisation, transfer to another organisation does not take into account how the transferred employee will behave in a new place of work, how their transfer will influence other employees or the image of the organisation

Source: author's own research

A true challenge for both management practitioners and academics is to develop objective methods of determining the effectiveness of training aimed at modelling ethical behaviour. The main problems lie in the proper identification of factors influencing the effectiveness of such training and the determination of their significance and factual impact in various environmental conditions.

References

5 Tips for Dealing with an Uncooperative Employee. 2016. *HR Specialist* 14 (2).

Aguilar, Melissa Klein. 2011. Anticorruption Trends: What You Should Expect in 2011. *Compliance Week* 8 (87): 11–12.

Armstrong, Michael. 2011. *Zarządzanie ludźmi. Praktyczny przewodnik dla menedżerów liniowych*. Poznań: Dom Wydawniczy Rebis.

Ball, Gail A., Linda Klebe Trevino, and Henry P. Sims Jr. 1992. Understanding Subordinate Reactions to Punishment Incidents: Perspectives From Justice and Social Affect. *Leadership Quarterly* 3 (4): 307–333.

Basińska, Joanna. 2015. Polityka antymobbingowa-obowiązki pracodawcy. 13 July. http://www.wglex.pl/polityka-antymobbingowa-obowiazki-praco-dawcy. Accessed 10 Oct 2016.

Bugdol, Marek. 2007. *Gry i zachowania nieetyczne w organizacji*. Warszawa: Wyd. Difin.

Burke, Michael J., Sue Ann Sarpy, Kristin Smith-Crowe, Suzanne Chan-Serafin, S. Rommel O. Salvador, and Gazi Islam. 2006. Relative Effectiveness of Worker Safety and Health Training Methods. *American Journal of Public Health* 96 (2): 315–324.

Cole, Nina D. 2008. The Effects of Differences in Explanations, Employee Attributions, Type of Infraction, and Discipline Severity on Perceived Fairness of Employee Discipline. *Canadian Journal of Administrative Sciences (Canadian Journal of Administrative Sciences)* 25 (2): 107–120.

Crafting Performance Measurement Systems to Reduce Corruption Risks in Complex Organizations: The Case of the World Bank. 2007. *Measuring Business Excellence* 11 (4).

Difficult Employee? Time for 'The Chat'. 2014. *Managing People at Work* 1 (7).

Eisenberger, Robert, Florence Stinglhamber, Christian Vandenberghe, Ivan L. Sucharski, and Linda Rhoades. 2002. Perceived Supervisor Support: Contributions to Perceived Organizational Support and Employee Retention. *Journal of Applied Psychology* 87 (3): 565–567.

Flaherty, Shane, and Simon A. Moss. 2007. The Impact of Personality and Team Context on the Relationship Between Workplace Injustice and Counterproductive Work Behavior. *Journal of Applied Social Psychology* 37 (11): 2549–2575.

Gladis, Steve. 2015. TD: Working with Difficult People. *Talent Development* 69 (1): 78–81.

Graham, Harold Thomas, and Eric R. Bennett. 1995. *Human Resources Management*. London: Pitman Publishing.

Grossman, Rebecca, and Eduardo Salas. 2011. The Transfer of Training: What Really Matters. *International Journal of Training & Development* 15 (2): 103–120.

Guffey, Cynthia J., and Marilyn M. Helms Dr. 2011. Effective Employee Discipline: A Case of the Internal Revenue Service. *Public Personnel Management* 30 (1): 111–127.

Haimann, Theo, and Raymond L. Hilgert. 1997. *Supervision. Concepts and Practice of Management*. Chicago: South-Western Publishing.

Jaeger, Jaclyn. 2011. The Dos and Don'ts of Corporate Hospitality. *Compliance Week* 8 (92): 20–21.

Jones, Martyn C., Karen Smith, and Derek W. Johnston. 2005. Exploring the Michigan Model: The Relationship of Personality, Managerial Support and Organizational Structure with Health Outcomes in Entrants to the Healthcare Environment. *Work & Stress* 19 (1): 1–22.

Kaushik, Shailja. 2014. Fixing Out-of-Order Behaviours. *Human Capital*, March.

Kelloway, E. Kevin, Lori Francis, Matthew Prosser, and James E. Cameron. 2010. Counterproductive Work Behavior as Protest. *Human Resource Management Review* 20 (1): 18–25.

King, Karen N., and Denise E. Wilcox. 2003. Employee-Proposed Discipline: How Well is it Working? *Public Personnel Management* 32 (2, Summer): 197–209.

Klotz, Anthony C., and Mark C. Bolino. 2013. Citizenship and Counterproductive Work Behavior: A Moral Licensing View. *Academy of Management Review* 38 (2): 292–306.

Kolasiński, B., ed. 2005. *Citizens' Anticorruption Charter*. Developed in the Appellate Public Prosecutor's Office, Version II amended. Szczecin, December.

Kurtz, Larry, and Rita Kucsan. 2009. Close Encounters: Using Scenario Training to Handle Difficult Employees. *Talent Development (T+D)* 63 (8): 28–30.

Laff, Michael. 2006. What Is Effective Training? *Talent Development (T+D)* 60 (6): 12–13.

Liff, Stewart. 2007. *CHAPTER 4: Dealing with Difficult People.* Managing Government Employees.

Lisiecka, Krystyna, and Iwona Burka. 2016. *Lean service w teorii i praktyce.* Katowice: Wyd. UE Katowice.

Liu, Zhen, and Meixin Xu. 2012. Preliminary Exploring the Influence of Person-Organization Fit on Counterproductive Work Behavior. *International Business & Management* 4 (2): 133–139.

Mayer, Steven J., and James S. Russell. 1987. Behavior Modeling Training in Organizations: Concerns and Conclusions. *Journal of Management* 1 (3): 21–40.

McCafferty, Dennis. 2014a. 13 Ways to Manage Difficult Employees. *CIO Insight*, 9/7/.

———. 2014b. How to Work Effectively With Difficult Colleagues. *Baseline*, 9/9/.

Miller, Laurence. 2008. *From Difficult to Disturbed: Understanding and Managing Dysfunctional Employees.* New York: AMACOM.

———. 2009. From Difficult to Disturbed: Understanding and Managing Dysfunctional Employees. *Personnel Psychology* 62 (1, Spring): 171–197.

Morley, Matt, Robert Hadley, and Brian F. Saulnier. 2011. What Lies Ahead for Anticorruption Laws. *World Trade: WT100* 24 (3): 32–33.

Podsakoff, Philip M., William H. Bommer, Nathan P. Podsakoff, and Scott B. Mackenzie. 2006. Relationships Between Leader Reward and Punishment Behavior and Subordinate Attitudes, Perceptions, and Behaviors: A Meta-Analytic Review of Existing and New Research. *Organizational Behavior & Human Decision Processes* 99 (2): 113–142.

Sawang, Sukanlaya. 2010. Moderation or Mediation? An Examination of the Role Perceived Managerial Support has on Job satisfaction and Psychological Strain. *Current Psychology* 29 (3): 247–256.

Schoen, Sterling H., and Douglas E. Durand. 1979. *Supervision. The Management of Organizational Resources.* New York: Prentice-Hall.

Seitz, Jamie, Jill Oeding, and Michael Wiese. 2015. Is It Ethical for the U.S. Government to Offer Financial Awards to Potential Whistleblowers of Financial Statement Fraud and Internal Control Violations? *Journal of Theoretical Accounting Research* 10 (2, Spring): 247–256.

Sherman, Andrew J., and R. Christopher Cook. 2011. International Mergers: How to Detect Corruption. *Journal of Corporate Accounting & Finance (Wiley)* 22 (6): 11–15.

Sidle, Stuard D. 2010. Counterproductive Work Behavior: Can It Sometimes Be Good to Be Bad? *Academy of Management Perspectives* 24 (3): 101–103.

Steele, Logan M., Tyler J. Mulhearn, Kelsey E. Medeiros, Logan L. Watts, Shane Connelly, and Michael D. Mumford. 2016. How Do We Know What Works? A Review and Critique of Current Practices in Ethics Training Evaluation. *Accountability in Research: Policies & Quality Assurance* 23 (6): 319–350.

Stoner, James A.F., R. Edward Freeman, Daniel R. Gilbert, and Jr. 2001. *Kierowanie*. Warszawa: PWE.

Taylor, Paul J., Darlene F. Russ-Eft, and Daniel W.L. Chan. 2005. "A Meta— Analytic Review of Behavior Modeling Training". *Journal of Applied Psychology*, nr 90 (4), 692.

The Breakroom. 2016. *Managing People at Work*, 3/1/ 3 (5).

The Economist. 23.01.2012.

The Standardization Act of 12 September 2002. cyt. za https://mfiles.pl/pl/index.php/Standaryzacja,Dz.U.2002.169.1386. Accessed 17 July 2016.

Think You Need to Fire a Difficult Employee? Document Your Warnings and Discipline. 2014. *HR Specialist: Employment Law* 44 (9).

Valentine, Sean. 2009. Ethics Training, Ethical Context, and Sales and Marketing Professionals' Satisfaction With Supervisors and Coworker. *Journal of Personal Selling & Sales Management* 29 (3, Summer): 227–242.

Wagner, Ellen J. 1991. *Sexual Harassment in the Workplace: How to Prevent, Investigate, and Resolve Problems in Your Organization*. New York: AMACOM.

Warren, Danielle E., Joseph P. Gaspar, and William S. Laufer. 2014. Is Formal Ethics Training Merely Cosmetic? A Study of Ethics Training and Ethical Organizational Culture. *Business Ethics Quarterly* 24 (1): 85–117.

Yang, Jixia, and James M. Diefendorff. 2009. The Relations of Daily Counterproductive Workplace Behavior with Emotions, Situational Antecedents, and Personality Moderators: A Diary Study in Hong Kong. *Personnel Psychology* 62 (2): 259–295.

Yarbrough, Jonathan W. 2015. How to Address Difficult Employee Issues. *Rural Telecom* 34 (5, Special section): 22–25.

Zabriskie, Kate. 2016. Why Your Employees Aren't Performing. *Government Executive*, 2/5/.

Zadjali, Mahir Al, and Christopher S. Wright. 2012. A New Paradigm of Corruption to Aid in Its Control and Dispel Its Sweet-spot Myth. *Journal of Leadership, Accountability & Ethics* 9 (1): 34.

[www1]. https://pl.wikipedia.org/wiki/Unifikacja_(maszynoznawstwo). Accessed 21 July 2016.

6

Conclusion

6.1 Limitations and Further Research

This book on work discipline does not have a uniform character; it is neither an academic analysis nor a how-to manual. On the one hand, it shows the current state of knowledge of work discipline, and on the other hand, its objective has been to present various practical possibilities of shaping and maintaining discipline. Also, it has been impossible to omit a short description of various types of unethical behaviour. The problem lies in that such behaviour requires specialist knowledge and, consequently, more detailed content. What this book presents is just a sketch, a small segment of research issues or problems with which both managers and employees have to cope today. Chapter 4 "Discipline and the Selected Manifestations of Employee Behaviour" does not contain a complete review of the literature on the subject.

The author wanted to look at discipline differently, more broadly than in the case of earlier research and practice. His intention was to show that discipline is not only a catalogue of punishments but that, in practice, an employee functions in some cultural environment which can foster the expression of attitudes and behaviour which, in turn, are accepted or not.

© The Author(s) 2018
M. Bugdol, *A Different Approach to Work Discipline*,
https://doi.org/10.1007/978-3-319-74008-9_6

The author's conclusion is that work discipline has a relational character. Employees behave differently under the influence of different people, expressed emotions or the quality of interaction. Their interaction with some people is momentary; with others, they have strong psycho-social ties. Such behaviour can be strengthened by strategic elements (objectives; remuneration systems favouring the achievement of objectives).

The presented review of discipline models is not and cannot be complete. Many different organisations will have developed their own original models of discipline which have not been mentioned in any publications. Although the number of publications on organisations without bosses is growing, little is known about discipline models used in them. It cannot be ruled out that some organisations without bosses have not given up the progressive discipline model.

The author wanted to show that organisations use various types of punishments, not only formal ones. We know very little about emotional punishment. The same is also true of the consequences of applying punishments and rewards alternately, especially if they are very strong. The research indicates a very sad conclusion, namely that in only one of the surveyed organisations, employees punished for quality mistakes were in fact guilty of making them. In the vast majority of cases, employees are punished for quality mistakes for which they are not responsible. This proves again the correctness of E. Deming's thesis that the majority of mistakes have a systemic character and the blame for them falls on management.

The book does not study the problem of fear and conformism, which is a dominant trait in many organisations. Fear prevents employees from breaching work discipline rules but, on the other hand, it is a paralysing force that can lead to serious financial problems (Volkswagen is a case in point) or even the downfall of an organisation.

The book does not explain how people management methods (e.g. employee assessment methods) influence work discipline. Such influence can be direct (e.g. employee assessment) or indirect (e.g. in occupational adaptation). This problem also deserves separate research and publications.

It seems that what considerably influences people management methods is an organisation's business perspective. If it is a long-term perspective, it can be assumed that the atmosphere in the workplace is not full of tension, is not oriented towards achieving financial objectives quickly. In such organisations, employee mobility is lower, more emphasis is put on developing and maintaining competences, and managers are rarely dismissed. Thus, it would be worth conducting some research into the influence of such a perspective on work discipline.

The book does not mention many other issues related to work discipline, but it may be a good introduction to further research. And the author will be very glad if managers find this book of some use in their everyday work (maybe the book will change their approach to various management methods).

Researchers specialising in work discipline are facing new challenges such as developing systems of responsibility for damage caused by artificial intelligence or establishing principles of cooperation between people and machines that will replace outsourced employees.

Blade Runner, directed by Ridley Scott, shows a group of robots who have escaped from an off-world colony to Earth. They know that they are about to be "retired". Fighting for survival, they commit many crimes, including murder. If technological progress allows robots to make independent decisions (based on accumulated experience), it will become necessary to determine criminal liability for acts committed not by machine engineers, but by state-of-the-art machines provided with artificial intelligence.

Another research area concerns establishing rules of cooperation in increasingly complex socio-technical systems. Some companies (e.g. Adidas) are giving up outsourcing. Work previously performed in China or Vietnam by cheap workers is being transferred back to Germany. Cheap labour is being replaced by modern technologies, allowing the manufacture of goods without human interference. The reason is very simple: both personnel and logistics costs are rising and transporting goods from China to Germany is becoming uneconomical. Furthermore, modern technologies make it possible to produce goods quickly, in accordance with customers' individual requirements. Thus work discipline is becoming more and more dependent on technological discipline connected with the maintenance of appropriate operating criteria. Another new challenge lies in guaranteeing a fast flow of information between people responsible for identifying customer and market requirements and programmers. Managers are increasingly going to wonder: who is to blame, the programme or the man? Is it a good idea to punish employees if an organisation's existence depends on them to a considerable degree (losing specialists to competitors constitutes a growing economic risk)?

6.2   Disciples and New Challenges

It would be a mistake to assume that the problem of the dehumanised and cruel treatment of employees is no longer topical. It is enough to consult current publications. For example, the *Guardian* (The Guardian 2016: 23437) reports that the well-known company Sport Direct implemented an inhumane work discipline system. Superiors could discipline and even fire employees for trivial and not necessarily rational reasons. An employee who received six black cards in a six-month period could be dismissed automatically. More than three thousand people had temporary employment contracts. They were frequently remunerated below the legally minimum wage. The work atmosphere was such that employees were afraid to use days off or holidays to which they were entitled. Employees were punished even for short work breaks or for drinking water. Some women claimed that their employment contracts had been extended in return for sexual favours. One employee even gave birth to a child in a company toilet. In 2016 the *Guardian* published another article disclosing the appalling work conditions in Amazon warehouses. Employees were penalised for taking medical leave. The stressful work conditions were caused by the permanent control and monitoring of employees. Low wages resulted in some employees camping in tents outside the company premises in order to save on public transport fares (www1).

It can be assumed that the problem of unfair treatment of employees will intensify. One of the reasons for formulating such a thesis is the current situation in the labour market. Employment and consequently labour relations are under the enormous influence of globalisation. The development of the freelancer market has caused unemployment in developed countries as work moves to Asia. The labour market is a "zero-sum game" (a Pakistani employee gets a job performed previously by somebody in Europe or the US; there are winners and losers). And it is young people who tend to lose in this game. There are more and more people referred to as "NEETS" (not in education, employment or training). The number of people with temporary employment contracts is growing as well (19.7 per cent in the US, which, according to the Mc Kinsley Global Institute, may rise to as much as 58 per cent in the near future). Almost every fifth job is to be outsourced.

Another noticeable phenomenon is the development of modern technologies influencing the level of employment and also forms of employee control. In some sectors (e.g. the medical and the catering sectors), the following two phenomena can be observed: a decrease in the number of available jobs and an increase in the scope of their monitoring (e.g. in Japan, more than 200 restaurants are managed by one person; computerised monitoring systems and automatised belts have been introduced).

The implementation of modern technologies influences work discipline to a considerable extent. On the one hand, supervisory functions are no longer performed by superiors, but by impersonal computer software, work-time recording systems, etc. On the other hand, it is employees who fulfil the role of supervisors of robots (e.g. in the automotive company Audi, employees determine workplaces for robots and fulfil the role of their supervisors).

References

The Guardian. 22.07.2016.
[www1]. https://www.theguardian.com/technology/2016/dec/11/amazon-accused-of-intolerable-conditions-at-scottish-warehouse. Accessed 11 Dec 2016.

Index

© The Author(s) 2018
M. Bugdol, *A Different Approach to Work Discipline*,
https://doi.org/10.1007/978-3-319-74008-9

Lightning Source UK Ltd.
Milton Keynes UK
UKHW02n1353020518
322005UK00003B/216/P